# MAY ALL YOUR FENCES HAVE GATES

..........................................................................

# May All Your

University of Iowa Press ᴪ Iowa City

# Fences Have Gates

..................................................................

ESSAYS ON THE DRAMA OF

# AUGUST WILSON

EDITED BY ALAN NADEL

University of Iowa Press, Iowa City 52242

Copyright © 1994 by the University of Iowa Press

Printed in the United States of America

Design by Richard Hendel

Printed on acid-free paper

Library of Congress Cataloging-in-Publication Data

May all your fences have gates: essays on the drama of August Wilson / edited by
Alan Nadel.

p.     cm.

Includes bibliographical references and index.

ISBN 0-87745-428-0, ISBN 0-87745-439-6 (paper)

1. Wilson, August—Criticism and interpretation. 2. Afro-Americans in literature.

I. Nadel, Alan, 1947–

PS3573.I45677Z78    1994

812'.54—dc20                                              93-34628

                                                                    CIP


98   97   96   95   94   C   5   4   3   2   1

98   97                   P   5   4   3   2

*This collection is dedicated*

*to the memory of my parents,*

PERCY and ADELE NADEL,

*who took me to the theater;*

*and to my daughter*

GLYNNIS PERKINS NADEL,

*who loves to perform*

# CONTENTS

Preface *by Alan Nadel*, ix

Introduction *by Alan Nadel*, 1

The History Lesson: Authenticity and Anachronism in
  August Wilson's Plays, 9
  *by Anne Flèche*

August Wilson's Burden: The Function of Neoclassical Jazz, 21
  *by Craig Werner*

Speaking of Ma Rainey / Talking about the Blues, 51
  *by Sandra Adell*

Filling the Time: Reading History in the Drama of August Wilson, 67
  *by John Timpane*

Boundaries, Logistics, and Identity: The Property of Metaphor in
  *Fences* and *Joe Turner's Come and Gone*, 86
  *by Alan Nadel*

Ghosts on the Piano: August Wilson and the Representation
  of Black American History, 105
  *by Michael Morales*

American History as "Loud Talking" in *Two Trains Running*, 116
  *by Mark William Rocha*

Romare Bearden, August Wilson, and the Traditions of
  African Performance, 133
  *by Joan Fishman*

The Ground on Which I Stand: August Wilson's Perspective

on African American Women, 150

*by Sandra G. Shannon*

August Wilson's Women, 165

*by Harry J. Elam, Jr.*

August Wilson's Gender Lesson, 183

*by Missy Dehn Kubitschek*

I Want a Black Director, 200

*by August Wilson*

"The Crookeds with the Straights": *Fences*, Race, and the

Politics of Adaptation, 205

*by Michael Awkward*

Annotated Bibliography of Works by and about August Wilson, 230

*by Sandra G. Shannon*

Notes on Contributors, 267

Index to the Plays, 269

**ALAN NADEL**

# Preface

..................................................................

When I was nine years old I saw Orson Welles—I think it was on "The Steve Allen Show"—perform Shylock's speech from *The Merchant of Venice.* I was so struck by the power of the speech and its rendition that I read the play. It was not typical fare for a fourth-grader, and I'm not sure what I got from the experience, but I do remember discovering that the play was not just about prejudice but about money and, I guess, about the ways in which they are connected. I also remember feeling that it was about a similar connection between money and love and about the problems of a smart woman in a stupid world, a woman who reminded me of the women played by Katharine Hepburn and Rosalind Russell in the old movies I loved to watch on television.

It was just about then that my parents took me to see Paul Muni in *Inherit the Wind,* a play based on the Scopes trial that tested the Tennessee law prohibiting the teaching of evolution. This too, as I understood it, was about the destructive power of prejudice and the need to resist it. The same themes were being played out that year (and perhaps ever since) across my television screen as court-ordered desegregation was pitting the courage of six-year-old children against the fears of the governor of Arkansas. It is impossible to assess the exact impact of these and of so many other events from 1956 and 1957 that remain vivid in my memory. But I know that that period marks a time when I became however crudely aware of the ways theater, film, even television constituted a gateway not only out to the vast suffering and success of others but also into my small personal sites of fear and fortitude, sites made slightly larger and more communal through my ability to recognize them elsewhere.

I think this explains my love of theater and the profound effect it has had on me over nearly four decades. And I would like to think that this explanation is implicit in the inscription August Wilson wrote on my copy of his plays: "May all your fences have gates." Everything we know of history is circumscribed by fences. From the walls of the womb and the bars of the crib to colonial maps and the Berlin Wall, we can chart human civilization in the dust or the shadow of fences, and thus the frame of the proscenium may possibly stand as the sign of history, that is, of the fence opened by the gateway of drama.

Literary criticism, one hopes, can also provide gateways through the proscenium arch to eliminate some barriers to understanding or open the written and the performed to new perspectives. That has been the goal of this collection. As such it represents my attempt to return in small part the great favor theater does for us all. And it represents my personal gratitude for the plays of August Wilson, which continually reconfirm the important social and historical power of drama.

My gratitude also goes to all the contributors for their fine essays and to Maryemma Graham, who served as the helpful respondent at the Modern Language Association session where this collection was born. Permissions were provided by the Bearden Foundation for the Bearden prints and by *Spin* magazine for August Wilson's essay. I also greatly appreciate the University of Iowa Press for being accessible, cooperative, and encouraging and for sending the manuscript to a superb copy editor, Jan McInroy.

Special thanks go to Emily Kretchmer, August Wilson's assistant during the time this book was compiled, for countless forms of help. And to my wife, Amy Perkins, with whom a running dialogue about theater and literature continues to invigorate rather than exhaust in ways that make projects such as this one *seem* possible and *become* rewarding.

Finally, to August: may all your gates open both ways.

# MAY ALL YOUR FENCES HAVE GATES

ALAN NADEL

# Introduction

．．．．．．．．．．．．．．．．．．．．．．．．．．．．．．．．．．．．．．．．．．．．．．．．．．．．．．．．．．

In less than a decade, August Wilson has become one of the most significant playwrights in the history of American theater and one of the most important contemporary African American writers. A prolific writer, Wilson began writing plays in the 1970s, and in the latter part of that decade he embarked upon an ambitious project to write a cycle of plays about African American life, one set in each decade of the twentieth century. He has now completed six plays in the cycle, five of which—*Ma Rainey's Black Bottom* (1984), *Fences* (1987), *Joe Turner's Come and Gone* (1988), *The Piano Lesson* (1990), and *Two Trains Running* (1992)—have run on Broadway in an eight-year period, and by the time *Two Trains* reached Broadway, Wilson was well into writing the seventh play. Clearly Wilson is one of the most productive of American dramatists and, equally, one of the most vigilant historicizers of African American experience. He is also, without question, the most lauded American playwright of the 1980s. His five Broadway productions have earned him, in eight brief years, four New York Drama Critics' Circle Awards (*Ma Rainey, Fences, Joe Turner, Piano Lesson*), two Drama Desk Awards (*Fences, Piano Lesson*), an Outer Critics Circle Award (*Fences*), five Tony nominations, one Tony (*Fences*), and two Pulitzer prizes (*Fences, Piano Lesson*).

As many have noted, however, Wilson's success could never have been predicted from his origins in poverty: He was raised by his mother and barely knew his (white) father. He grew up as one of six children in a two-room, cold-water flat located in the Pittsburgh Hill district (the area, it has been suggested, that inspired the television series *Hill Street Blues*). He dropped out of high school after being unjustly accused of plagiarizing a report on Napoleon. Subsequently, he worked in marginal jobs.

During the 1960s he also wrote poetry and became involved in the Black Power movement. These two interests—writing and political action—intersected when he cofounded a black activist theater company in Pittsburgh. In 1978 he moved to St. Paul, where he wrote scripts for exhibitions at the Science Museum of Minnesota and became involved with the Playwrights'

Center in Minneapolis. At that point in his life, he began to concentrate his energies on the cycle of American dramas focused on black life in the twentieth century, from which all of his subsequent plays have come. The first, *Jitney*, set in 1971, was produced at the Allegheny Repertory Theater. The second, *Ma Rainey*, won a national competition run by the National Playwrights Conference that gave it a staged reading at the O'Neill Theater in Connecticut, where it caught the attention of the conference director, Lloyd Richards, who was the artistic director of the Yale Repertory Theater and the dean of the Yale School of Drama. *Ma Rainey* and all of Wilson's subsequent plays were directed by Richards and premiered at the Yale Rep.

..................

When I met August Wilson, during the New York previews of *Two Trains Running*, he told me about an occasion on which he had wandered into a bar in Boston, to discover not only from the composition of the crowd but also from its general demeanor (not to mention his difficulty in getting the bartender's attention), that it was a de facto whites-only bar. Under the circumstances, Wilson wanted merely to finish his drink and leave expeditiously. Then he heard rhythm and blues coming from the jukebox, and it changed his attitude. He began to savor his drink slowly and to make elbow room for himself at the crowded bar where he had been squeezed back. "You can't say," he reasoned, "that you want my music here but you don't want me."

In many ways, this story may be seen as a metaphor for Wilson's dramatic enterprise. Establishing himself over the past decade as the leading playwright in contemporary American theater, Wilson has created elbow room at the bar by making visible the connection between African American culture and the dominant white culture that has taken it for granted. This enterprise is as problematic as is the unique piano in *The Piano Lesson*, on the surface of which was carved by Boy Willie's and Berniece's great-grandfather the images of their slave ancestors. In antebellum America, their great-grandmother and their grandfather had been traded for that piano; their father had died to retrieve it. It was white property paid for with black blood, and as such it was the historical reminder of the time in America when blacks held the status of property. It was also the only substantial record of the family's history and talent, a history of living as property and of dying for it, of making art only within the white venue, upon the white instrument. Berniece, haunted by the piano's history, cannot play it, and Boy Willie, eager for a down payment on part of the land his ancestors used to work, wants to sell it.

Berniece, we could say, wants to hide from history and Boy Willie wants to get rid of it. Wilson, however, wants to rewrite it, even if he has to use traditionally white instruments, even if he has to resurrect some ugly ghosts, for the alternative, it would seem, is to deny African Americans their art and their history. The risk Wilson takes is large, for demanding recognition from the dominant culture can easily be viewed as validating the values that were responsible for repressing and denying the voices of minorities, the rights of minorities, even the very humanity of minorities. Making elbow room at the bar can easily be interpreted as wanting the approval of those people at the bar, or wanting to be accepted by their standards. The truth is, of course, that "their standards," as their choice of music proved, were not their own. They had already adopted Wilson's standards and lied about it in their history. Wilson therefore was not asking acceptance but asserting a right given him by the music—the right to make them confront the hypocrisy of their history, the errors in the stories they were telling themselves about who they were.

That is why, I think, Wilson has developed, in his cycle of plays, a pointedly historical project. In these fictionalized histories or historically specific fictions, he is presenting versions of American time no less distorted than those myriad representations that traditionally pass for America's "common" past and "common" culture—from western movies to national holidays, from Dixie worship to Elvis worship—and in many ways he is presenting accuracies never noticed before.

Since every aspect of a culture, potentially, has a history and equally can be absorbed or erased by other historical narratives, Wilson's project lays forth an array of histories, in consort and conflict. An African American's understanding of his or her location in spiritual time, for example, is confounded by the competing cosmologies of largely obscured African ritual and highly visible but dysfunctional Christian dogma. As Sandra Adell insightfully explains, the prolonged waiting in *Ma Rainey* is a form of spiritual ennui that marks the death of God and emphasizes the Nietzschean quality of the blues: "The blues is what excites the will-to-power of those beings who would otherwise lack the power to will beyond the narrow and racially defined spheres of their existence. In the absence of the God of Christianity, the blues is what *em*-powers them." Adell and John Timpane both make clear, moreover, that the biography—the personal history—of Gertrude "Ma" Rainey is implicated not only in the history of blues music but also in the history of recording technology and the history of marketing.

Competing histories, Timpane points out, also operate in *Fences*, which focuses on the shift between the time when professional sports was seen as a certain dead end for blacks to the time when it was seen as one of the very few avenues of opportunity. History, then, is not merely a chronicle of shifts but a series of sites in which one historical narrative has silenced others. These sites, Timpane stresses, can be noticed only retrospectively, and thus, as Anne Flèche points out, Wilson is engaged in a conscious anachronism, in order to create "ironic parables about anachronism."

But it is exactly Wilson's point that one person's anachronism is another's history. In my essay, for example, I point out that although the people in the 1911 Pittsburgh boardinghouse in *Joe Turner's Come and Gone* are described as the sons and daughters of newly freed slaves, they are more like the newly freed slaves themselves, still the children of a double diaspora—first from Africa and then from the South—and the half-century since Emancipation has done little to change their situation. In *Joe Turner*, too, the history of American capitalism and technology—deeply intertwined with one version of the history of the city of Pittsburgh—is represented as significantly separate from the stories of the blacks, all of whom in one way or another are still looking for a starting place of the sort repeatedly provided for successive waves of European emigrants since the end of the Civil War.

This history of emigration and of Pittsburgh is one about which the dominant culture has heard little, Wilson's work suggests, perhaps because it was not capable of listening. And it is possible to see Wilson's work, therefore, as representing not the history of events but rather the history of the act of listening. Focusing on *Two Trains Running*, Mark Rocha makes clear the ways in which Wilson works to construct an audience capable of hearing different histories by employing a form of "loud talking" common in black culture. This means speaking to an ostensive audience in a manner intended to be overheard by a third party, for whom the instruction is actually intended. In *Two Trains*, particularly, the white theater audience, as object of the loud talking, is indirectly being given angry lessons in a nonconfrontational manner.

Such nonconfrontational confrontation Craig Werner compares to the neoclassical innovations of Wynton Marsalis's jazz, viewing Wilson's plays as a "call for new responses to the jazz possibilities of African American life." With Werner's insights into jazz paradigms in mind, we are better able, I think, to appreciate the ensemble quality of Wilson's plays, the ways in which they often seem to favor interaction over the Aristotelian idea of "plot."

*Ma Rainey*, of course, is explicitly about a blues ensemble and the ways it fails, finally, to play together. Under the surveillance and control of the dominant culture's economic, legal, and mechanical technologies, the musicians are forced to reject all of their individual visions and versions in the interest of preserving the integrity of the authorized version of their music. But in the play the intervention of that authority destroys the community from which the music originated. These circumstances become particularly cogent in the light of Werner's astute examination of American jazz: "While the awareness of Euro-American and popular musical forms helped jazz attract an interracial audience, its creative vitality results in large part from the combination of the blues insistence on the immediacy of felt experience and the gospel insistence on a vision of individual and communal transcendence that transforms the meaning of immediate experience."

This perspective also helps us understand, I think, the ways in which the other plays draw on Euro-American dramatic forms, only to reinvent them, sometimes very subtly, as in the case of *Fences*, or more overtly, as in *Joe Turner*, *Piano Lesson*, and *Two Trains*. Even if *Fences* has a tragic hero who in many ways resembles Arthur Miller's Willy Loman, Wilson greatly revises Miller's consciously neo-Aristotelian objective, for Troy Maxson's activities become valorized as a form of responsibility to his family, and the fence he builds creates a site, I argue, on which three generations of his progeny become a community. If he was too strong a soloist, to return to the jazz paradigm, then he was also a very influential one, for the reconciliation of the family and the resolution of the play come when his son, Cory, and his daughter, Raynell, in duet, sing Troy's blues.

Both *Joe Turner* and *Two Trains*, similarly, may resemble Eugene O'Neill's *The Iceman Cometh*, and *Piano Lesson* may have much in common with Miller's *The Price*, in which a pair of adult siblings debate the disposition of a harp that is a family heirloom. But the profound difference is that in Wilson's plays the community is both the source of the dramatic tension and its product. Because these plays all resemble structurally a jazz set as much as they do a Euro-American play, we are confronted not with protagonists and antagonists but rather with the tension of interpretive energy, as a community of players play off one another's solos. If they tend at times to play variations on recognizable themes, the synergy of the interaction creates unexpected and exciting results. These interactions are exciting not in the way that a tragic death is but in the way that a Duke Ellington or a John Coltrane finale is. The disparate strains, the subversive chord structures, the competitive rhythms, having been given their freedom from the copyrighted version and the initial collaborative circumstance, remarkably unite, in spite of and because of their freedom and individual power, to create an unimagined and, even at the outset of the number, unimaginable new version.

Visual art has been influential for Wilson in similar ways; both *Piano Lesson* and *Joe Turner* were inspired by specific works by Romare Bearden, who, like Wynton Marsalis, could be considered a subversive neoclassicist. Joan Fishman details the extensive connection between Wilson and Bearden that includes their admiration for jazz, their collagist techniques, their attempt to reinvest the African American scene with elements and icons from its African origins, and their strong interest in African ritual and religion.

At the end of *Fences*, for example, Gabriel performs a miracle with a ritual dance that emphasizes African religion as a source of his power in the same way that Western religion is the source of his name. And Risa, in *Two Trains*, has performed a ritual scarification of her legs that, Harry Elam notes, "calls attention to Western standards of beauty." As Michael Morales has shown, *Piano Lesson* and *Joe Turner* employ African rituals in ways that challenge the premises of the American naturalist tradition with a form of ritual theater. The piano, according to Morales, affirms African culture and thought by serving as a mnemonic device that transmits oral history, like those used by several African civilizations, and it is also a sacred ancestral altar, like the one that provides a link for the Yoruba to dead spirits. *Joe Turner*, too, is a highly ritualistic drama that, according to Missy Dehn Kubitschek, "addresses African Americans' attempt to recover wholeness in the face of European attempts to control and possess their spirituality." Kubitschek identifies Bertha and Bynum as African American spiritual workers who make clear the importance of individual shamans and community rituals.

Kubitschek makes these points in the interest of exploring Wilson's depiction of gender relations. She stresses the significance of the fact that in the play male and female shamans "share rituals and ritual space; African American spirituality does not assume or enforce separate spheres." In general, Wilson's drama demonstrates the preferability of a model of gender relations, based on non-European traditions, that allows for "overlapping spheres" of influence, which promotes community interaction, as opposed to a European "separate spheres" model, which inhibits it.

Although, as Sandra Shannon has pointed out, Wilson writes male-centered plays which rarely include more than one adult woman, his female characters have attracted a great deal of attention. They collectively show, Shannon argues, his "coming to grips with the depth and diversity of African American womanhood." From the independent Ma Rainey to the enigmatic and self-mutilated Risa, Wilson's women are all, in one way or another, represented as

nurturers. What differentiates them is how they interpret the concept of nurturing, how they invest their nurturing energies, and what sacrifices they have
to make in the process, for Wilson's world is always necessarily one of scarcity
and limitation. The improvisational possibilities are limited—as they are for
the blues or for the carvings on the ancestral piano—by a history of depriva-
tion, sorrow, and loss. These limitations are perhaps even greater for black
women than for black men, and Wilson's recognition of this has been noted by
Elam, who points out that Wilson's females "press against historical limitations,
recognizing and confronting the additional burdens placed upon them by gender." Nevertheless, Elam argues, these independent women who assert feminist
positions "either through their own volition or as the result of external social
pressures, ultimately conform to traditional gender roles and historical expectations." One has only to think of Troy Maxson's extraordinary baseball skills, of
course, to realize that Wilson's men also face unreasonable burdens and limitations, that they too are often forced to conform to traditional roles (or, like
Gabriel, be exiled to the asylum). Elam's essay makes us aware, however, of the
ways in which Wilson demonstrates that black men frequently are part of the
limitation felt by black women, although the reverse is much less often the case.

Both Kubitschek and Elam point implicitly to the politics of gender relations in Wilson's work, which participates in the general politics of representation. To invoke literal ghosts and angels, to make Troy Maxson's battle with
death and Boy Willie's battle with Sutter's ghost literal rather than figurative,
is, I argue, a political statement located in the historical specificity of African
American experience, because that experience emerged out of historical conditions in which the humanity of blacks was figurative. As the Dred Scott
and Fugitive Slave Law decisions confirmed, a black could be treated *as if*
he or she were human, so long as that behavior did not interfere with someone else's legal claim that the black was property, in which case the literal—
the letter of the law—abrogated all claims for black humanity.

The politics of representation has affected debates not only over *how* black
experience should be represented on the stage but also over *who* should represent it. Wilson's articulate demand for a black director for the film version
of *Fences*, reprinted here, raises provocative suggestions about ethnic difference, as it functions within the historically specific conditions of late-twentieth-century America. In teasing out the implications of Wilson's argument,
Michael Awkward wonders why, if black Americans are able to gain formal
mastery over the icons of Europe, white Americans should be incapable of a
similar mastery of black style. The implicit rigidity of boundaries—racial

and other—Awkward further argues, is exactly what *Fences* critiques, being a play "infused with the poetics of boundary breaking." Awkward, in other words, is both calling for a propaganda machine to educate white Americans ,to the ethos of black experience (in the same way that black Americans are educated to white experience) and praising Wilson's plays for being such machines—although questioning the logic of Wilson's demand for a black director. In a powerful indictment of the politics of tokenism, however, Awkward ultimately affirms the political validity of Wilson's demand.

When I discussed Awkward's essay with Wilson, he told me about a white theater student at Yale who was upset when Wilson announced that he would not accept a white director for the film; the student said that it placed an arbitrary limitation on what he could do. "Good for you," Wilson responded. "Now you know what it feels like." In the ironies and paradoxes that mark whatever it is that we might call the "American" experience—in so many ways tugged and tripped up on all sides of its multicolored lines and lineages by the race it keeps running away from—we could say that that young white drama student became just a bit more qualified to direct the film *Fences* by virtue of his discovering it was something he would *never* do, regardless of his talent. The price of understanding Troy Maxson, in other words, is realizing that one would never use that understanding in a way commensurate with one's greatest talents and dreams.

Realizing anything less would not provide the necessary understanding, because, as Wilson told Bill Moyers, "blacks know more about whites in white culture and white life than whites know about blacks. We *have* to know because our survival depends on it. White people's survival does not depend on knowing blacks." If adapting to white culture is the means for surviving, then the myriad sites of the black grafting onto the trunk of white America can be traced as a history of survival, but such a tracing will produce a very different picture of the tree, identified by a varied pattern of flourishing eruptions against a background trunk that is everywhere, but only in the negative. Drama may be the positive process of drawing that pattern against negation. In Wilson's hands, it may be the process, moreover, of reminding Euro-American drama of its sacred origins and communal charge; in our hands, it may be the process by which we come to understand how history is made out of its representations, and the process by which we can measure how well we've been represented historically, by us, to us, and for us.

The complexity of that process, through the brilliance of August Wilson, this collection of essays explores.

**ANNE FLECHE**

# The History Lesson: Authenticity and Anachronism in August Wilson's Plays

........................................................

At the end of August Wilson's 1990 play, *The Piano Lesson*, something spooky/funny happens: Boy Willie invokes the ghost of Sutter, his family's slave master, and the ghost, unseen, struggles with Boy Willie and throws him down the stairs. It's a surprising, daring moment, breathtakingly ironic. Boy Willie opens the play too, knocking loudly on the door, waking everyone up. Waking the Dead is Wilson's specialty, and you can feel his identification with Boy Willie: "Hey Berniece . . . if you and Maretha don't keep playing on that piano . . . ain't no telling . . . me and Sutter both liable to come back" (108). The exorcism and the promise to return are now Wilson's recognizable signature,[1] but in *Piano Lesson* there is also a strong personal touch, a felt hand of the teacher, something urgent in the familiar. Even the play's title underscores Wilson's general emphasis on learning and teaching. ("I ain't studying you," his characters keep saying. It's a put-down that suggests they're indifferent, they aren't looking for an argument—though, of course, they are.) The literal presence of a white slaveowner's ghost is a heavy reminder that Wilson's history lesson isn't all black, it's chiaroscuro. Sutter is like the undead, the vampire from some expressionist film, who has come to prey on the people who don't believe he's there.

By this fourth play in his series of decade-by-decade period plays of black life in twentieth-century Pittsburgh,[2] Wilson must have a good idea what the problems are. The realistic conventions he uses—the past tense of the action, the naturalistic dialogue, the conflict erupting at the end into some kind of catharsis—with his sense of humor, have drawn to him an audience of willing, admiring believers. And he interweaves slice-of-life realism with African styles, from blood rituals to blues, that keep things moving in a more playful, less linear rhythm than realism does. But—and I think the ending of *The Piano Lesson*, among other things, shows this—the ghosts of realism remain, in various forms, the faith in some recoverable truth, some stable referent, some singular wholeness or touchstone of identity. Behind and before Wilson's African American "history" plays, there is still the referent of a dominant (white) history; any new lesson will be about the lesson you have already learned without knowing it. This is a serious problem for Wilson's dramatic history, however: Can he write plays about an African American "history" that do not, somehow, get swallowed up in the dominant historical voice? Can he write plays about his own "history" without simultaneously betraying it?

Wilson's plays set up duels between dual forces representing the conflict between going over old ground and starting anew. Boy Willie's argument throughout *Piano Lesson* has been with his sister, Berniece, who wants the piano in the parlor to be preserved as a reminder of the family's past. He wants to sell it so that he can buy the land on which their family worked as slaves. In Boy Willie's struggle with the ghostly slave master, the piano, which Berniece is playing, becomes a medium, a conjuring instrument. By invoking the spirits of Boy Willie's own ancestors, it exorcises, at least temporarily, the ghost of the master. The piano has seemed to be the source of contention in the play, but in the end the struggle is between not brother and sister but their family and Sutter. It settles the question of what to do about the piano. This grappling with the white ghost of the slave-owning past is symbolized as *voice* in Wilson's plays—as song, instrument, music, rhythm, style. And this voice, while it wrestles with the duality of black and white, past and present (or future), doesn't solve or obliterate these oppositions; it drives a wedge between them, keeping them *separate*, making distinctions—as at the end of *Piano Lesson*, when Sutter's ghost disappears but is not absorbed or destroyed. As Boy Willie says, both he and Sutter might come back at any time. Only "playing" the piano will keep the duelists apart.

The dualities in Wilson's plays, then, point to the underlying historical problem. Modernist theories of drama recognized the difficulty of constructing "modern" plays that would have a "ritual" significance of the sort found in Greek drama. George Lukács, in his 1914 essay "The Sociology of Modern Drama," wrote that only when "rational" drama re-acquires the "quality of mystical religious emotion" can you have a "drama" with a "unifying foundation." Lukács questioned drama as a useful genre for rendering "the modern man" or "the whole man." "The dramatic and the characteristic aspect of modern man do not coincide."[3] More recently, Peter Szondi has lamented

Brecht's rejection of Aristotelian dramatic principles as "a renunciation of dramatic form."[4] Lukács pointed out very early then a problem that continues to trouble twentieth-century theorists of the drama, the problem of historical consciousness. The drama of a unifying sensibility can still be achieved, Lukács says, but with a difference. "This meta-rational, indissoluble sensibility could never again escape the mark of consciousness, of being *a posteriori*; never could it be once more the unifying enveloping atmosphere of all things."[5] For Lukács, this anachronistic "wholeness" is now inseparable from the drama, as Brecht's alienated, self-conscious rewriting of Aristotle has demonstrated. And Lukács was also perhaps the first to see the need for "theory" to fill the gap.

> Since the vital centre of character and the intersecting point of man and his destiny do not necessarily coincide, supplemental theory is brought in to contrive a dramatic linkage of the two. . . . For this reason men's convictions, their ideologies, are of the highest artistic importance.[6]

Whether or not the reader agrees with Lukács's concerns about dramatic form and the "drama of individualism," Lukács does point to the deep connections between theory and theater, ideology and drama. The problem isn't only, as Derrida has argued in his essays on Artaud, that drama is the very type of belatedness and repetition. Dramatic representation has its own ghostly history of ritual and communal identification to contend with, a "double" more mysteriously "present" than any actor onstage. And the history of modern drama is a perpetual rehearsal for the final exorcism of that *a posteriori* historical consciousness, which is its raison d'être: If drama could somehow enter the present, if it could change history instead of narrating it, what kind of a theater would we have? Brecht sought to provide change, and he made drama more narrative than ever. He *emphasized* the duality of character/actor instead of trying to erase it. In this way real historical people were put onstage, to narrate the lives of their characters. It's hard to imagine a theater without a historical consciousness, without a theatrical antecedent, without a memory.[7]

Still, there is something vaguely disturbing about the inevitable comparisons between Wilson and, say, Miller, O'Neill, or Williams: Are these critics being consciously ironic?[8] *Joe Turner's Come and Gone* is compared to Melville, or to *The Iceman Cometh*, and you hear—despite protestations to the contrary—an invocation of a heroic literary past that historicizes Wilson and makes him a reference point on a time line. He is being placed, anachronistically, in the nineteenth century or the first half of the twentieth (he was born in 1945), but aren't his own anachronistic plays, themselves, like ironic parables about anachronism? When Wilson says he is writing a cycle of plays revisiting recent U. S. history from an African American perspective, it sounds, at first, naive: What should this "history" look like? But when you read or watch Wilson's plays, especially *Ma Rainey's Black Bottom* and *Joe Turner's Come and Gone*, you see what's new about them. The plays don't quite buy in to the notion of history as raw data; they represent history as something they're in pursuit of. This "history" isn't—and other writers have pointed this out[9]—merely cumulative or linear. History is a moment Wilson's characters can never catch up with; they have to keep going back and starting again.

*Joe Turner's Come and Gone* works this idea into its title. It seems conscious of O'Neill, in fact, in the punning title, so similar to that of *The Iceman Cometh*, the period (1911—O'Neill's play is set in 1912), and its boarding-house setting (*Iceman* is set in a bar/flophouse). And *Iceman*'s explicit concern is precisely with the inability of its characters to inhabit the present. Stuck happily in an alcoholic time warp, they make attempts to sober up and leave the bar—to enter history—that result in the loss of their historical consciousness, and so of their differentiation as characters. They become robots. The intersection with historical time is viewed as a death/climax, a fall out of irony into immobility. The desire of O'Neill's characters to go out of the bar and to act, to become real, to be *authentic*, is killing. "Never have art and life been farther apart than at the moment they seem to be reconciled," de Man remarks in his essay "The Rhetoric of Temporality"; for "to know inauthenticity is not the same as to be authentic."[10] *Iceman* works out the idea that the merging of self and consciousness, of what de Man calls the "empirical" and the "ironic" selves, results in the end of consciousness. I have discussed elsewhere some of the implications of such an idea for the drama,[11] but my purpose here is to place O'Neill as a part of the history of Wilson's drama (*not* as a companion in "greatness") and O'Neill's reflections on drama and history as a mirror for Wilson's own concerns. In giving voice to an unrepresented "history," Wilson has to quote "history," to set it apart from "life" or "reality." "Art" and "history" are inseparable, mutually reinforcing. The art of history evokes a history of art.

The calculated historical displacement of Wilson's dramas, then, makes the "historical" or "historicizing" project ironic, as *Joe Turner*'s echoes of O'Neill suggest (and, at least in the larger picture of dramatic history, I think, develop). Slavery's persistence into an era ostensibly post-manumission is anachronism par excellence, but Wilson's plays show, if anything, that slavery isn't "historical" or time-bound, or even continuous. It's something that starts all over again wherever oppression is elided or forgotten. The historical consciousness, far from being a dramatic *problem* or limitation, as it was for Lukács, is what Wilson works with; it's probably why he moved from poetry toward the drama. As Lukács pointed out, the problem of history is bound up with the problem of a "modern" drama, closely related to its concerns with character and identity. Where else but in drama could Wilson play out the counterpoint between a dominant history and an improvisational one that seems fated to return to the dominant? Opera, perhaps: "Authentic" has its musical meaning, "to range upward from the keynote."

But there is danger in this historical ahistorical approach: Slavery can become abstracted. In making the "past" ironic, part of a *consciousness* of "the past" instead of something he's "mastered," Wilson could come close to *erasing* slave history. It's a fine line we walk between historical consciousness and historical blindness, a point made tellingly (perhaps autobiographically) by de Man:

> And since interpretation is nothing but the possibility of error, by claiming that a certain degree of blindness is part of the specificity of all literature we also reaffirm the absolute dependence of the interpretation on the text and of the text on the interpretation.[12]

Drama, no less than history, is bound to a past that it continually reasserts through its interpretations, a past whose interpretation re-forms both its matter and its technique. If we ever really exorcise the ghost of that past, history, like the drama, might be exorcised with it. The question of originality or authenticity gets to the heart of Wilson's dramatic project; no wonder it's a recurring theme in his plays.

In *Joe Turner's Come and Gone*, the boardinghouse is a way station for freed slaves trying to find a place to begin. Like *Ma Rainey* and *The Piano Lesson*, the play is composed of comings and goings, continual overlapping narratives, a string of expository scenes where everything has the quality of an announcement (one of the major characters is named Herald). The absence of any kind of suspense or surprise in the dialogue is striking, as if all the characters already know the answer to their questions, and that they would meet at this same spot—or another one like it—again. Herald Loomis hires the "People Finder," Rutherford Selig, the son and grandson of slave traders and catchers, to find his lost wife. But Bertha, the wife of Seth, who owns the boardinghouse, explains these miraculous returns as calculated departures:

> Folks plan on leaving plan by Selig's timing. They wait till he get ready to go, then they hitch a ride on his wagon. Then he charge folks a dollar to tell them where he took them. Now, that's the truth of Rutherford Selig. This old People Finding business is for the birds. He ain't never found nobody he ain't took away. (42)

Selig "finds" people as part of an elaborate shell game in which loss and gain are equally under his control. "You can call him a People Finder if you want to," Bertha says, but his authenticity derives from his authoritative power, not the other way around. (The word "authentic" itself derives from the Greek words for "master" and "accomplish" and is akin to a Sanskrit word meaning "he gains." As for Selig, his name means "blessed," as well as "deceased" or "late." It's the root word for "seligkeit," "salvation.") Herald Loomis does find his wife, Martha, via Selig, but this too is the opposite of a reunion: He was only looking for her to say good-bye. *Joe Turner's Come and Gone* is about misplaced persons, and when Martha shows up she's like a ghost (her new name is "Pentecost"), and it's too late for her and Loomis; he is already dead for her. ("So I killed you in my heart" [90].) This scene seems to *define* anachronism (literally, "to be late"), as does the rest of the play, with its African rituals and sacrifices and its wandering ex-slaves, "cut off from memory," as Wilson's play note puts it. "You got your time coming," Bertha tells Mattie Campbell, another boarder (75), but Mattie tells Loomis, "Seem like all I do is start over" (76). "He don't work nowhere," Seth says of Loomis (32). "Just go out and come back. Go out and come back." Like Selig's "finder" scam, the efforts of the characters to move and join seem like an expense with no net return. Herald Loomis "frees" himself in the end, says good-bye to Martha, gives her their child, and runs off—this time joined by Mattie. The children, Reuben and Zonia, imagine what it feels like to be dead ("Like being sleep only you don't know nothing and can't move no more" [81]), and when they say good-bye, there is another of Wilson's spooky moments when the boy says to Zonia (who is now his "girl"), "When I get grown, I come looking for you" (84). Even the meetings and joinings have the feeling of déjà vu, of an uncanny already lost foundness.

So far, interestingly, readers of Wilson tend not to question his project or its conception of history. The plays are, indeed, often analyzed by their relation to linear time: "The source of Herald Loomis' struggle lies in the past: he has to disown the burden of the past in order to gain strength for his new start in life. Troy Maxson's problem [in *Fences*] lies in the future, in his inevitable fate of being mortal." [13] Ching assumes a present tense for the two plays that makes it possible to point them backward or forward, to isolate (and to blame) past and future time. Rich's review of *The Piano Lesson* is especially complicated in its description of Wilson's history as that which is neither a "serial" nor a "textbook timeline" but (something just as universal) "a dynamic heritage haunting a people to the bone." [14] Wilson's "history," as Rich sees it, is only disruptive in its capacity to "pour out, with its full range of pain and triumph and mystery, at any time, anywhere, in any humble voice." That is, it's oral, a marginalized, a suppressed "history," but it's all there, waiting to pour. The difference between Rich's "dynamic heritage" and his "textbook timeline" has less to do with their notion of what history *means* than with its mode of transmission. "Oral" history may be different in kind from "textbook" history—but Rich doesn't go into that. His sense of the uniqueness of Wilson's history is a difficult act to sustain. In interviews, Wilson himself doesn't give up his facts. He tends to deflect allegorical readings and to concentrate on the literal. He doesn't ratify his plays. [15]

Yet isn't the complicated interweaving of art with history Wilson's main concern? How could he not be sensitive to the ways in which the art of history represents its own interests? If his elusive answers to the interviewers are his way of avoiding the historical typing that goes on around him, they also have the effect of distancing him from the plays, so that, in an eerie way, their "story" seems objective after all. His art seems thus to escape (or to transcend) consciousness and to join the timelessness of "art" that some of his admirers are trying to push him into. Wilson is in danger of becoming authenticated as Great Literature. And that's a trap, as his first successful play shows he knows.

In *Ma Rainey's Black Bottom*, the first-written play in the series, Wilson takes on directly the importance of improvisation and the problem of authority and authenticity. The play is set in a recording studio where Ma Rainey and her band arrive, rehearse, and record some songs for a pair of white men (one of whom is Ma's manager). It suggests, in the course of things, that spontaneity and improvisation give over their authority once they have been recorded; that authenticity and instinct, once captured, are irrevocably lost; and that the authentic voice is a thing of the present, an extension of the self, not the expression of a recoverable history. So it isn't surprising, after all, to have a play written about a famous singer in which she appears, and sings, as herself. As Ma Rainey says, the blues didn't originate with her, "The blues always been there" (83). Her singing isn't something already formed but something formed in the *act*—"You sing 'cause that's a way of understanding life" (82). Ma doesn't seem to care too much about the recording session, and delays things, including the signing of the release forms, to get her nephew paid, her car fixed, her Coke. But once she signs the release forms she has no more authority here, and she knows it. "They don't care nothing about me. All they want is my voice. . . . As soon as they get my voice down on them recording machines, then it's just like if I'd be some whore and they roll over and put their pants on. Ain't got no use for me then" (79).

The suggestive connections between power and sex are clear, as they are in the title of *Joe Turner's Come and Gone*, and more explicitly oppressive; but Ma Rainey has a philosophical attitude: These men respect money, they tolerate her because she makes them money, it's nothing personal. When she walks in, there is an amusing moment. Ma tells her manager, Irvin, to explain to a policeman who she is, and when Irvin (who seems to have trouble remembering the performers' names) says, "Ma Rainey," she blows up: "Madame Rainey! Get it straight!" (49). Her name isn't so much a name as a form of address (and there's a pun on her lesbianism, too). When she tells Irvin off later, and describes her singing as an instinct he knows nothing about, she speaks of herself in the third person: "What you all say don't count with me. You understand? Ma listens to her heart. Ma listens to the voice inside her. That's what counts with Ma" (63).

There is never any question here of an "authentic" Ma Rainey—we know we're getting a rehearsal, and a recording, and when Ma finally sings "Ma Rainey's Black Bottom," near the end of the play, the version we get to hear is not the one that gets recorded. The song itself is a funny, sexy tease in which the climax occurs during the instrumental interlude.

> They say your black bottom is really good
> Come on and show me your black bottom
> I want to learn that dance.
>
> .     .     .     .     .     .     .
>
> (Instrumental break)
> I done showed you all my black bottom
> You ought to learn that dance. (86)

Anyone who admires Wilson's plays for their "authenticity" ought to learn that dance too. It's not possible to capture an authentic voice and have it too, and Wilson seems to know this—he keeps coming back to the keynote. When Ma Rainey signs those forms, giving up the rights to her voice, and gets paid, along with her musicians, and we see how little they get, it's shocking. In the play note, Wilson refers to betrayal and being cheated. ("Somewhere the moon has fallen through a window and broken into thirty pieces of silver" [xv]—Judas's price, which is also a reminder of Joseph's sale into slavery by his brothers.) This image is strongly associated with Levee, the trumpeter who works on instinct and kills Toledo, the piano-playing intellectual and historian. Toledo articulates a "history" in which the African betrays himself by imitating the master: "We done sold ourselves to the white man in order to be like him. . . . We's imitation white men" (94). He keeps arguing for a kind of historical fatalism, and he is murdered over a shoe, because he can't see where Levee's thwarted—and improvisational—talent is taking things. Just before he kills Toledo, Levee throws away the money he has been paid for songs written but not recorded. And he can't bear Toledo's insinuation, that he himself has already *been sold*. But it is clear that Ma has been sold short too, just as her speech about whoring says. Wilson never suggests that these characters have done anything to deserve what's happening to them. *Ma Rainey* doesn't hold out much hope for black entrepreneurship. The play's last line, when Cutler tells Slow Drag to "get Mr. Irvin down here," however you read it, is angry, and chilling. The (white) man in the control booth opened the play, and the (white) manager is going to tidy things up. Just before the blackout, Levee's trumpet is heard, "blowing pain and warning" (111). It's a warning about many things, and I think it's a different warning for black and white audiences. Levee's trumpet brings anachronism and authenticity together, in a wail that is (anachronistically) outside the play, "struggling for the highest possibilities," yes, but as Wilson notes in the same breath, "muted." African American history for Wilson is taking place in an unseen present, and what his anachronistic plays show is that it is already accompanied by the shadow-presence of a dominant "history." There is no original or authentic or solo voice to be celebrated; history, like the blues, "always been there." Toledo's historical analysis does have a point: "Now, what's the colored man gonna do with himself? That's what we waiting to find out. But first we gotta know we the leftovers. Now, who knows that? . . . But we don't know that we been took and made history out of"

(57–58). Theoretically, Toledo holds out the possibility of original action based on the denial of the past. For him African Americans are simply outside history, the "leftovers." But he very interestingly cancels out the optimistic/fatalistic humanism in this historical view with the notion that history has already included black history; it hasn't excluded it at all: "We been took and made history out of." A dominant history plays with authority underneath any African improvisation. In *Joe Turner* the song invokes this dominantly; in *Ma Rainey* it's the voice recorded, trapped, and we watch this happening. In *The Piano Lesson* it comes back, like a refrain, or an angel to be wrestled with, his master's voice that *gives* authenticity even to this other history. This song has its tonic, no matter how well or how long it improvises. Wilson ironizes history, avoiding any attempt at a present or summing-up, and he knows, I think, that his anachronism doesn't provide a solution to the problem he starts with, the problem of his "history" as a conscious *a posteriori*, a track that's running two trains all the way down the line.

...................

## NOTES

I am grateful to Laura Tanner, James Krasner, and Celeste Goodridge for their helpful readings of this essay.

1. This is particularly noticeable in the later-written works, in fact, such as *Joe Turner's Come and Gone* (1988; produced 1986) and *Two Trains Running* (1991; produced 1990), as well as *The Piano Lesson* (1990; produced 1987).

2. "August Wilson has vowed to write one play about each decade of black American life in this century" (Rich, Review of *The Piano Lesson*, p. 25). Cf. Wilson: "What you end up with is a kind of review, or re-examination, of history" (Powers, "Interview," p. 52).

3. Lukács, "Sociology," pp. 435–36.

4. Szondi, *Theory*, p. 70.

5. Lukács, "Sociology," p. 436.

6. Ibid., pp. 436–37.

7. Brecht saw drama's ideological power in its constant restaging of its own "history": familiar patterns replicated by the machine of the "apparatus." "Society absorbs via the apparatus whatever it needs in order to reproduce itself. . . . Art is merchandise, only to be manufactured by the means of production (apparati). An opera can only be written for the opera" (Brecht, pp. 34–35). And Lukács's and Szondi's assumptions about drama's suitability for the "modern" age (and vice versa) show how wedded *they* are to a *tradition* of dramatic representation.

8. For example, Frank Rich, of the *New York Times*, compares *Ma Rainey* to O'Neill (specifically *Iceman*), Hansberry, and Miller; *Fences* to Miller (and the set designer to Joe Mielziner, who designed the set for *Death of a Salesman*); and *Joe Turner* to O'Neill (again *Iceman*) and Melville. Shannon also compares *Ma Rainey* to *Iceman*. The tradition is never referred to, as far as I can see, with irony.

9. Rich, Review of *The Piano Lesson*, p. 25; Ching, "Wrestling," p. 70.

10. de Man, *Blindness and Insight*, pp. 218, 214.

11. In my book manuscript, "Mimetic Disillusion: Eugene O'Neill, Tennessee Williams, and U.S. Dramatic Realism," chapter 3, I argue that *The Iceman Cometh* opposes realistic time (implicit in the play's rhetoric of capitalism and revolution) with the ironic double of a self that can exist only in language and that Hickey demonstrates to the other characters the impossibility of fusing "tomorrow" with "today" in the moment of a historical gesture. Such an anti-Aristotelian view of "character," I suggest, might have particular resonance with American audiences in the era just before World War II.

12. de Man, *Blindness and Insight*, p. 141.

13. Ching, "Wrestling," p. 71.

14. Rich, Review of *The Piano Lesson*, p. 25.

15. "The importance of history to me," Wilson says in a 1984 interview, "is simply to find out who you are and where you've been" (Powers, "Interview," p. 52). Selig he explains this way: "The fact that his father was a 'People Finder' who worked for the plantation bosses and caught runaway slaves has no bearing on Selig's character. That was his job. That was something he did and got paid for" (ibid., p. 53). When the interviewer—on this occasion, Kim Powers—implies that a play written in the *present* might complicate Wilson's project, Wilson answers with a notion of history as something already historicized, something with a past; he doesn't suggest how *he* historicizes: "A play set in 1984 would still have to contain historical elements. . . . The play I write about the '60's will be about what happened prior to the '60's, its historical antecedents" (ibid., pp. 52–53).

..................

## WORKS CITED

Brecht, Bertolt. *Brecht on Theatre*. Translated by John Willett. New York: Hill and Wang, 1964.

Ching, Mei-Ling, "Wrestling against History." *Theater* 19, no. 3 (1988): 70–71.

de Man, Paul. *Blindness and Insight: Essays in the Rhetoric of Contemporary Criticism*. 2d ed., Rev. Minneapolis: University of Minnesota Press, 1983.

Derrida, Jacques. *Writing and Difference.* Translated by Alan Bass. Chicago: University of Chicago Press, 1978.

Lukács, George. "The Sociology of Modern Drama." Translated by Lee Baxandall. In *The Theory of the Modern Stage: An Introduction to Modern Theatre and Drama*, edited by Eric Bentley, pp. 425–50. New York: Penguin, 1968. Reprint 1983.

Powers, Kim. "An Interview with August Wilson." *Theater* 16, no. 1 (1984): 50–55.

Rich, Frank. Review of *Fences. New York Times*, 7 May 1985, sec. C, p. 7, col 1.

———. Review of *Joe Turner's Come and Gone. New York Times*, 6 May 1986, sec. C, p. 17, col. 2.

———. Review of *Ma Rainey's Black Bottom. New York Times*, 11 April 1984, sec. C, p. 19, col. 1.

———. Review of *The Piano Lesson. New York Times*, 10 December 1987, sec. C, p. 25, col. 4.

Shannon, Sandra G. "The Long Wait: August Wilson's *Ma Rainey's Black Bottom*," *Black American Literature Forum* 25, no. 1 (1991): 135–46.

Szondi, Peter. *Theory of the Modern Drama.* Edited and translated by Michael Hays. Minneapolis: University of Minnesota Press, 1987.

Wilson, August. *Joe Turner's Come and Gone.* New York: New American Library, Plume, 1988.

———. *Ma Rainey's Black Bottom.* New York: New American Library, Plume, 1985.

———. *The Piano Lesson.* New York: New American Library, Plume, 1990.

———. *Two Trains Running. Theater* 22, no. 1 (1991): 40–72.

CRAIG WERNER

# August Wilson's Burden: The Function of Neoclassical Jazz

....................................................

## JAZZ CODA: IN THE TRADITION

*The end is in the beginning and lies far ahead.*
—*Ralph Ellison*, Invisible Man

*For here there are warriors and saints. Here there is hope refreshing itself, quickening into life. Here there is a drumbeat fueled by the blood of Africa. And through it all there are the lessons, the wounds of history. There are always and only two trains running. There is life and there is death. Each of us ride them both. To live life with dignity, to celebrate and accept responsibility for your presence in the world is all that can be asked of anyone.*
—*August Wilson*, Two Trains Running

*Are you sure, sweetheart, that you want to be well?*
—*Toni Cade Bambara*, The Salt Eaters

In *Two Trains Running*, August Wilson offers a healing vision, a jazz response to the call of black men and women bearing their burdens, singing their blues: Sterling with his gangsta rap; Risa with her self-scarred legs.

Remembering the sources: Aunt Ester, whose living spirit carries three centuries of jazz voices down the wind, who asks only that we throw our money in the river, let the devil be. That we *use* our past to envision our future.

The "we" is as limited and limiting as we believe.

...................

## AUGUST WILSON AND BLACK MUSIC

Playing the changes in a jazz voice grounded in gospel and the blues, Wilson revoices both African American and Euro-American expressive traditions in a heroic attempt to heal the wounds that devastate individuals and communities as we near the end of the twentieth century. Highly aware of the tension between received notions of "universality" and the specific circumstances of African American communities, Wilson crafts a vision closely related to the "neoclassical" jazz of Wynton Marsalis. As Paul Carter Harrison has demonstrated, Wilson (like Marsalis) expresses a profound appreciation and knowledge of black music as serious art. Both Wilson and Marsalis actively seek a broad audience for their work and emphasize the need for a mastery of their craft based on serious study and discipline. Wilson differs from Marsalis, however, in his awareness that the tradition, if it is to remain *functional*, must remain aware of, and responsive to, the changing circumstances of communities with little knowledge of, or interest in, "classical" aesthetics.

In her meditation on Thelonious Monk as a source of literary aesthetics, Wanda Coleman describes the "chilling" situation of African American writers at the end of the 1980s: "To escape economic slavery the Black artist is forced to turn his/her back on Black heritage and adapt to White tastes/ sensibilities in order to make money (in this case, money is synonymous with freedom but not power)."[1] Coleman insists that conscious use of the jazz tradition provides the best foundation for a meaningful response to the crisis of African American communal memory during the Reagan/Bush era: "By relegating Jazz (and the Jazz principle) to obscurity, the people who give birth to it are kept in a position of economic and cultural inferiority. And the *quality* of one's work has *nuthin'* to do with it." Coleman's conclusion that "to recognize is to empower"[2] echoes bell hooks's observations concerning the centrality of cultural expression to communal health: "There was in the traditional southern racially segregated black community a concern with racial uplift that continually promoted recognition of the need for artistic expressiveness and cultural production."[3] Alain Locke and many other intellectuals of the Harlem Renaissance emphasized the importance of art as a means of changing white attitudes. Near the end of "The New Negro," Locke wrote: "The especially cultural recognition they [the artists and writers of the Harlem Renaissance] win should in turn prove the key to that revaluation of the Negro which must precede or accompany any considerable further betterment of race relationships."[4] Having experienced the failure of masterworks such as *Invisible Man* and *Song of Solomon* to spark real change in the conditions of oppression in poor black communities, hooks emphasizes African aesthetic traditions as a source of political and psychological resistance within black communities: "Art was seen as intrinsically serving a political function. Whatever African Americans created in music, dance, poetry, painting, etc., it was regarded as testimony, bearing witness, challenging racist thinking which suggested that black folks were not fully human, were uncivilized, and that the measure of this was our collective failure to create 'great art.'"[5]

As Coleman suggests, both approaches to the function of art are problematic. On the one hand, it has become clear that individual black artists and works can attain financial and critical acceptance without generating any benefits for poor black communities. On the other hand, writers and, to a lesser extent, musicians who direct their work primarily to black audiences often have difficulty supporting themselves economically, which in turn limits their ability to support social change. Given this situation, one of the primary challenges facing highly "successful" writers such as Toni Morrison, Alice Walker, and Wilson is developing ways of using their positions of relative "freedom" (though not, as Coleman notes, of power) to locate new possibilities for themselves and for the communities that they are forced, without concern for their individual preference, to "represent."

The dilemma of successful black artists was complicated by forces at work within the African American community during the 1970s and 1980s. Even as writers (Morrison, Walker), critics (Gates, Houston Baker), and musicians (Prince, Michael Jackson) attained unprecedented levels of popular success, conditions in many African American communities deteriorated seriously. Generated by the post–Civil Rights Movement ability of black individuals to move out of the ghetto[6] and by the polarization of wealth resulting from Reagan-era taxation policies,[7] this deterioration contributed to a growing physical separation between middle-class and poor black communities. This division in turn intensified the cultural fragmentation of Afro-America. Whereas artists such as Duke Ellington and Ralph Ellison, both of whom enjoyed considerable mainstream recognition, could assume a shared base of cultural references with the larger black community—particularly those relating to the black church and the blues—contemporary black artists confront a more difficult situation.

The implications of this situation can be seen in the juxtaposition of two highly visible forms of 1980s black cultural expression: the novels of Toni Morrison, Alice Walker, Gloria Naylor, and Terry McMillan; and rap music, particularly that created by young black men from poor urban communities. Although their differences are at least as striking as their similarities, black women's novels exemplify the potential of direct engagement with the cultural mainstream. Novels exploring African American history, the specific circumstances of black women, and, increasingly, the problems of black professionals in middle-class America have attracted favorable attention within academia and the publishing industry. Despite their enthusiastic reception by educated blacks and whites, however, these novelists have little following among younger blacks from poor economic backgrounds, especially young black men who have been denied even basic reading skills in an underfunded and indifferent school system.[8] Media stereotypes to the contrary, the lack of literacy does not indicate that young blacks have acquiesced in their dehumanization. Rather, they have developed innovative cultural forms, most notably rap, to express their rage against both the oppressive white system and what many perceive as the indifference of the black middle class; rappers such as N.W.A., Ice Cube, and Naughty by Nature ridicule what they see as irrelevant standards of "culture" and "decency." Perhaps the most disturbing signs of the fragmentation of African American culture are the dehumanizing images of women in many raps. Reflecting the impact of economic force, the fundamental division seems to follow class, rather than gender, lines, as evidenced by the relatively strong awareness of the specific situations of black women in the novels of John Edgar Wideman and Leon Forrest. The fact that the rappers show no awareness of, rather than conscious contempt for, the work of the novelists emphasizes the historically unprecedented fragmentation of the black audience. The high level of white interest in and economic support for *both* the novelists and the rappers simply places a final ironic twist on the situation confronting artists such as Wilson who are determined to heal the wounds of the African American community.

....................

## FUNCTIONALITY AND THE JAZZ IMPULSE

Adding her voice to a critical tradition extending at least as far back as W. E. B. Du Bois's *The Souls of Black Folk*, Coleman suggests that overcoming the divisions within black America requires a high level of awareness of the connections between literary and oral traditions: "There was no effective way to discuss Black language without interjecting Black music."[9] As Paul Carter Harrison demonstrates, just such a sense of language-as-music and music-as-language is perhaps the most salient characteristic of "August Wilson's Blues Poetics." More specifically, Harrison views Wilson's drama as a variation on the "modal" jazz pioneered by Miles Davis during the 1950s: "As an expressive strategy in blues and jazz improvisations, the modal distribution of related and nonrelated ideas often revivifies the familiar story with new illumination."[10]

Before Harrison's formulation can be usefully applied to Wilson's "healing song," it will be helpful to examine several issues regarding the meaning of jazz in African American culture. Despite significant differences in interpretive perspective, theorists such as hooks, Ellison, Amiri Baraka, Ben Sidran, and Robert Farris Thompson agree that throughout the African diaspora, cultural production is viewed in terms of *functionality*; rather than serving as a respite from or an alternative to everyday reality, art is intricately involved with the daily lives of individuals and communities. Thompson's list of aesthetic practices linking diaspora communities culminates in "*songs and dances of social allusion* (music which, however danceable and 'swinging,' remorselessly contrasts social imperfections against implied criteria for perfect living)."[11] On occasion, the social function may be obvious, as in Ben Sidran's description of the revolutionary implications of black music:

Each man developed his own "cry" and his own "personal sound." The development of "cries" was thus more than a stylization; it became the basis on which a group of individuals could join together, commit a social act, and remain individuals throughout, and this in the face of overt suppression. It has been suggested that the social act of music was at all times more than it seemed within the black culture. Further, to the extent the black man was involved with black music, he was involved with the black revolution. Black music was itself revolutionary, if only because it maintained a non-Western orientation in the realms of perception and communication.[12]

Although art may occasionally transmit a specifically political "message," the underlying meanings of functionality are more subtle and elusive. Reflecting the importance of the ancestors in West African societies, black music encodes memories of historical events and personal experiences omitted from or distorted by the written documentation of European American cultural memory. As Coleman notes, "If one defines art as memory, then Black music (or music infused with/infected by blackness) gives me *my* memory."[13] Transmitting such memory to the present, music provides organizing rhythms for daily life. Whether "political"—as in the use of gospel music to provide organization, inspiration, and courage during the Civil Rights Movement—or "personal"—as in the use of music in courtship—black music helps maintain a sense of African difference within a hostile cultural context.

It should be emphasized that, especially within the jazz tradition, this assertion of difference does not entail a repudiation of European influences or traditions. Discussing the impact of African traditions on the Caribbean in terms applicable (to different degrees) to other New World multicultures, Antonio Benitez-Rojo highlights the coexistence—*not* the synthesis—of multiple decentered energies, including those European energies grounded in relatively rigid binary concepts. As hooks observes, jazz plays a central role in developing concepts of freedom appropriate to these energies. Revolutionary jazz, writes hooks, resists any attempt to reduce the complexity of African American experience: "Avant-garde jazz musicians, grappling with artistic expressivity that demanded experimentation, resisted restrictive mandates about their work, whether they were imposed by a white public saying their work was not really music or a black public which wanted to see more overt links between that work and political struggle."[14] Developing primarily in urban settings where blacks were forced into proximity with various cultural traditions, jazz plays a crucial role in opening the African American tradition to new energies, including those associated with the European American "masters." Since the beginning of the twentieth century, jazz has drawn on the European American orchestral tradition and mainstream American popular music, as well as those forms reflecting the worldviews of poor black communities: the harsh realism of the blues and the visionary community of gospel music.

Providing a useful set of terms for discussing Wilson's negotiation of these issues, Ellison defines the jazz impulse as a way of defining/creating the self in relationship to community and tradition. Applicable to any form of cultural expression, the jazz impulse encourages the entry of new ideas, new *vision*, into the tradition. Ellison writes:

> True jazz is an art of individual assertion within and against the group. Each true jazz moment (as distinct from the uninspired commercial performance) springs from a contest in which each artist challenges all the rest; each solo flight, or improvisation, represents (like the successive canvases of a painter) a definition of his identity: as individual, as member of the collectivity and as a link in the chain of tradition.[15]

Or, as Coleman revoices Ellison's definition: "THE KEY/history + vision + craft = transcendence."[16]

As Coleman's emphasis on "history" intimates, almost all successful jazz is grounded in what Ellison calls the "blues impulse." Before one can hope to create a meaningful new vision of individual or communal identity, the artist must acknowledge the full complexity of his/her experience. In his classic essay on Richard Wright, Ellison defines the blues impulse as "an impulse to keep the painful details and episodes of a brutal experience alive in one's aching consciousness, to finger its jagged grain, and to transcend it, not by the consolation of philosophy but by squeezing from it a near-tragic, near-comic lyricism."[17] Although the blues impulse is based on intensely individual feelings, these feelings can be traced in part to the brutal racist context experienced in some form by almost all blacks. Substituting the less philosophical term "affirmation" for Ellison's idea of "transcendence," Albert Murray emphasizes that, especially when his/her call elicits a response from a community that confirms a shared experience, the blues artist becomes "an agent of affirmation and continuity in the face of adversity."[18] Both the individual expression and the affirmative, and self-affirming, response of the community are crucial to the blues dynamic. Seen in relation to the blues impulse, the jazz impulse provides a way of exploring implications, of realizing the relational possibilities of the self, and of expanding consciousness (of self and community) through a process of continual improvisation.

What has been less clearly recognized in discussions of African American aesthetics is the way in which both the blues and the jazz impulses are grounded in the "gospel impulse,"[19] which centers on what Coleman's formulation refers to as "vision." The foundations of African American cultural expression lie in the call and response forms of the sacred tradition; in the twentieth century, the gospel church provides the institutional setting for the communal affirmation of individual experience. As Amiri Baraka (Leroi Jones) notes in *Blues People*, both the call and response structure of the secular work songs and the a-a-b form of the classic blues can be traced to sacred forms which encode West African understandings of the nature of self, community, and spiritual energy. If the blues impulse can be described as a three-stage secular process—brutal experience, lyrical expression, affirmation—then the gospel impulse can be described in parallel terms derived from the sacred vocabularies of the African American church—the burden, bearing witness, and the vision of (universal) salvation. Bearing witness to his/her experience of the "burden," the gospel artist—possessed by a "Spirit" that transcends human categorization—communicates a vision affirming the possibility of salvation for any person willing to engage in the process. Whether phrased as "burden" or "brutal experience," as "near-tragic, near-comic lyricism" or as "bearing witness," as existential "affirmation" or spiritual "vision," the blues/gospel process provides a foundation for the jazz artist's exploration of new possibilities for self and community. To summarize, awareness of the blues and gospel roots highlights two central functions of the jazz impulse: *clarifying (blues) realities* and *envisioning (gospel) possibilities*. The most successful jazz performances, then, articulate these issues in response to the specific historical context of the ever-changing moment.

Before the widespread integration of the black middle class into mainstream institutions, numerous jazz-oriented African American artists—Miles Davis, Duke Ellington, Ralph Ellison, Billie Holiday, Gwendolyn Brooks—were able to forge styles that commanded respect in both affluent European American and relatively disadvantaged African American settings. Their immaculate clothes, polished speech, proper manners, and understanding of European American traditions were not intended, nor understood, as a betrayal of any element of the broader black community. The problem today facing Wilson, Marsalis, and Morrison, among others, derives from the fragmented context that, to a disturbing degree, forecloses the cultural space occupied by Ellington, Ellison, and Davis. Change, of course, is nothing new for jazz artists. Derived from the Yoruba concept of *itutu* or "the correct way you represent yourself to a human being"[20] and parallel, as Murray notes, to Ernest Hemingway's "grace under pressure,"[21] the idea of "cool" exemplified by Miles Davis places a central value on the ability to negotiate unpredictable, and uncontrollable, changes in social, economic, and political conditions.

Nevertheless, the specific conditions of the 1980s and 1990s do present unique challenges for artists who desire to reach a broad audience, within and beyond the black community. As noted above, black musicians and writers today must confront a situation in which middle-class/academic/literary (and feminist-informed) and poor/street/oral (and predominantly male) perspectives *appear* to be in open conflict with one another. Unlike Ellington and Brooks, who could address a privileged (and at that time almost exclusively white) audience for purposes of economic reward and "serious" critical attention without surrendering their connection with the larger black community (including those "organic intellectuals" who provide "serious" responses outside the network of formal cultural institutions), Wilson and Marsalis find themselves in a context where success with one group too often entails rejection by the other. With crucial differences in understanding and application, both have responded to the situation by creating what might be called a "neoclassical" voicing of the jazz impulse.

## WYNTON MARSALIS AND NEOCLASSICISM

In part because of his award-winning recordings of trumpet concertos by Haydn, Mozart, and other European composers, Marsalis has been seen by both supporters and detractors as the leading figure in a "neoclassical" movement determined to "save" jazz from the perceived chaos of the free jazz movement of the 1960s and 1970s. Jazz drummer and critic Stanley Crouch articulates the values and intentions of the neoclassical movement in his provocative liner notes to Marsalis's jazz albums, especially *Black Codes from the Underground* (1985), *The Majesty of the Blues* (1989), the three volumes of *Soul Gestures in the South* (1991), and *Blue Interlude* (1992). Emphasizing the balance between composition and improvisation as a means of exploring the relationship between individual and community within the tradition, Crouch offers Marsalis as an exemplar of jazz as high art:

> Wynton Marsalis continues to make even more explicit those human vistas of jazz that exemplify its ongoing revitalization. That revitalization calls upon the best of the art and reinterprets it with affection and adventure of the sort that corresponds to the serious listener's mood for a classic. Marsalis is quite successfully working at a vision in which there is an organic relationship between the power of the jazz pen and the members of his group.[22]

Insisting on conscious understanding of tradition—whether European or African in origin—Crouch quotes Marsalis's belief that "in order to understand the meaning of an art form, you have to find out what the great-est artists have in common."[23] Perhaps the single most important attribute of the greatest African American artists for Marsalis is their repudiation of any contemporary manifestation of the "black codes" that deprived "chattels of anything other than what was necessary to maintain their positions as talking work animals."[24] Assuming a high humanist stance, Marsalis views his as an alternative to both racism and the vulgarization of contemporary culture:

> Black codes mean a lot of things. Anything that reduces potential, that pushes your taste down to an obvious, animal level. Anything that makes you think less significance is *more* enjoyable. Anything that keeps you on the surface. The way they depict women in rock videos—black codes. People gobbling up junk food when they can afford something better—black codes. The argument that illiteracy is valid in a technological world—black codes. People who equate ignorance with soulfulness—defi-nitely black codes. The overall quality of every true artist's work is a rebel-lion against black codes.[25]

Marsalis's neoclassicism should not be confused with an uncritical accep-tance of European American standards. Crouch emphasizes the importance of both blues-based African American and classical European traditions to Marsalis's developing conception of great art:

> Marsalis arrived in jazz with both a technical fluidity that had little prece-dent and an acknowledged authority in European concert music that no jazz musician before him had ever possessed. At the same time the trum-peter was critical of his own jazz work and of the obstacles to learning how to play jazz. Coming from New Orleans, he was immersed in the blues tra-dition, but having grown up during the fusion era, he had no awareness of the importance of the blues to jazz. Though well schooled in harmony, he knew little about how to apply it during an improvisation, and worried over his ability to swing on the level of the art's masters, living or dead. But he was a man ready to endure the isolation and the feeling of impotence that are inevitable when one chooses to learn formidable amounts of information.[26]

Drawing on his classical training to analyze the blues as a response to "the central chords of Western harmony," Marsalis shares Wanda Coleman's inter-est in Thelonious Monk as an artistic ancestor who both developed a nu-anced approach to composition and recognized that "the European approach was not sufficient for what he wanted to do."[27] In his treatment of the jazz classics—exemplified by his brilliantly humorous rendition of Monk's "Think of One"—Marsalis makes it clear that his neoclassicism cannot be reduced to a preference for highbrow, European, or conventional "classical" music. Moreover, as Francis Davis argues, Marsalis's classical albums have effectively exhausted the repertoire of interesting trumpet concertos.[28]

Nor is Marsalis unaware of the links between the "classical jazzmen" and the African American community. Recorded on Marsalis's *The Majesty of the Blues*, Crouch's jazz sermon "Premature Autopsies" invokes Ellington as Marsalis's stylistic ancestor, a profoundly intellectual figure "willing to face the majesty of their heritage and endure the slow, painful development of serious study." Celebrating the courage which allowed Ellington to overcome "the pain and the agony and the self-doubt and the disappointment" inherent in his attempt to articulate the "majesty he heard coming from the musicians of all hues and from all levels of training," Crouch concludes with a reminder that the roots of a functional African American art lie in the continuing relationship between artist and community: "This noble sound, this thing of majesty, this art, so battered but so ready for battle, it just might lift you high enough in the understanding of human life to let you know in no uncertain terms why that marvelous Washingtonian, Edward Kennedy Ellington, NEVER came off the road."[29]

Despite Crouch's eloquent promotion/defense of Marsalis, the broader critical reception of his work raises serious questions concerning Marsalis's adaptation of the Ellingtonian style. In a 1982 review, Greg Tate sounded what has become the leitmotif of attacks on the neoclassical movement: "Because jazz was once a music defined as much by brinkmanship—social and aesthetic—as by virtuosic refinement, the music's current hidebound swing toward bop and post-bop revivalism has to be seen as not only regenerative but reactionary."[30] Although Tate concludes the passage with the qualifier "but necessary," his use of the term "reactionary" implies that neoclassicism, at least indirectly, supports the neoconservative agenda of the Reagan/Bush administrations. Such criticism results in part from the willingness of his most ardent defenders to support neoconservative attacks on cultural pluralism. An extreme example of the neoconservative construction of Marsalis's neoclassicism—unfortunately echoed in numerous mass media celebrations of the movement—can be found in Ted Gioia's *The Imperfect Art: Reflections and Jazz and Modern Culture*. Trivializing Gunther Schuller's analytical concern with the "third stream" synthesis of jazz and classical traditions, Gioia dismisses critics who "take [Marsalis] to task for not progressing beyond existing jazz conventions."[31] Gioia concludes with a nostalgic invocation of a (largely mythical) common language destroyed by a pluralism he constructs as hostile to civilized standards of excellence and moral values:

> The abundance of schools and styles has led to the all but complete disappearance of a common language, a common set of standards, a shared notion of good and bad. In the absence of these things, the continued health of the art form lies in doubt. The benefits of pluralism threaten to collapse into the uncertainties of relativism.[32]

Blaming fragmentation on aesthetic exploration (rather than a hostile political and economic environment), Gioia laments "the collapse of the jazz world into countless schools and tendencies, each unable to communicate with those outside its own small world."[33] Gioia bases much of his argument on an almost entirely inaccurate image of the experimental jazz tradition as an "avant-garde" that "delights in lengthy solo performances by instruments once thought to be incapable of sustaining interest without a group."[34] Such a formulation strongly suggests that Gioia has not actually listened to the leading experimentalists of the past two decades: David Murray, Muhal Richard Abrams, John Carter, Anthony Davis, Anthony Braxton, or the Art Ensemble of Chicago, all of whom combine composition and improvisation. Casting the neoclassicist as a rebel conducting "his lonely pursuit for form and order," Gioia concludes with a celebration of "musical perfection—almost Platonic in nature"[35] that echoes the neoconservative attribution of artistic excellence solely to the Greco-Roman tradition. The irony of this attitude in jazz criticism should be obvious. As John Gennart and McDonald Smith Moore have demonstrated in different contexts, during the 1910s and 1920s the classical tradition, strongly associated with Victorian constructions of morality, was continually invoked in attacks *against* "classical jazz."

Inasmuch as criticism of Marsalis's neoclassicism focuses on the larger cultural debate, it is at least partially undeserved; Marsalis clearly has no wish to contribute to any form of neoconservatism that would adversely affect black communities. Nonetheless, his public statements at times seem to endorse neoconservative "cultural pathology" interpretation of inner city problems. Commenting on the 1992 Los Angeles riot, Marsalis sympathized with the underlying frustration: "I've been hustled by the police. You grow up in this society as a black, you get that." His subsequent analysis, however, reveals the limits of Marsalis's identification with, and understanding of, street perspectives: "But the greatest menace in the black community is not the police. It's all these young black men who beat up old ladies and kids. Whenever you elevate hoodlums to heroes, you've got trouble. When you look at that looting, by blacks *and* whites, that wasn't a protest. They wanted TV sets."[36] Presented without extensive contextual and historical qualification, such statements encourage neoconservative appropriation of Marsalis.

The language of the debate over neoconservatism recurs frequently in criticism of Marsalis's neoclassical approach. Francis Davis, for example, views neoclassicism as an attempt to impose "a rigid code of attitudes" on performers, showing "little tolerance for those who play by a looser set of rules."[37] Echoing Davis's suspicion that Wynton and his brother Branford "may be musical reactionaries who are fooling even themselves into believing they are radicals,"[38] Carlos Figueroa contrasts David Murray's traditionalism with Marsalis's neoclassicism:

> Murray goes about the business of being himself with a fervor and dedication truly worthy of the art form in which he has chosen to express his world view. Mention is made of this choice because it stands in stark contrast to the one made by many of his younger compatriots in the music who seem to be content with recapturing and recapitulating the sounds and stylings (both musical and sartorial) of their musical forebears.[39]

Similarly, Gary Giddins acknowledges Marsalis's "complete instrumental mastery, reverence for the complexities of jazz improvisation, and sartorial elegance on the bandstand" but concludes that "Marsalis hasn't found his own voice."[40] Both Giddins and Figueroa insist on individual style as fundamental to the visionary function of jazz. Figueroa writes: "To be sure, Murray's music is solidly in the tradition; his approach has been to blaze a fresh trail through the woods as opposed to trodding a path already delineated."[41]

Even as Martin Williams emphasizes the dialectic between innovation and consolidation in the jazz tradition, he observes that Marsalis's reverence for standards has rarely been a hallmark of leading African American jazz performers: "The most obviously outstanding young black players are (so far) doing nothing truly new. That has certainly never happened in jazz before: in the past, the kind of musical conservatism they represent has largely been the white man's burden."[42] Similarly, Ronald Radano emphasizes that while "for its innovators [neoclassicism] is an expression of the *Black Codes* that identify African American artistic greatness," the celebration of the movement in cover stories in *Time* and the *New York Times Magazine* threatens to repress the more visionary currents of jazz: "for its challengers in improvised, experimental music, it is often seen as a travesty of the flexibility that is said to characterize black music."[43]

Perhaps the most satisfactory response to such criticism focuses not on the jazz artist's role as visionary but on his/her relationship with the actual community/audience. Gary Giddins focuses on Marsalis's desire to broaden the audience for *both* neoclassical and experimental jazz: "Not unlike the popularizers of swing in the 1930s and soul in the 1950s, musicians such as Marsalis are needed to restore order, replenish melody, revitalize the beat, loot the tradition for whatever works, and *expand the audience*."[44] Caustically observing that "you know it's ability to play that classical shit which gives him so-called legitimacy" and signifying on "how slick a hustle these brothers have pulled in mainstreaming their models for middle-American consumption," Greg Tate nevertheless recognizes that the real measure of the neoclassicists' success is not the content of their work but their ability to make "sociocultural breakthroughs equal to the aesthetic ones of their mentors."[45] Responding to Marsalis as both potential inspiration and cautionary example, the remainder of this essay will place August Wilson's plays in the forefront of a jazz-inflected movement to envision the nature of such breakthroughs.

................

## WILSON, UNIVERSALISM, AND JAZZ NEOCLASSICISM

In literary criticism, the neoclassical discourse focuses largely on the concept of "universalism," the idea that certain themes, images, and/or techniques express fundamentally "human" concerns that transcend the limitations of any particular set of circumstances. The implications of this discourse, which consistently associates the "universals" with the specific experiences of white males of relatively privileged social standing, are by now a well-known story to scholars of African American and women's literature. Within this institutionally established discourse, only those black writers whose work can be presented in terms of the "universals"—Ellison is perhaps the most obvious example—receive "serious" (if extraordinarily narrow) attention and financial rewards. As early distrust of Ellison among the aggressively anti-universalist writers associated with the black arts movement demonstrates, such success can create difficulties for a jazz writer seeking to engage in a call and response with the community.

As Wilson's plays demonstrate, however, visionary jazz cannot simply accept or reject "universalism." In an interview with Bill Moyers, Wilson expresses values reminiscent of Marsalis's neoclassicism:

> I was writing about black America—the specifics of the play are about black America. But there is something larger at work. A painter, when asked to comment on his work, once said, "I try to explore in terms of the life I know best those things which are common to all culture." So while the specifics of the play are black, the commonalities of culture are larger realities in the play. You have father-son conflict, you have husband-wife conflict—all these things are universal.[46]

Avoiding the trap revealed in Marsalis's comments on the Los Angeles disturbance, however, Wilson emphasizes the presence of "universal" values in black communities where neoconservatives see only a pathological absence of culture. Emphasizing the centrality of the blues to his understanding of universal truths, Wilson describes his own struggle against racist notions of universality:

> There was a nobility to the lives of blacks in America which I didn't always see. At that time I was living in a rooming house in Pittsburgh. After I discovered the blues, I began to look at the people in the house a little differently than I had before. I began to see a value in their lives that I simply hadn't seen before. I discovered a beauty and a nobility in their struggle to survive. I began to understand the fact that the avenues for participation in society were closed to these people and that their ambitions had been thwarted, whatever they may have been. The mere fact that they were still able to make this music was a testament to the resiliency of their spirit.

When Moyers adds, "Which everyday life squashed," Wilson provides the necessary corrective: "Attempted to squash because the spirit was resilient and strong and still is."[47]

Wilson's concerns parallel those of George Kent, whose essays on Gwendolyn Brooks, Langston Hughes, and Ralph Ellison articulate a nuanced response to simplistic understandings of "universalism." Seeking what he calls a "legitimate universalism," Kent advances the idea of a "subjective correlative" as an alternative to the appropriation of T. S. Eliot's "objective correlative" by academically powerful and politically conservative New Critics. Focusing on Brooks's poetry, Kent rejects the idea of "universalism" as "a reach for some preexisting Western universal to be arrived at by reducing the tensions inherent in the black experience." Although such reduction might attract a white audience seeking an accessible, comforting, or perhaps simply comprehensible image of black experience, it inevitably reduces the ability of art to address the tensions dividing African American communities. Like Wilson, however, Kent emphasizes the presence of "universal" concerns *in black experience*:

> [This] universalism derives, instead, from complete projection of a situation or experience's *space* and *vibrations* (going down deep, not transcending). Even where a preexisting universal may be paraphrasable, the true roots of the poet's universalism are in her power of enforcing the illusion that the vibrations from the space her imagination has encircled are captured and focused with all the power and significance which the raw materials afforded.[48]

The core of August Wilson's success lies precisely in his nuanced treatment of "universal" themes in relation to the particular and changing conditions of black life.

As Wilson has frequently observed, the fullest expression of black life at any time can be found in the community's music:

> I listen to the music of the particular period that I'm working on. Inside the music are clues to what is happening with the people. I don't know that much about contemporary music, so if I were going to write a play set in 1980, I would go and listen to the music, particularly music that blacks are making, and find out what their ideas and attitudes are about the situation, and about the time in which they live.[49]

Wilson's preface to *Ma Rainey's Black Bottom* applies this approach to Chicago in 1927. Focusing on the Great Migration of blacks from the rural South to the urban North, Wilson emphasizes the play's concern with "their values, their attitudes, and particularly their music." Defining the music of the 1920s as "music that breathes and touches. That connects," Wilson locates "universal" virtues in the music's response to potentially cataclysmic change in the specific circumstances of black life: "The men and women who make this music have learned it from the narrow crooked streets of East St. Louis, or the streets of the city's South Side, and the Alabama or Mississippi roots have been strangled by the northern manners and customs of free men of definite and sincere worth." Wilson concludes with a reminder of the importance of functionality to the "men for whom this music often lies at the forefront of their conscience and concerns. Thus they are laid open to be consumed by it: its warmth and redress, its braggadocio and roughly poignant comments, its vision and prayer, which would instruct and allow them to reconnect, to reassemble and gird up for the next battle in which they would be both victim and the ten thousand slain."[50]

If the musical power of Wilson's work derives from this profound sense of African American music, its commercial success derives in large part from his equally sure knowledge of, and interest in, the concerns of "classical" American theater, particularly that of Eugene O'Neill. Wilson employs numerous themes and motifs familiar to theater audiences who are grounded in the post-O'Neill tradition, which includes Tennessee Williams, Sam Shepard, Lillian Hellman, Lanford Wilson, Beth Henley, and many others. Among these are the disruption of the surface of family life by repressed or buried secrets, the blurring of the line separating "psychological" and "physical" realities, and the use of transformation of everyday diction and syntax into a heightened vernacular poetry. Wilson's approach recalls Ellison's comparison of T. S. Eliot and Louis Armstrong. Emphasizing Eliot's and Armstrong's parallel interest in "the artful juxtapositioning of earlier styles," Ellison observes that the jazz tradition makes no distinction between the sources of those styles. Both Eliot's juxtaposition of ragtime and Shakespeare in "The Waste Land" and Coltrane's modal revoicing of "Chim Chim Cheree" can be viewed as antecedents of Wilson's combination of Robert Johnson and O'Neill, who himself drew on African American traditions. Perhaps the most important reason that Wilson has attracted relatively little harsh criticism of the sort directed against Marsalis is that he clearly understands the principle behind Ellison's caution that the Eliot-Armstrong analogy "is not a matter of giving the music fine airs—it doesn't need them—but of saying that whatever touches our highly conscious creators of culture" will be treated with equal seriousness in their work.[51] Combining a firm belief in the transcendent virtue of art with his awareness of the presence of these virtues in African American vernacular traditions, Wilson's description of the carvings on the piano in *The Piano Lesson* sums up his neoclassical perspective: "The carvings are rendered with a grace and power of invention that lifts them out of the realm of craftsmanship and into the realm of art."[52]

....................

## WILSON AS JAZZ VISIONARY: FIVE IMPROVISATIONS

In *The Repeating Island*, Antonio Benitez-Rojo explores the "chaotic"—in the scientific sense of a complex system with multiple states of potential equilibrium—interaction of European binary systems with Native American, Asian, and African traditions. Rather than subordinating one sensibility to the other (illegitimate universalism) or creating a synthesis that reduces the tensions created by the juxtaposition (a mulatto or mestizo aesthetic), Benitez-Rojo recommends a polyrhythmic literature which can be read "as a stream of texts in flight, in intense differentiation among themselves and within whose complex coexistence there are vague regularities, usually paradoxical."[53] In addition to "ironizing a set of values taken as universal," polyrhythmic texts "communicate their own turbulence, their own clash, and their own void, the swirling black hold of social violence produced by the *encomienda* and the plantation, that is, their otherness, their peripheral asymmetry with regard to the West."[54] Derived in large part from the African traditions which generated gospel, blues, and jazz, Benitez-Rojo's polyrhythmic culture provides a useful point of reference for discussion of Wilson's jazz neoclassicism.

Because the concept of the organizing thesis derives primarily from European analytical traditions, criticism organized around a central proposition risks repressing the chaotic potential—and thereby subverting part of the functionality—of polyrhythmic texts, such as Wilson's plays. To this point, this essay's examination of jazz neoclassicism and the fragmentation of contemporary African American cultural discourse has been structured to accord with the Eurocentric conventions of the academic tradition. As Benitez-Rojo observes, the point of polyrhythmic discourse is not to destroy or replace binary discourses but to understand them as part of a larger chaotic context in which other voices sound freely. This formulation suggests the appropriateness of an additional, not an alternative, critical methodology based on the polyrhythmic formal structures of the oral tradition. The remainder of this essay represents my polyrhythmic response to a sequence of interrelated calls that I hear in Wilson's major plays. Rather than attempting to demonstrate thematic consistency or support a thesis, I will present a series of "improvisational" responses to Wilson's visions of the universal themes—life and death, men and women, success and failure—in black America, the specific source and focus of his jazz-inflected voice.

Responding to Harrison's description of Wilson's plays, my improvisations follow a "modal structure" founded on the "distribution of related and non-related ideas." From *Ma Rainey's Black Bottom* through *Two Trains Running*, many of Wilson's most interesting and powerful passages juxtapose ideas to clarify the function of black music, understood as both cultural resource and economic commodity, as a response to the chaotic fragmentation of African

American communities. Resonating with the "intense differentiation" of African American experience between people and across time, Wilson's jazz call envisions the transformation of "vague" and "paradoxical" regularities into the foundation for a healthy and healing community.

...................

## MA RAINEY AND THE DEVIL

The black metafiction that provides the title for August Wilson's first major play, *Ma Rainey's Black Bottom*, realizes the process it describes, calling on later black artists to maintain blues realism in a system designed to steal their voices: "I done showed you all my black bottom / You ought to learn that dance" (70). There's no self-delusion in Ma's assessment of the white folks' "love" for her: "They don't care nothing about me. All they want is my voice. Well, I done learned that, and they gonna treat me like I want to be treated no matter how much it hurt them" (64). And there's no self-delusion in Wilson's response. Knowing full well that the devil is a "White fellow . . . got on good clothes and everything. Standing there with a clipboard in his hand" (*Fences*, 117), Wilson knows that plenty of black folks, especially the men hellhounded out of the church by their own demons, their ambitions, share Levee's response: "The only thing I ask about the devil . . . to see him coming so I can sell him this one [soul] I got" (34).

The market's still active.

So it comes down to a battle over which of the "two versions" of "Ma Rainey's Black Bottom" we're going to hear. But before we can answer that, we need to know what "we" means, who we are. Grounded in the deep blues, Cutler tells Levee not to confuse the white man's version with reality: "It ain't what you say, or what Mr. Irvin say . . . it's what Ma say that counts" (28). Slow Drag, the bass player in charge of the black bottom of the sound, gives his amen: "Ma say what happens with her" (28). Toledo, the only literate member of the band, provides an Afrocentric critique of Levee's willingness to sell his soul, to play the songs he thinks the white man wants to hear: "As long as he looks to white folks for approval . . . then he ain't never gonna find out who he is and what he's about. He's just gonna be about what white folks want him to be about" (29). It's not even a matter of being what the white folks want him to be; the devil's satisfied to control the question, set the terms of the contract.

And make no mistake. The devil sets the terms for anyone who wants, who needs, the money or the fame, or the good reviews. The devil lies to

Levee and Levee kills Toledo for telling him the truth: "We done sold Africa for the price of tomatoes. We done sold ourselves to the white man in order to be like him. Look at the way you dressed. . . . That ain't African. That's the white man" (78). But Ma tells a deeper truth, a black variation of a neoclassical riff on the transcendent value of art: "White folks don't understand about the blues. They hear it come out, but they don't know how it got there. They don't understand that's life's way of talking. You don't sing to feel better. You sing cause that's a way of understanding life" (67).

For Ma's people—and make no mistake, "the colored folks made Ma a star" (78)—understanding develops through call and response. As Sterling Brown sang in "Ma Rainey," the people respond to Ma's response to the call of their own burdens, their lived blues. The process requires each individual not to seek a synthesis, to deny the extreme aspects of his/her own experience, but to assert his/her subjectivity in response to other, equally personal and potentially extreme, assertions of experience. Call and response is African American analysis: a process that, by admitting diverse voices and diverse experiences, approximates "universality" more clearly than any individual analysis. The communal critique of Levee takes its force from the convergence of Cutler's voice with Slow Drag's and Toledo's. Toledo's blood is Wilson's amen.

...............

## GABRIEL'S TRUMPET AND THE BLACK WOMEN'S BLUES

When Ma Rainey talks about the blues, they're the black folks blues. When, three decades later, the characters in *Fences* live the blues, they live black *men's* blues and black *women's* blues. Wilson's most classically tragic play, *Fences* explores what that means in a world where jazz—the source of new visions—has fallen into desperate hustles and calls without response.

Troy and Bono, the black men who carry the South in their blood and on their backs, have heard the walking blues in their fathers' lives. Bono's father was "just moving on through. Searching out the New Land" (146); Troy's father "felt a responsibility toward us. . . . without that responsibility he could have walked off and left us . . . made his own way" (147). Like the tormented figures in D. H. Lawrence's *Studies in Classic American Literature*, in flight from oppression and women and civilization and sometimes just responsibility, black men with the walking blues reach out for freedom or nature or truth or money or a visionary gospel city in the North, a "different idea of myself" (163) or even just "second base" (164). Betraying his father and his son and, most basically, Rose, Troy voices his betrayal as a profoundly American black man's blues: "Rose, you're not listening to me. I'm trying the best I can to explain it to you. It's not easy for me to admit that I been standing in the same place for eighteen years" (164–65).

Rose has been standing beside him through every one of those years, every one of those days. Calling out in a world where men still leave—male rappers have only recently begun to acknowledge the idea of responsibility—where black women's blues echo without response, Rose's monologue responds to the calls of Toni Morrison and Alice Walker and Gloria Naylor and the real women in the lives of real men:

> I been standing with you! I been right here with you, Troy. I got a life too. I gave eighteen years of my life to stand in the same spot with you. Don't you think I ever wanted other things? . . . You not the only one who's got wants and needs. But I held on to you, Troy. I took all my feelings, my wants and needs, my dreams and I buried them inside you. I planted a seed and watched it and prayed over it. I planted myself inside you and waited to bloom. And it didn't take me no eighteen years to find out the soil was hard and rocky and it wasn't never gonna bloom. But I held on to you, Troy. I held you tighter. (165)

So Troy forgets the source, loses what he loves. Rose. Corey, whose own blues propel him to the military. The shadow of Vietnam hangs heavy over the play.

What can the jazz-man say? For Lyons, jazz starts out as an "idea of being" rather than "the actual practice of the music" (115). Only after he gives up on the quick hit, the devil's bargain, does Lyons begin to understand the blues that may make jazz possible: "I'm still playing. It still helps me to get out of bed in the morning. As long as it do that I'm gonna be right there playing and trying to make some sense out of it" (187).

And finally, Gabriel, name echoing with the myth of Louis Armstrong. Pursued by hellhounds, a victim of the last war, determined to tell Saint Peter when it's time to open the gate, Gabriel combines the blues and gospel dimensions of the jazz impulse. He knows "the devil's strong" (144); he knows Lyons is living in the white man's "jungle" (145); he loves and honors Rose. Risking the madness that Dostoevski and Ellison and Melville and Morrison encountered in the universal and absolutely specific depths of human experience, Gabriel transforms his burden, the burden of his family and his community, into visionary jazz: "There is a weight of impossible description that falls away and leaves him bare and exposed to a frightful realization. It is a trauma that a sane and normal mind would be unable to withstand" (192). Rather than surrendering to madness or walking away, Gabriel points back to Africa with a "slow, strange dance, eerie and life-giving. A dance of atavistic signature and ritual." When Lyons attempts to embrace him, Gabriel howls—"an attempt at song, or perhaps a song turning back into itself in an attempt at speech"—which opens the "gates of heaven" (192). Wilson bears witness to Gabriel's jazz vision, his burden and his call. In neoclassical jazz, tragedy is a fragmented world where no one responds.

And remember the cost of accepting, however brilliantly, the fragmentation: Charlie Parker. Remember that the black women never accepted it, even as they felt it most deeply. Gospel jazz-women, sources: Aretha, Nina Simone, Rose. Remember the sources, remember that the world wasn't always the way it is.

...............

## AFRICA AND THE MEMORY OF THE WIND

Remember the source of division. When the world split. In two. When Joe Turner, "brother of the governor of the great sovereign state of Tennessee, swooped down on us and grabbed everybody there" (269). Bynum knows that devil: "What he wanted was your song. He wanted to have that song to be his" (270). That's how the blues, the men's blues and the women's blues, were born: "Joe Turner split us up. Joe Turner turned the world upside-down" (273).

*Joe Turner's Come and Gone* reaches farther back than *Fences*, or even *Ma Rainey's Black Bottom*. Back to a world where Jeremy considers withdrawing from the devil's game: "I don't play no contest, Mr. Bynum. Had one of them white fellows cure me of that" (219). Faced with the "realities" of the labor market where he has to pay the devil to keep his job, Jeremy walks on, bluesman in a world where the responses, of communities and individuals, haven't yet been fixed. This is the core of jazz neoclassicism. Not to turn to the past for answers. But to seek the moments when the answers hadn't been provided, when the calls and responses were still open.

*Joe Turner's Come and Gone* resonates with Loomis's vision of the ancestors, the bones walking across the water, turning into the black people walking out their blues. Seeking reunion with Martha Pentecost, black woman and gospel spirit, Loomis lives the forces creating jazz: "A man driven not by the hellhounds that seemingly bay at his heels, but by his search for a world that speaks to something about himself. He is unable to harmonize the forces that swirl around him, and seeks to recreate the world into one that contains his image" (216). Or, as Bynum phrases it, "Now, I can look at you, Mr. Loomis, and see you a man who done forgot his song. Forgot how to sing it" (267). The birth of tragedy—Ma Rainey's and Nietzsche's and Robert Johnson's—is the loss of a world where "All you got to do is sing it. Then you be free" (287).

The song is on the wind. Where the children, Reuben and Zonia, setting out to sing their own versions of the male/female blues, can still hear the call and response between Bynum and the ancestors: "First he say something . . . and the wind it say back to him" (275). With his deep memories of Africa, his communion with the ancestors, his memories of his father's "Healing Song," Bynum understands the burden of the individual, the jazz artist, who passes the tradition on to the community in a chaotically changing world:

> That song was hard to carry. I fought against it. Didn't want to accept that song. I tried to find my daddy to give him back the song. But I found out it wasn't his song. It was my song. It had come from way deep inside me. I looked long back in memory and gathered up pieces and snatches of things to make that song. I was making it up out of myself. (268)

And, like all African art, the song *worked*: "And that song helped me on the road" (268). The song of the wind, materializing into Miss Mabel, who helps Reuben: "She says, 'Didn't you promise Eugene something?' Then she hit me with her cane. She say, 'Let them pigeons go.' Then she hit me again" (276). The ancestor—conceived as spirit or memory or magic or even neurons firing, an echo in mind—commands respect for the ancestors; responsibility to the community; reverence before the symbols of the spirit. Demands that we live up to our promises. Commands freedom. The ancestors as source of moral direction. The grandmother as manifestation of the moral energy in the universe, the one who knows that there are times when you just plain *do right* or you ain't a man, much less a human being (and the voices of the *orisha*, the ancestors, the elders resound with a blues humor filled with all *kinds* of double meanings, in theory and practice).

And think what difference it would have made had white folks, white men, ever dealt with the simple question: "Didn't you promise something?"

Bynum knows that, in the world, as it is, he can no longer hope for a response to his father's "Healing Song." So he sings a "Binding Song" for the black men and black women falling away from the gospel vision, from

Bertha, who holds the community together as it forgets what Bynum knows, grows deaf to the voices on the wind: "Bertha moves about the kitchen as though blessing it and chasing away the huge sadness that seems to envelop it. It is a dance and demonstration of her own magic, her own remedy that is centuries old and to which she is connected by the muscles of her heart and the blood's memory" (283).

## PLAYING THE CHANGES

As always, there's a white man "going around to all the colored people's houses looking to buy up musical instruments. He'd buy anything. Drums. Guitars. Harmonicas. Pianos" (11). As always, there's the piano, the one Berniece and Boy Willie's father died for, "the story of our whole family" (45): white folks and money and the threat of black blood. A house full of ghosts, a family full of ghosts. An American obsession: Hawthorne and Henry James, Poe and Charles Chesnutt, Faulkner and David Bradley, Eugene O'Neill, Toni Morrison. Ancestors. The past burdens the present.

While the present closes paths, circumscribes responses. Yet and still, Wining Boy "give that piano up. That was the best thing that ever happened to me, getting rid of that piano. That piano got so big and I'm carrying it around on my back. I don't wish that on nobody. See, you think it's all fun being a recording star. Got to carrying that piano around and man did I get slow." Playing for money, the devil's game, forecloses possibilities, fixes your options: "I'm walking around with that piano. Alright. Now, there ain't but so many places you can go. Only so many road wide enough for you and that piano" (41). Haunted, Berniece seconds the emotion: "When my mama died I shut the top on that piano and I ain't never opened it since. I was only playing it for her. . . . say when I played it she could hear my daddy talking to her. I used to think them pictures came alive and walked through the house. Sometime late at night I could hear my mama talking to them. I said that wasn't gonna happen to me. I don't play that piano cause I don't want to wake them spirits. They never be walking around in this house" (70). Above all, Berniece hopes to shield Maretha: "She got a chance I didn't have. I ain't gonna burden her with that piano" (70).

As if it were possible. Because, like it or not, the spirits are in the house, the voices on the wind. The only question is on what terms. As always, the devil, Sutter's ghost, defines what it means to be a man. Boy Willie learns the lesson well: "They mistreat me I mistreat them right back. Ain't no difference in me and the white man" (38). A different phrasing: They're both willing to kill to own, to control. The ghosts of the yellow dog: Morrison's Seven Days. From the crossroads where the Southern cross the Dog. Yellow, white turning black, and black turning white. Boy Willie's "Bible say an eye for an eye, a tooth for a tooth, and a life for a life" (89). Like Morrison's Pilate, Maretha, already living the black women's blues, sees that ghost: Boy Willie threatening Wining Boy, his doubled self, locked together with Sutter's ghost in "a life-and-death struggle fraught with perils and faultless terror" (106). Berniece has seen it before, suffered it, borne the burden like Margaret Walker's Vyry, Morrison's Dorcas, Naylor's Lorraine: "You're all alike. All this thieving and killing and thieving and killing. And what it ever lead to? More killing and more thieving. I ain't never seen it come to nothing. People getting burned up. People getting shot. People falling down their wells. It don't never stop" (52).

But the cycle of violence is, *can be*, broken. Berniece, growing into herself as ancestor, returns, remembers, sings: "It is an old urge to song that is both a commandment and a plea. With each repetition it gains in strength. It is intended as an exorcism and a dressing for battle. A rustle of wind blowing across two continents" (106). The wind crying out for the ancestors and the self: "I want you to help me . . . Mama Berniece . . . Mama Esther . . . Papa Boy Charles . . . Mama Ola" (107). Men and women. The song come down from Mama Ola, who "polished this piano with her tears for seventeen years. For seventeen years she rubbed on it till her hands bled. Then she rubbed the blood in . . . mixed it up with the rest of the blood on it."

Down at the crossroads, the place where we "cultivate the art of recognizing significant communications, knowing what is truth and what is falsehood, or else the lessons of the crossroads—the point where doors open or close, where persons have to make decisions that may forever after affect their lives—will be lost."[55] Home of Esu, the interpreter, of Legba, home of the devil. The phrasing makes all the difference. And the universal lesson to be learned from the piano is that the past, the African past, the slave past, the free past, never dies. We can lock the energies up, carve them into wood and try to forget, contain, repress them. We can let them kill us. Or we can go down to the crossroads for the power to exorcise the devil, casting out "the spirit of one James Sutter" (104) in the name of the ancestors as well as the Holy Spirit. Go down to the crossroads where, as Wining Boy knows, the ancestors sing: "I done been to where the Southern cross the Yellow Dog and called out their names. They talk back to you, too" (34). The crossroads where the ancestors, like the piano, *function*, give themselves to the present as sources of power: "I can't say how they talked to nobody else. But to me it just filled me up in a strange sort of way to be standing there on that spot. I didn't want to leave. It felt like the longer I stood there the bigger I got" (35). Boy Willie believes, responds: "They like the wind you can't see them. But sometimes you be in trouble they might be around to help you" (86). The song on the wind, the song Berniece sings, binds, creates the possibility of healing; Sutter's ghost exorcised, Maretha and Boy Willie hug, the black man and black woman reconcile, respond.

*The Piano Lesson* teaches us that art—even, or especially, the neoclassical art of an economically successful playwright who looks at the community he grew up in, the community he writes about, and knows "most of it is no longer there"—must be *functional*.[56] Wilson sketches a process, responds to the call of a desperately fragmented world. What we make of it is, the ancestors willing, up to us.

.................

## JAZZ CODA

Structured like a jam session—the voices entering, echoing, calling, responding, never quite resolving, improvising on the changing times—*Two Trains* revoices Wilson's concerns in response to the world of Malcolm X and Martin Luther King, a world where "they killed the dreamer" (52), a world where the music is locked up in a broken jukebox that "ain't gonna do nothing but break again if they do fix it" (56). A world where the spirit's in danger of being subdivided, part for the dead Prophet in a coffin full of hundred-dollar bills, part for ancient Aunt Ester, who asks only that you throw your money in the river, *if* you want to get right with yourself, if you really want to be healed.

A world where Sterling, twenty years before N.W.A., celebrates the gangsta vision: "That's all a man need is a pocketful of money, a cadillac and a good woman" (67). Where Risa, daughter of Gloria Naylor or Toni Morrison or Leon Forrest or Gayl Jones, takes a razor blade to her own legs, her own soul, to survive in a world that has no earthly idea of her name.

Sterling sets out to kill the devil: the Alberts who yet and still and always steal his money and his dreams. But he never makes it to the devil's door. Instead, he turns to Aunt Ester, daughter of the *orisha*, sister of Morrison's Pilate and Bambara's Minnie Ransom, who asks simply: "Are you sure, sweetheart, that you want to be well?" What turns Sterling's steps toward the healer, what empowers him to break the cycle of violence, to turn away from the devil's game, is Risa's voice: "I didn't know it mattered to nobody. I heard you calling me" (68). For Sterling and Risa, the future seems possible.

Reconciling but not resolving, Wilson offers us his vision: a binding song for desperate times.

..................

## NOTES

1. Coleman, "On Theloniousism," p. 69.

2. Ibid., p. 74.

3. hooks, *Yearning*, p. 105.

4. Locke, "New Negro," p. 15.

5. hooks, *Yearning*, p. 105.

6. W. J. Wilson, *The Truly Disadvantaged.*

7. Phillips, *Politics of Rich and Poor.*

8. Kozol, *Savage Inequalities.*

9. Coleman, "On Theloniousism," p. 68.

10. Harrison, "August Wilson's Blues Poetics," p. 306.

11. Thompson, *Flash of the Spirit*, p. xiii.

12. Sidran, *Black Talk*, p. 14.

13. Coleman, "On Theloniousism," p. 78.

14. hooks, *Yearning*, p. 109.

15. Ellison, *Shadow and Act*, p. 234.

16. Coleman, "On Theloniousism," p. 68.

17. Ellison, *Shadow and Act*, pp. 78–79.

18. Murray, *Stomping the Blues*, p. 38.

19. Werner, "James Baldwin," pp. 113–15.

20. Thompson, *Flash of the Spirit*, p. 13.

21. Murray, *The Hero and the Blues*, pp. 35–43.

22. Crouch, *Blue Interlude*, p. 1.

23. Crouch, *Majesty of the Blues*, p. 6.

24. Crouch, *Black Codes*, p. 4.

25. Ibid., p. 8.

26. Crouch, *Blue Interlude*, p. 1.

27. Crouch, *Majesty of the Blues*, p. 6.

28. Davis, *In the Moment*, p. 30.

29. Crouch, *Majesty of the Blues*, p. 10.

30. Tate, *Flyboy in the Buttermilk*, p. 45.

31. Gioia, *Imperfect Art*, p. 73.

32. Ibid., p. 74.

33. Ibid., p. 84.

34. Ibid., p. 77.

35. Ibid., p. 94.

36. Quoted in Brady, "In Step with Wynton Marsalis."

37. Davis, *In the Moment*, p. 29.

38. Ibid., p. 40.

39. Figueroa, *Ming's Samba*, liner notes.

40. Giddins, *Rhythmm-a-ning*, p. 158.

41. Figueroa, *Ming's Samba*, p. 6.

42. Williams, *Jazz in Its Time*, p. 46.

43. Radano, *Jazz Recast*.

44. Giddins, *Rhythmm-a-ning*, p. 161.

45. Tate, *Flyboy in the Buttermilk*, p. 52.

46. Moyers, *World of Ideas*, p. 177.

47. Ibid., p. 169.

48. Kent, *Blackness and Western Culture*, p. 112.

49. Moyers, *World of Ideas*, p. 168.

50. A. Wilson, *Three Plays*, pp. 10–11.

51. Ellison, *Shadow and Act*, p. 221.

52. A. Wilson, *The Piano Lesson*, p. xvii.

53. Benitez-Rojo, *The Repeating Island*, p. 27.

54. Ibid., p. 26.

55. Thompson, *Flash of the Spirit*, p. 19.

56. Moyers, *World of Ideas*, p. 171.

................

## WORKS CITED

Bambara, Toni Cade. *The Salt Eaters*. New York: Random House, 1980.

Baraka, Amiri [as LeRoi Jones]. *Blues People: Negro Music in White America*. New York: Morrow, 1963.

Benitez-Rojo, Antonio. *The Repeating Island: The Caribbean and the Postmodern Perspective*. Translated by James E. Maraniss. Durham: Duke University Press, 1992.

Brady, James. "In Step with Wynton Marsalis." *Parade Magazine*, 16 August 1992, p. 18.

Coleman, Wanda. "On Theloniousism." *Caliban* 4 (1988): 67–79.

Crouch, Stanley. Liner notes to Wynton Marsalis, *Black Codes from the Underground*. Columbia CK 43651 (1985).

―――. Liner notes to Wynton Marsalis, *Blue Interlude*. Columbia CK 48729 (1992).

―――. Liner notes to Wynton Marsalis, *Levee Low Moan. Soul Gestures in the South*. Columbia CK 47975 (1991).

―――. Liner notes to Wynton Marsalis, *The Majesty of the Blues*. Columbia CK 45091 (1989).

―――. Liner notes to Wynton Marsalis, *Thick in the South. Soul Gestures in the South*. Columbia CK 47977 (1991).

―――. Liner notes to Wynton Marsalis, *Uptown Ruler. Soul Gestures in the South*. Columbia CK 47976 (1991).

Davis, Francis. *In the Moment: Jazz in the 1980s*. New York: Oxford University Press, 1986.

Ellison, Ralph. *Invisible Man*. 1952. Reprint. New York: Vintage, 1989.

―――. *Shadow and Act*. 1964. Reprint. New York: Signet, 1966.

Figueroa, Carlos. Liner notes to David Murray, *Ming's Samba*. Columbia CK 45834 (1989).

Giddins, Gary. *Rhythmm-a-ning: Jazz Tradition and Innovation in the 80's*. New York: Oxford University Press, 1986.

Gioia, Ted. *The Imperfect Art: Reflections and Jazz and Modern Culture*. New York: Oxford University Press, 1988.

Harrison, Paul Carter. "August Wilson's Blues Poetics." In *Three Plays*, by August Wilson. Pittsburgh: University of Pittsburgh Press, 1991.

hooks, bell. *Yearning: Race, Gender, and Cultural Politics*. Boston: South End Press, 1990.

Kent, George. *Blackness and the Adventure of Western Culture*. Chicago: Third World Press, 1972.

Kozol, Jonathan. *Savage Inequalities*. New York: Crown, 1991.

Locke, Alain. "The New Negro." In *The New Negro*, edited by Alain Locke, 1925. Reprint. New York: Atheneum, 1968.

Moyers, Bill. *A World of Ideas*. New York: Doubleday, 1989.

Murray, Albert. *The Hero and the Blues*. Columbia: University of Missouri Press, 1973.

―――. *Stomping the Blues*. 1976. Reprint. New York: Vintage, 1982.

Phillips, Kevin. *The Politics of Rich and Poor: Wealth and the American Electorate in the Reagan Aftermath*. New York: Random House, 1990.

Sidran, Ben. *Black Talk*. 1971. New York: Da Capo, 1981.

Tate, Greg. *Flyboy in the Buttermilk: Essays on Contemporary America*. New York: Simon and Schuster, 1992.

Thompson, Robert Farris. *Flash of the Spirit: African and Afro-American Art and Philosophy*. New York: Random House, 1983.

Werner, Craig. "James Baldwin: Politics and the Gospel Impulse." *New Politics*, no. 6 (Winter 1989): 106–24.

Williams, Martin. *Jazz in Its Time*. New York: Oxford University Press, 1989.

Wilson, August. *The Piano Lesson*. New York: New American Library, Plume, 1990.

————. *Three Plays*. Pittsburgh: University of Pittsburgh Press, 1991.

————. "Two Trains Running." *Theater* 22, no. 1 (Winter 1991): 40–72.

Wilson, William Julius. *The Truly Disadvantaged*. Chicago: University of Chicago Press, 1987.

SANDRA ADELL

# Speaking of Ma Rainey / Talking about the Blues

······················································

I've traveled 'Til I'm tired

And I ain't satisfied

I've traveled 'til I'm tired

And I ain't satisfied

If I don't find my sweet man

I'll ramble 'til I die

Ah Lawdy Lawd Lawd Lawdy

Lawd Lawdy Lawd lawd Lawd

Ah Lawdy Lawd lawd lawdy

Lawd lawdy lawd lawd lawd

Lawd lawdy Lawd Lawd Lawd

Lawd Lawdy lawd lawd lawd

—"Slow Drivin' Moan" by
Gertrude (Ma) Rainey

Oh Ma Rainey

Sing yo' song;

Now you's back

Whah you belong,

Git way inside us,

Keep us strong.

—Sterling Brown

August Wilson's drama receives its strongest impulses from what Houston Baker has called the "blues matrix"—that metaphorical space where down-home folk like Boy Willie, Wining Boy, and Doaker in *The Piano Lesson*, Bynum in *Joe Turner's Come and Gone*, and Madame Ma Rainey in *Ma*

*Rainey's Black Bottom* all reside. Each of these characters serves as a kind of repository for a musical tradition that Wilson considers crucial to the development of the historical perspective he needs in order to write. In a 1989 interview with Bill Moyers, Wilson explained why the blues are so important for his work:

> The blues are important primarily because they contain the cultural responses of blacks in America to the situation that they find themselves in. Contained in the blues is a philosophical system at work. You get the ideas and attitudes of the people as part of the oral tradition. This is a way of passing along information. If you're going to tell someone a story, and if you want to keep information alive, you have to make it memorable so that the person hearing it will go tell someone else. This is how it stays alive. The music provides you an emotional reference for the information, and it is sanctioned by the community in the sense that if someone sings the song, other people sing the song. They keep it alive because they sanction the information that it contains.[1]

Like the blues singer, Wilson keeps *his* story alive by improvising on a theme: the theme of displaced Southern black people struggling to survive in a hostile Northern urban environment. Wilson makes his story memorable by elaborating a philosophical system in which music becomes the metaphysical activity par excellence. Music is tied to understanding in a most primordial way, one that evades any logical explanation. This is the point Ma Rainey makes when she complains to Cutler about how badly white folks have misunderstood what it means to sing the blues:

> White folks don't understand about the blues. They hear it come out, but they don't know how it got there. They don't understand that's life's way of talking. You don't sing to feel better. You sing 'cause that's a way of understanding life. (82)

It is also a way of securing for one's *self* a temporary reprieve from the forces of oppression with which each of Wilson's characters must always contend. And it is through the figure of Ma Rainey that Wilson most strongly articulates the possibility for grounding this kind of self-possession in the rituals and soulful rhythms of those low-down dirty gut-bucket blues.

*Ma Rainey's Black Bottom* is the first of what August Wilson has referred to as a "cycle of history plays," which he hopes will "stand as a record of Black experience over the past hundred years." Set in a Chicago recording studio in 1927, this two-act play attempts to explore, among other things, the tensions arising out of a conflict between a traditional vaudeville-based down-home blues aesthetic and a new, more fast-paced and urbane style of the blues. It also presents a powerful and persuasive image of the woman who was called the Mother of the Blues.

Gertrude "Ma" Rainey was born on April 26, 1886, in Columbus, Georgia. According to one source, she made her theater debut in 1900 in a talent show called "The Bunch of Blackberries." Four years later she married William "Pa" Rainey with whom she spent many years traveling and performing on the Southern minstrel and vaudeville show circuit. By the 1920s when she began to record for Paramount records, she had already become the most popular female down-home blues singer in the country. For the folk down home and the down-home folk up North, Ma Rainey represented the epitome of black female wealth, power, and sensuality.[2] She had her own group of musicians, a spectacular wardrobe, and for a while, her own touring bus. She also had a strong voice that could project her raunchy lyrics, without the aid of a megaphone, over the music and the noise of the crowds who regularly attended her blues performances.

An important feature of Ma Rainey's performances was a large cardboard replica of a Victrola, from which she emerged, extravagantly attired in a sequined gown and a necklace made of twenty-dollar gold pieces, singing her big recorded hit, "Moonshine Blues."[3] This part of her stage performance most certainly must have symbolized for Ma Rainey's audiences her great success as a recording star, but in *Ma Rainey's Black Bottom* it becomes, at least implicitly, the technical instrument that detaches the down-home blues singer from the domain of the blues tradition. The Victrola makes it possible for Ma Rainey's voice to be heard in places other than the great circus tents where she usually performs. One no longer has to *be there* to experience Ma Rainey coming out of the Victrola; all one needs is a phonograph record. The phonograph record reproduces the sound of Ma Rainey singing the blues and, to borrow a phrase from Walter Benjamin, it "enables the original to meet the beholder halfway."[4] What it cannot reproduce is what Benjamin, in "The Work of Art in the Age of Mechanical Reproduction," refers to as the "aura" or the presence, in space and time, that guarantees an object—be it a painting, a choral performance, or a staged performance—its uniqueness and singularity.

According to Benjamin, the "aura" of a work of art is what "withers" in the age of mechanical reproduction:

> That which withers in the age of mechanical reproduction is the aura of the work of art. This is a symptomatic process whose significance points beyond the realm of art. One might generalize by saying: the technique of reproduction detaches the reproduced object from the domain of tradition. By making many reproductions it substitutes a plurality of copies for a unique existence. And in permitting the reproduction to meet the beholder or listener in his own particular situation, it reactivates the object reproduced. These two processes lead to a tremendous shattering of tradition which is the obverse of the contemporary crisis and renewal of mankind. Both processes are intimately connected with the contemporary mass movements. Their most powerful agent is the film. Its social significance, particularly in its most positive form, is inconceivable without its destructive, cathartic aspect, that is, the liquidation of the traditional value of the cultural heritage.[5]

One might also generalize by saying that the second most powerful agent is the phonograph record. Like the film, the phonograph record is designed for its own reproducibility and marketability rather than for the transmission of the "traditional value of the cultural heritage."[6] In that sense, the phonograph record, like the film, does indeed lead to a "tremendous shattering of tradition." What Benjamin argues in his essay and what August Wilson dramatizes in *Ma Rainey's Black Bottom* is that the age of mechanical reproduction reduces everything within the aesthetic domain to a simple matter of supply and demand. And by the time Ma Rainey is scheduled to record her "Black Bottom Blues," that demand, especially among her loyal displaced downhome fans, has already translated into enormous profits for the two white entrepreneurs, Irvin and Sturdyvant, who control the techniques of reproduction and the "recording machines." What they cannot control—and this becomes obvious during the first moments of the play—is Ma Rainey, upon whose cooperation those enormous profits necessarily rely.

Ma Rainey does not cooperate with Irvin and Sturdyvant. Fully aware of the extent to which she is being exploited, Ma Rainey uses her exploitation to her advantage whenever she can. To cite just one example, although she does not deliberately disrupt Irvin and Sturdyvant's plan to run the recording session "just like clockwork," when she finally arrives at the studio she takes advantage of the commotion caused by the automobile accident that detained her to gain the upper hand. Ignoring Irvin's remarks about her tardiness, Ma Rainey insists that he talk to the policeman who is trying to arrest her for hitting a taxi driver and set him straight about who she is:

*Ma Rainey:* Tell the men [*sic*] who he's messing with!
*Policeman:* Do you know this lady?
*Ma Rainey:* Just tell the man who I am! That's all you gotta do.
*Policeman:* Lady, will you let me talk, huh?
*Ma Rainey:* Tell the man who I am!
*Irvin:* Wait a minute . . . wait a minute! Let me handle it. Ma, will you let me handle it?
*Ma Rainey:* Tell him who he's messing with!
*Irvin:* Okay! Okay! Give me a chance! Officer, this is one of our recording artists . . . Ma Rainey.
*Ma Rainey:* Madame Rainey! Get it straight! Madame Rainey! Talking about taking me to jail! (49)

Unintimidated by the threat of arrest, Ma Rainey refuses to "await her verb," as Hortense Spillers might put it. Ma Rainey does not ask, "Who am I?" Ma Rainey demands instead that the world be informed about who she *is*—a social *and* sexual subject who, as the drama unfolds, continuously challenges the presumed authority of the white men and the black men who make up her immediate environment. She is, as blues singer, what Spillers calls "a metaphor of commanding female sexuality . . . who celebrates, chides, embraces, inquires into, *controls* her womanhood through the eloquence of form that she both makes use of and brings into being" (emphasis added).[7] That control, however, is negotiable. For Ma Rainey, it has an exchange value, particularly insofar as her managers are concerned. She exchanges the rights to her voice for a right that is denied most other blacks, including her musicians: the right to be treated as she wants to be treated. But, as she makes clear to Cutler, her lead musician, she has no illusions about the limits of that control. Ma Rainey knows that she gets her way because she has something that Irvin and Sturdyvant want—her voice. She knows that Irvin and Sturdyvant lack any real commitment to her, her music, or the blues tradition and that they will put up with her only as long as it is profitable for them to record her songs.

They don't care nothing about me. All they want is my voice. Well, I done learned that, and they gonna treat me like I want to be treated no matter how much it hurt them. They back there now call me all kinds of names . . . calling me everything but a child of god. But they can't do nothing else. They ain't got what they wanted yet. As soon as they get my voice down on them recording machines, then it's just like if I'd be some whore and they roll over and put their pants on. Ain't got no use for me then. (79)

This is what the trumpet player Levee fails to comprehend when he talks about leaving Ma Rainey and getting his own band together and making records for Irvin and Sturdyvant. Levee wants to be like Ma Rainey. He believes that the white men respect her and that all he has to do to make them respect him is to turn over a good profit. Yet unlike Ma Rainey, who knows that it was black people and not white people who made her a star, Levee relies on Irvin and Sturdyvant to give him his break. Ma Rainey, on the other hand, has learned, after long years of performing on the Southern circuit, how to manipulate the powers that be. She has also learned to place a higher value on the blues tradition and all that it implies than on its technical innovations and mechanical reproduction. For example, when Irvin balks about not having enough time to let her stuttering nephew Sylvester record the lead-in lines to her "Black Bottom Blues," Ma Rainey does not hesitate to remind him that this recording session is something she does not need to do. She can easily return to her Southern tour, where over the years she has cultivated large numbers of loyal fans:

> If you wanna make a record, you gonna find time. I ain't playing with you, Irvin. I can walk out of here and go back to my tour. I got plenty fans. I don't need to go through all of this. Just go and get the boy a microphone. (74)

Ma Rainey doesn't need to go through the performance-inhibiting ordeal of a recording session because she remains solidly grounded in the tradition out of which her music evolved. Her *contract* is not with Irvin and Sturdyvant; it is with the people, the down-home folk who identify most closely with her brand of the blues. Her "Black Bottom" belongs to them, and she refuses to give it up to anyone else unless she gets something in return. As the last line of her "Moonshine Blues" goes, "You got to fetch it with you when you come." And when Irvin comes out of the control booth after the recording session with Sturdyvant's crooked deal to pay Sylvester with part of the money he owes her, Ma Rainey sends Irvin right back to fetch the boy's pay, then makes him and Sturdyvant beg her to sign the release forms.

*Sturdyvant:* Hey, Ma . . . come on, sign the forms, huh?

*Irvin:* Ma . . . come on now.

*Ma Rainey:* Get your coat, Sylvester. Irvin, where's my car?

*Irvin:* It's right out front, Ma. Here . . . I got the keys right here. Come on, sign the forms, huh?

*Ma Rainey:* Irvin, give me my car keys!

*Irvin:* Sure, Ma . . . just sign the forms, huh?

*(He gives her the keys, expecting a trade-off.)*

*Ma Rainey:* Send them to my address and I'll get around to them.

*Irvin:* Come on, Ma . . . I took care of everything, right? I straightened everything out. (106)

Ma Rainey signs. Just before she makes her exit she signs, but by that time she has gotten everything she can out of Irvin and Sturdyvant and their recording machines, including the satisfaction of making them put everything on hold, of making them wait.

*Ma Rainey's Black Bottom* is structured around the *act* of waiting and its consequences for her four black musicians, for whom waiting seems to be a condition of their being: waiting to play a halfway decent gig; waiting to get paid, in cash, when they do play a gig; waiting to have just one mo' good time; waiting for a good woman to help ease their trouble-in-mind; waiting for Ma Rainey to sing her "Black Bottom Blues."

Sandra Shannon has commented on how the act of waiting is crucial for establishing the tensions that culminate in Levee's murderous act at the end of the play. In "The Long Wait: August Wilson's *Ma Rainey's Black Bottom,*" Shannon argues that Wilson makes us all wait for Ma Rainey in order to focus more closely on the musicians as they wait for Ma Rainey to arrive:

Capitalizing on the knowledge that both the reader and the viewer subconsciously expect the sassy blues singer to grace the stage at any moment, Wilson manages to upstage her entrance by focusing instead upon seemingly trivial conversations among her band members. Not only does Wilson make the rehearsal group wait for Ma Rainey, but he strategically places the audience on hold as well. Subconsciously they experience, in some measure, the frustration of waiting and its accompanying effects upon the cast. As a result of the delay, what they learn about the various idiosyncrasies of the troubled group serves as a context for understanding their motives when they are finally in the company of Ma Rainey.[8]

What we learn is that each of the musicians has a story to tell, and that embedded in these stories are clues to why they interact with each other the way they do. We also learn that, with the exception of Levee, each of the musicians is strongly committed to doing things Ma Rainey's way. As Cutler and Slow Drag remind the rebellious Levee, who insists on doing things Irvin and Sturdyvant's way, when it comes to her music or her *self*, what Irvin and Sturdyvant want doesn't matter: Ma Rainey will alway have the final say.

> *Cutler:* Levee, the sooner you understand it ain't what you say, or what
> Mr. Irvin say . . . it's what Ma say that counts.
> *Slow Drag:* Don't nobody say when it come to Ma. She's gonna do what
> she wants to do. Ma says what happens with her.
> *Levee:* Hell, the man's the one putting out the record! He's gonna put out
> what he wanna put out!
> *Slow Drag:* He's gonna put out what Ma want him to put out! (37)

Consequently, although Wilson does indeed manage to upstage her entrance, his strategy does not close off the possibility of rendering Ma Rainey powerfully present even in her absence. In fact, her *presence* causes everyone, and especially Sturdyvant, a great deal of anxiety long before she arrives on the scene.

Sturdyvant would rather not deal with blacks under any circumstances and finds it particularly irritating to have to put up with one who comports herself as if she were a queen. As he helps Irvin test the studio's sound equipment for the one o'clock recording session, Sturdyvant continually reminds Irvin that it is his responsibility to keep Ma Rainey in line.

> *Sturdyvant:* She's your responsibility. I'm not putting up with any Royal
> Highness . . . Queen of the Blues bullshit!
> *Irvin:* Mother of the Blues, Mel. Mother of the Blues.
> *Sturdyvant:* I don't care what she calls herself. I'm not putting up with it.
> I just want to get her in here . . . record those songs on that list . . . and
> get her out. Just like clockwork, huh?
> *Irvin:* Like clockwork, Mel. You just stay out of the way and let me
> handle it. (18)

And for the most part, Sturdyvant does stay out of the way, in the control booth, while Irvin tries to handle a situation that, from the moment the musicians arrive without Ma Rainey, becomes increasingly chaotic. There is confusion about the songs the group is supposed to record. Irvin hands Cutler, who can't even read, a list that is different from the one Ma Rainey told him they would be recording. According to Toledo, the only member of the group who can read, Irvin's list includes four songs instead of six and one of them is Bessie Smith's version of "Moonshine Blues." It also includes Levee's *and* Ma Rainey's versions of "Black Bottom Blues." To further complicate matters, Levee refuses to rehearse the music on the list because he feels that it is outdated and requires a different kind of band, a jug band. This leads to a heated discussion about whether or not this style of music can be called art.

> *Levee:* You ain't gotta rehearse that . . . ain't nothing but old jug-band music. They need one of them jug bands for this.
> *Slow Drag:* Don't make me no difference. Long as we get paid.
> *Levee:* That ain't what I'm talking about, nigger. I'm talking about art!
> *Slow Drag:* What's drawing got to do with it?
> *Levee:* Where you get this nigger from, Cutler? He sound like one of the Alabama niggers.
> *Cutler:* Slow Drag's all right. It's you talking all that weird shit about art. Just play the piece, nigger. You wanna be one of them . . . what you call . . . virtuoso or something, you in the wrong place. You ain't no Buddy Bolden or King Oliver . . . you just an old trumpet player come a dime a dozen. Talking about art. (25–26)

But it is about art. It's about an art that is being divested of its Being, for the three-and-a-half-minute mechanically reproduced sound of the blues will always lack the presence, in time and space, of the "unique existence" that assures its authenticity.[9] What is at stake, especially for the folk down home, is not just a musical style but a way of being, a way of understanding, defining, and improvising upon a world from which the Christian God had disappeared long before those white men *waited* 'til Levee's daddy went to Natchez to buy that seed and fertilizer and then came to Levee's daddy's house when Levee wasn't nothin' but about eight years old and had to do with his mama "any way they wanted" and Levee tried to save her *'cause God couldn't since he was already dead* and one of those white men cut him so bad that his mama had to carry him two miles to keep him from dying too and his daddy came back and acted like didn't nothin' happen and even sold his land to one of those white men and then moved out of that county and *waited* and then went back and got four of them before the other four or five got him (68).

*Hear me talkin' now people. I'm talkin' about the BLUES!*

Levee's got the blues! Levee's got the blues so bad that he thinks he learned from his father's example how to handle the white man. When Cutler and Slow Drag criticize him for the way he "yessirs" Sturdyvant, and Toledo accuses him of being "spooked up with the white man" like everyone else, Levee tries to defend himself by insisting that his daddy's actions taught him what to do:

> I seen my daddy go up and grin in this cracker's face . . . smile in his face and sell him his land. All the while he's planning how he's gonna get him and what he's gonna do to him. That taught me how to handle them. So you all just back up and leave Levee alone about the white man. I can smile and say yessir to whoever I please. I got time coming to me. You all just leave Levee alone about the white man. (70)

What Levee forgets is that his daddy did not smile and yessir the white man in order to get something from him. He did it in order to do something to him, and he carried his plan out to the bitter end. A true warrior, Memphis Green learned how to do what his son cannot. He learned how to live with his "head in the lion's mouth," as the enigmatic grandfather in Ralph Ellison's *Invisible Man* puts it. He did what the grandfather advised Ellison's protagonist's father to do. He overcame 'em with yeses, undermined 'em with grins, and agreed 'em to death and destruction before they destroyed him.[10] What Memphis Green didn't do was what the grandfather in *Invisible Man* insisted in his dying breath that *his* son must do: "Learn it to the young-uns."[11] Memphis Green couldn't learn it to his "youngun": his time ran out just a bit too soon. Consequently, Levee lets his personal ambition dictate how to do battle with his oppressors. In so doing, he reverses his father's smile-and-sell strategy and substitutes compliance for subversiveness. Levee believes that all he has to do to make his way to the top of an industry already dominated by the immutable figure of the Mother of the Blues is yessir and smile and sell Sturdyvant a few of his songs. His strategy fails. Sturdyvant agrees to buy Levee's compositions—for five dollars apiece—but refuses to let him record them because he doesn't "think they'd sell like Ma's records" (108). When Levee objects, Sturdyvant shoves five dollars in his pocket for the song he's already given him. And as Sturdyvant leaves the room, he lets the door slam in Levee's face. This makes Levee *mad*. However, instead of confronting the real enemy, Levee displaces his anger and resentment—first onto Cutler, who tries to persuade him, through his story of Reverend Gates, not to expect respect from white men, and then onto Toledo, who makes the mistake of stepping on one of his brand-new shoes.

Cutler's story is a familiar one, one that Toledo insists isn't worth telling since it has already been told "a hundred times" (97). A black preacher takes a train to visit a sick relative and ends up, through no fault of his own, in a no-(black)man's-land surrounded by a group of white men who have nothing better to do than terrorize and humiliate him (97). What Cutler tries to make Levee see is that it is foolish for a black person to expect to be respected by people who won't even respect a "man of God" if he happens to be black. But all Cutler succeeds in doing is making Levee even *madder* than he already is. As far as Levee is concerned, Cutler's story is proof enough that this God that Cutler is so fond of is "a white man's God" who "don't pay niggers no mind. In fact . . . God hate niggers! Hate them with all the fury in his heart" (98). As Levee's own fury intensifies, so do his blasphemous attacks on God. This in turn provokes a bloody battle between the two men. Toledo and Slow Drag break it up just as Levee pulls a knife on Cutler and dares "Cutler's God" to come and save him:

> Cutler's God! Come on and save this nigger! Come on and save him like you did my mama! Save him like you did my mama! I heard her when she called you! I heard her when she said, "Lord, have mercy! Jesus, help me! Please, God, have mercy on me, Lord Jesus, help me!" And did you turn your back? Did you turn your back, motherfucker? Did you turn your back? (Levee *becomes so caught up in his dialogue with God that he forgets about* Cutler *and begins to stab upward in the air, trying to reach God.*)
> Come on! Come on and turn your back on me! Turn your back on me! Come on! Where is you? Come on and turn your back on me! Turn your back on me, motherfucker! I'll cut your heart out! Come on, turn your back on me! Come on! What's the matter? Where is you? Come on and turn your back on me! Come on, what you scared of? Turn your back on me! Come on! Coward, motherfucker! (100)

Cutler's God can't come. Cutler's God is the Christian God, and that God had already been pronounced dead by another *madman*, Nietzsche's madman who, in *The Gay Science*, went running around the marketplace with his lit lantern looking for Him. When the people in the marketplace laughed at him for seeking a God they had long ago ceased to believe in, Nietzsche's madman proclaimed his death and said that *we* have killed him: "God is dead. God remains dead. And we have killed him. How shall we, the murderers of all murderers, comfort ourselves? What was holiest and most powerful of all that the world has yet owned has bled to death under our *knives*" (emphasis added).[12] The bloody knives of unbelief killed God once. Now Levee is trying to conjure him up in order to make him bleed all over again. The difference is that this time the potential murderer "of all murderers" is not an unbeliever. Levee believes in God as much as Cutler does. What Levee has lost faith in is the idea of God as the "holiest and most powerful of all that the world has yet owned." In that sense, Levee stands in the shadow of Nietzsche's most "uncanny guest," nihilism, or what Martin Heidegger in "The Word of Nietzsche: 'God is Dead'" calls, after Nietzsche, the ongoing historical event of the "devaluing of the highest values up to now."[13]

Heidegger defines the highest values as the suprasensory world, which is subsumed under the name God, and the true, the good, and the beautiful. These values

> are already devaluing themselves through the emerging of the insight that the ideal world is not and is never to be realized within the real world. The obligatory character of the highest values begins to totter. The question arises: Of what avail are these highest values if they do not simultaneously render secure the warrant and the ways and means for a realization of the goals posited in them?[14]

For the nihilist these values are of no avail once their "obligatory character" and their authority begin to totter. That does not imply that in the face of this "tottering of the dominion of prior values," the world falls into decline and decay. The world remains, but it lacks the essential something that must occupy the authoritative realm which is preserved despite the fact that God is absent from it. As Heidegger explains,

> if God in the sense of the Christian god has disappeared from his authoritative position in the suprasensory world, then this authoritative place itself is still always preserved, even though as that which has become empty. The now-empty authoritative realm of the suprasensory and the ideal world can still be adhered to. What is more, the empty place demands to be occupied anew and to have the god now vanished from it replaced by something else.[15]

August Wilson's Ma Rainey also recognizes the importance of replacing that now-empty realm with something else. However, unlike Toledo, who in the first act suggests that the gods be reconceptualized and named according to African traditions, Ma Rainey turns away from the theological altogether. Using the idiom of the blues tradition, Ma Rainey explains to Cutler and Toledo how her music helps to fill that space:

> *Ma Rainey:* The blues help you get out of bed in the morning. You get up knowing you ain't alone. There's something else in the world. Something's been added by that song. This be an empty world without the blues. I take that emptiness and try to fill it up with something.
> *Toledo:* You fill it up with something the people can't be without, Ma. That's why they call you the Mother of the Blues. You fill up that emptiness in a way ain't nobody ever thought of doing before. And now they can't be without it.
> *Ma Rainey:* I ain't started the blues way of singing. The blues always been there.
> *Cutler:* In the church sometimes you find that way of singing. They got blues in the church.
> *Ma Rainey:* They say I started it . . . but I didn't. I just helped it out. Filled up that empty space a little bit. That's all. (83)

The blues is what excites the will-to-power of those beings who would otherwise lack the power to will beyond the narrow and racially defined spheres of their existence. In the absence of the God of Christianity, the blues is what *em*-powers them to seek their truth in a "dimension of happening" that transcends the value-laden realities of the everyday. Ma Rainey's *truth* is her song transformed into a communal act. In that sense, she has much in common with Dionysius whom Nietzsche, in *The Birth of Tragedy*, credits with having broken the "spell of individuation" that governs the artistic energies of the Apollonian, or the plastic arts, and opening the way for the symbolic expression of what he feels is at the heart of all human experience: the tragic.[16] Nietzsche writes that while Dionysian art "wishes to convince us of the eternal joy of existence," it urges us to seek it "not in phenomena, but behind them" in order to recognize, without fear, that

> all that comes into being must be ready for a sorrowful end; we are forced to look into the terrors of the individual existence—yet we are not to

become rigid with fear: a metaphysical comfort tears us momentarily from the bustle of the changing figures. We are really for a brief moment primordial being itself, feeling its raging desire for existence and joy in existence; the struggle, the pain, the destruction of phenomena; now appear necessary to us, in view of the excess of countless forms of existence which force and push one another into life, in view of the exuberant fertility of the universal will. We are pierced by the maddening sting of these pains just when we have become, as it were, one with the infinite primordial joy in existence, and when we anticipate, in Dionysian ecstasy, the indestructibility and eternity of this joy. In spite of fear and pity, we are the happy living beings, not as individuals, but as the *one* living being, with whose creative joy we are united.[17]

What Nietzsche had in mind when he developed his concepts of the Apollonian and the Dionysian was tragedy as it is manifest in the works of Richard Wagner. But he could just as easily have been talking about the blues. For the spirit of Dionysius is transfigured onto Ma Rainey, whose music celebrates and mourns—many of her songs are called "moans"—one of the most tragic cultures of the modern age. Furthermore, Ma Rainey's music is valued only insofar as it links her with her people in a communal "bond of kinship" signaled by her name. Levee breaks out of that bond and separates himself from his immediate "kin" when, in the second act, he deliberately provokes Ma Rainey until she fires him just before she leaves.

Afterwards, while the musicians wait in the bandroom for Sturdyvant to pay them their twenty-five dollars each, Slow Drag offers to show Levee a card trick just "to be nice" (104). Levee refuses Slow Drag's friendly gesture, thus further alienating himself from the group. Toledo plays the game instead and pulls the six of diamonds, which, in the end, proves to be his unlucky card. After having "done been through life" and "made [his] marks," Toledo ends up the target of Levee's terribly misguided "warrior spirit" (91).

August Wilson has described the "warrior spirit" as a refusal to accept the limitations of a racist society and a "willingness to battle, even to death" the forces that threaten existence in a real and immediate way.[18] He feels that throughout the play Levee is guided by the "warrior spirit" despite the fact that he progresses toward the wrong target. Toledo posed no threat to Levee. If anything, Toledo simply forced him to confront his own ignorance about music and about what it means to be a struggling musician in a business that is being controlled by white men. He also showed him how little he understands "the basic understanding of everything" (31). But *Ma Rainey's Black Bottom* is very much in the tragic mode. And tragedy demands that someone be sacrificed. Tragedy insists that someone must die.

## NOTES

1. Moyers, *World of Ideas*, p. 168.
2. Hazel Carby deals with the relationship between power, sexuality, and the Classic Blues singers in "'It Jus Be's Dat Way Sometime': The Sexual Politics of Women's Blues," an essay that has been recently reprinted in *Unequal Sisters: A Multicultural Reader in U.S. Women's History* (New York: Routledge, 1990), pp. 238–49.
3. Titon, *Early Downhome Blues*, p. 208.
4. Benjamin, "Work of Art," p. 218.
5. Ibid., p. 221.
6. See ibid., p. 244, n. 7, for Benjamin's discussion of the social significance of the relation between the technique of film production, mechanical reproduction, and mass distribution.
7. Spillers, "Interstices," p. 87.
8. Shannon, "Long Wait," p. 139.
9. Benjamin, "Work of Art," p. 220.
10. Ellison, *Invisible Man*, p. 16.
11. Ibid.
12. Nietzsche, *Portable Nietzsche*, pp. 95–96.
13. Heidegger, "Word of Nietzsche," p. 61.
14. Heidegger defines the realm of the suprasensory as the "true and genuinely real world." It contrasts with the sensory world or the "world down here" with its "vale of tears" in that it promises "everlasting bliss in the beyond" (ibid., p. 61).
15. Ibid., p. 69.
16. Nietzsche, *Birth of Tragedy*, p. 100.
17. Ibid., p. 104.
18. Moyers, *World of Ideas*, p. 179.

## WORKS CITED

Benjamin, Walter. *Illuminations*. Edited by Hannah Arendt. New York: Schocken Books, 1976.

Ellison, Ralph. *Invisible Man*. New York: Vintage, 1972.

Heidegger, Martin. *The Question Concerning Technology and Other Essays*. Translated by William Lovitt. New York: Harper and Row, 1977.

Moyers, Bill. *A World of Ideas: Conversations with Thoughtful Men and Women about American Life Today and the Ideas Shaping Our Future*. New York: Doubleday, 1989.

Nietzsche, Friedrich. *The Birth of Tragedy and the Case of Wagner*. New York: Vintage, 1967.

———. *The Portable Nietzsche*. Edited by Walter Kaufmann. New York: Viking, 1982.

Shannon, Sandra G. "The Long Wait: August Wilson's *Ma Rainey's Black Bottom*." *Black American Literature Forum* 25, no. 1 (1991): 135–46.

Spillers, Hortense. "Interstices: A Small Drama of Words." In *Pleasure and Danger: Exploring Female Sexuality*, edited by Carole S. Vance, pp. 73–100. Boston: Routledge and Kegan Paul, 1984.

Titon, Jeff. *Early Downhome Blues*. Urbana: University of Illinois Press, 1979.

Wilson, August. *Ma Rainey's Black Bottom*. New York: New American Library, Plume, 1985.

JOHN TIMPANE

# Filling the Time: Reading History in the Drama of August Wilson

· · · · · · · · · · · · · · · · · · · · · · · · · · · · · · · · · · · · · · · · · · · · · · · · · · · · · · · · · · ·

Do the excluded and the empowered read history differently? This question is brought to mind by the dramatic practice of August Wilson. In his plays, Wilson portrays individual lives in relation to moments of subtle yet decisive historical change. Finding they cannot live without reference to the change, these characters evolve various ways of reading it. Knowing the change and its significance is complicated by their position and their wishes.

In a Wilson drama, history passes in the form not of a progress but of a crisis of reading. In plays such as *Fences* and *Ma Rainey's Black Bottom*, the audience guesses that a historical change has occurred not because they see the *Augenblick* itself—the "durationless instant" that traditional philosophy has found so elusive—but because they can compare the way different characters read their worlds. Despite mounting evidence that an old way of reading is no longer adequate, one or more characters refuse to give it up. Indeed, they cannot give it up. Reading equals a way of life. Character is reading is fate.

Troy Maxson and Ma Rainey construct their identities based on their relation to a particular social and historic change; they would not be where and who they are had not the change occurred. Yet this relation is tragically ironic for both of them: This change, which they personally helped create, (Troy in baseball and Ma Rainey in popular music) ultimately disenfranchises them at the same time that it signals expanded opportunities for other people like them. Not fully knowing, they have sacrificed themselves so that the change can happen. At some level, however, each does know, making necessary some powerful self-deception in order to survive. Knowing the change and their own role in it, they are now forced to deny it. The violence created by the ensuing mental conflict is mostly potential in both plays: the sacrifice has already happened, and each is *post facto* in his or her own life.

Being *post facto*, Troy and Ma Rainey call on the audience to search for the *factum* itself, to become readers and to gauge differences in reading. What they read is not only how individual lives are lived and lost but also how we and they read changes in time. That is a complex matter.

..................

## SPECIOUS PRESENT, MANUFACTURED PAST

In the first volume of *Principles of Psychology*, William James turns to the question of our consciousness of time. "What," he writes, "is the *original* of our experience of pastness, from whence we get the meaning of the term?"[1] Constantly, we perceive a past time and the events now *in* the past; the question is, from what vantage point do we experience the movement of time—or, more precisely, since time does not move, the change from present to past? These questions lead James to his consideration of the "specious present," called "specious" because it is so vanishingly short—James himself wrote that only its latter boundary should be called the real "present."[2] The specious present was not to be confused with the "conscious present," a larger construct we are constantly building out of sense impressions and memory. James, Bertrand Russell, and others concluded that, in the words of C. W. K. Mundle, "time" itself "is a notion we construct from temporal relations which are sense-given."[3] Like many important mental processes, this construction is continual, lightning-fast, and invisible to the constructor.

And that is the main point—human consciousness of time is a matter of perception, a tissue of memory, expectation, cultural conditioning. Likewise, an audience's sense of the "pastness" and "presentness" of a dramatic situation involves manipulated memories, manufactured expectations, artificial conditioning. With lightning calibrations, an audience constantly triangulates its present situation with the past, present, and likely future situations predicated by the words and actions in the play. Since these events take place in "real" time, we can experience them much as we experience events outside the theater. But since these events predicate fictive realities occurring in a "stage time," we are alienated from them and forced to judge.

An excellent example lies in Wilson's plays, which appeal to the audience's sense of pastness as a dramatic given. Far from being simply "setting," this appeal forces us to become critical readers. Our irrevocable separation from these pasts alienates us from the manner in which Ma Rainey, in 1927

Chicago, or Troy Maxson, in 1957 Pittsburgh, constructs the "present." We learn about their "times" what is normally invisible to us about our own: how much our sense of the present depends on what we want and where we stand, on wishes and position. We learn precisely what is specious about the present.

Michel Foucault has little to say about how we perceive time—and much to say about how we read and write about it. Following Nietzsche's lead, Foucault explored the concept of history as just such a species of reading. Nietzsche saw the traditional European institution called "history" as a lie riddled with circularity, self-interest, and the will to power. He rejected it in favor of "genealogy," a way of reading the past that does not seek to reduce it to a "story" or to explain it in terms that validate the present. Genealogy does not "demonstrate that the past actively exists in the present"; rather, it identifies "the errors, the false appraisals, the faulty calculations" that accrete to form the assemblage of accidents called the past.[4]

Foucault's target is Nietzsche's target: the old idea that historical change is a "flow," somehow "seamless," proceeding inevitably toward that self-fulfilling prophecy, the present moment. In *Archaeology of Knowledge*, Foucault rejected a reading of history concerned with "continuities, transitions, anticipations, and foreshadowings," replacing it with an archaeology that "is much more willing . . . to speak of discontinuities, ruptures, gaps, entirely new forms of positivity, and of sudden redistributions."[5] Foucault portrayed his new historical project as being "willing" to acknowledge what the high priests of the old history were "reticent" to speak of—a present composed of fragments, a life created by disjunction rather than by continuities.

····················

## A TIME CALLED TOO EARLY

In the prefatorial piece "The Play," Wilson locates *Fences* in a "big-city neighborhood" of an eastern industrial town—probably Pittsburgh—in 1957. In 1957, "the Milwaukee Braves won the World Series, and the hot winds of change that would make the sixties a turbulent, racing, dangerous, and provocative decade had not yet begun to blow full."[6] The year 1957, as Wilson does not mean us to forget, was the year of Little Rock, when Eisenhower reluctantly ordered regular army paratroops to prevent interference with court-ordered racial integration at Little Rock Central High School. That was the year of H.R. 6127, the Civil Rights Act of 1957, passed after virulent debate and filibuster in the Senate. Texas, Tennessee, Delaware,

Maryland, and other states were in the throes of court-ordered desegregation; Little Rock stood out because of the prospect that state and federal troops might face each other. The winds of change blew both hot and cold. The possibility of new positivities coexisted with the fact of ancient recalcitrance. Only three weeks before Little Rock, Ku Klux Klan members had castrated a black man outside of Zion, Alabama. And Louis "Satchmo" Armstrong, in a public gesture that attracted both widespread praise and widespread blame, canceled a much-publicized tour of the USSR, saying that "the way they are treating my people in the South, the government can go to hell. . . . It's getting almost so bad, a colored man hasn't got any country."

In *Fences*, baseball operates metonymically, as a metaphoric stand-in for the troubled changes of 1957. Much of the action takes place just before the Milwaukee Braves' victory over the New York Yankees in the 1957 World Series. That victory signified a year of many changes in baseball, changes that reflected the social upheavals of 1957. One change, very much in progress, was the emergence of the black ballplayer. Black players had played prominent roles in previous World Series—Willie Mays in the 1954 series and Jackie Robinson in the Brooklyn Dodgers' victory over the Yankees in 1955. Milwaukee was the first non–New York team led by a black star to win a World Series. Hank Aaron, the most powerful hitter in baseball history, played alongside Eddie Mathews, white and a great slugger, and alongside three excellent white pitchers: Warren Spahn, Bob Buhl, and Lew Burdette. Because of the quick rise to prominence of Mays, Aaron, Roberto Clemente, and Frank Robinson, the question was no longer whether blacks would play but whether they could become leaders. As the success of the Braves portended, the answer was yes: Aaron led the league in power statistics, hit a home run on the last day of the season to give the Braves the pennant, rampaged through Yankee pitching to give his team the World Series, and won the National League Most Valuable Player Award for 1957.

Yet the Braves were far from being a truly integrated team, and integration was far from complete in baseball. Though blacks had been playing in the major leagues since 1947, it would take until 1959 for each major league team to have at least one black player. Behind the grudging, piecemeal process of integration in sports lies a Foucaultian "disjunction"—World War II—and a resultant "redistribution": the postwar move west. Hard times in postwar Boston meant dwindling patronage for the Boston Braves, so the team moved west to Milwaukee in 1953. In 1957, the Dodgers left Brooklyn for Los Angeles, and the New York Giants left for San Francisco. In so doing, these teams mirrored an accelerating westward shift in the center of population. Further, the war probably created new social potential (to this day not completely realized) for women and blacks. For baseball, all this meant new teams, new audiences, and new pressures to tap at last the large pool of talented black players. The National League led in this regard. Indeed, it was not until Frank Robinson was traded from the Cincinnati Reds to the Baltimore Orioles and won the Triple Crown in 1966 that a black player dominated American League pitching the way Mays, Clemente, and Aaron had done in the National League.

Changes in baseball and changes in American life complicate the ability of anyone who, like Troy, bases his assumptions about reality on the facts of a prewar world. In the first scene of *Fences*, Troy pits his reading of things against those of Bono, Rose, and Lyons. Troy intersperses lies with truths, claiming he has seen and contended with Death and the devil. Rose challenges the way Troy presents these tales: "Anything you can't understand, you want to call it the devil" (14). Rose and Bono are a chorus parenthesizing Troy's insistence on his reading:

> *Rose:* Times have changed since you was playing baseball, Troy. That was
> before the war. Times have changed a lot since then.
> *Troy:* How in hell they done changed?
> *Rose:* They got lots of colored boys playing ball now. Baseball and football.
> *Bono:* You right about that, Rose. Times have changed, Troy. You done
> come along too early.
> *Troy:* There ought not never have been no time called too early! (9)

James calls the present "a saddle-back . . . from which we look in two directions into time."[7] Throughout *Fences*, Troy Maxson straddles this saddle-back, constantly constructing a present selectively out of memory (the past) and desire (the future).

Desire figures most clearly in his conflict with his son, Cory. Troy is affronted by Cory's desire to try out before a college football recruiter from North Carolina. Troy's own sport, and the source of his personal language of metaphors, is baseball; Cory's choice of football galls him. American popular culture has forgotten that integration had come to major league football long before Jackie Robinson signed a baseball contract. Fritz Pollard had played with the Akron Indians beginning in 1919, and black players played professional football until 1933, when the disruption of the Depression made football a whites-only sport for thirteen years.

As with baseball, this redistribution was tied to the postwar westward push. The National Football League (NFL) had originally centered in the Midwest, gradually adding franchises in eastern industrial centers. Long-standing interest in starting a franchise on the West Coast was realized when the Cleveland Rams moved to Los Angeles after the war. A rival league, the All-American Football Conference (AAFC), started up in 1946. Though the two leagues would soon merge, the AAFC forced some innovative moves, including the initiation of western franchises (the Los Angeles Dons and the San Francisco 49ers) and the signing of black players. That same year, the Los Angeles Rams signed Kenny Washington and Woody Strode, and the Cleveland Browns signed Bill Willis and Marion Motley. Motley became a record-breaking rusher, beginning a strong tradition of black running backs that included Joe Perry, who, while playing for the San Francisco 49ers and Baltimore Colts, broke all rushing records through the 1950s. (His heir-apparent was Jim Brown.) By 1953, a black collegiate running back, J. C. Caroline of the University of Illinois, had broken the hallowed records of "Red" Grange, a white runner of the 1920s and 1930s. By the late 1950s, black athletes had established a prominence in football that at least equaled the standing of Mays, Aaron, and the Robinsons in baseball.[8]

With the stronger tradition of integration, football was on the verge of becoming a truly national sport in 1957. Cory believes, as Troy does not, that a talented black athlete can get a chance. This disagreement emerges when they discuss Roberto Clemente, now in his third year with the local baseball club, the Pittsburgh Pirates.

> *Troy:* I ain't thinking about the Pirates. Got an all-white team. Got that boy . . . that Puerto Rican boy . . . Clemente. Don't even half-play him. That boy could be something if they give him a chance. Play him one day and sit him on the bench the next.
> *Cory:* He gets a lot of chances to play.
> *Troy:* I'm talking about playing regular. Playing every day so you can get your timing. That's what I'm talking about.
> *Cory:* They got some white guys on the team that don't play every day. You can't play everybody at the same time.
> *Troy:* If they got a white fellow sitting on the bench . . . you can bet your last dollar he can't play! The colored guy got to be twice as good before he get on the team. That's why I don't want you to get all tied up in them sports. Man on the team and what it get him? They got colored

on the team and don't use them. Same as not having them. All them
teams the same.

*Cory:* The Braves got Hank Aaron and Wes Covington. Hank Aaron hit
two home runs today. That makes forty-three.

*Troy:* Hank Aaron ain't nobody. (33–34)

Far beyond baseball, the ulterior difference here is over whether a change has
occurred in American society. Generational differences indicate a difference
in reading. All Cory knows are the achievements of Aaron (who would hit
forty-four home runs in 1957), Covington, and Clemente; these seem incon-
trovertible evidence that his dreams have a foundation.

What Troy knows is his own frustration as a great player in the Negro
Leagues. His success was also his self-sacrifice: The Negro Leagues began to
die as soon as black players began to be accepted in numbers into professional
baseball.[9] What killed Troy's career was, ironically, the *advent* of integrated
baseball. Although he is clearly aware of these facts, and clearly damaged by
them, Troy insists that history is continuous, that what was once true is still
true. Cory assumes that what is true is new—that there is now a new form of
positivity, a sudden redistribution—and this assumption on Cory's part out-
rages his father. For one the gap signifies the death he constantly pits himself
against, and for the other it signifies a life in the future, liberated from his father's limitations. Granted, Troy's knowing dictum that "the colored guy got
to be twice as good before he get on the team" was quite true in 1957 and is
still a widely shared perception today. But Cory is not arguing that his chance
is likely; he is arguing that it is possible.

Troy gives many names to his resistance. Compassion is one. As he says to
Rose, "I got sense enough not to let my boy get hurt over playing no sports"
(39). Jealousy is another. Cory is getting a chance while he is still young,
whereas even in 1947 Troy was "too old to play in the major leagues" (39).
Both these "reasons" are versions of his resistance to reading the change that
is making Clemente and Aaron into national heroes. Both Troy's compassion
for his son and his jealousy of him are ways to deny his own death.

Here, we may remember one of Foucault's more disturbing claims: that
the traditional view of history as a seamless continuity really disguised the
quest to construct the self as authoritative, continuous, integrated, and eternal. In *Archaeology of Knowledge* he pictures the outraged author crying,
"'Must I suppose that in my discourse I can have no survival? And that in
speaking I am not banishing my death, but actually establishing it?'"[10] For

Troy, to acknowledge the possibility of Cory's success is to acknowledge that his own time has passed. Thus his repression of a fact that would have been available to any avid baseball fan in Pittsburgh—that Roberto Clemente really is getting a chance to play. Clemente had 543 at-bats in 1956 and 451 in 1957.[11] Thus his claim that Aaron is "nobody." Note the extreme care with which Wilson has placed the action of the third act: quite late in September 1957, seemingly to show that reality takes no heed of Troy's judgments. Aaron would win the home-run and runs-batted-in titles, earning him the Most Valuable Player Award. Clemente would go on to 3,000 hits and the Hall of Fame.

. . . . . . . . . . . . . . . . .

## LEFTOVERS

Like Troy Maxson, Ma Rainey refuses in order to survive. As one of the first great prominent black female jazz singers to sing with a band, Ma, like Troy, bestrides a moment of disjunction between a present way and a past way.[12] Ma Rainey was the first female blues singer to enjoy widespread popularity through recording: from 1923 to 1929, she recorded almost one hundred sides. Her innovation was to pitch the blues against a large-band accompaniment. She sang a style of "down-home" blues in which the vocal line closely followed the accompaniment. Her style carried many of the trappings of its Southern sideshow past—including the "tent call" at the beginning of a tune, a convention that the stuttering Sylvester is called on to reproduce in the studio.

Recording was both ascent and eclipse. Though quite popular in the South, Ma's records did not move as well in the Northern cities, and her popularity faded before the rise of Bessie Smith. Six years younger than Rainey, Smith began recording the same year, in 1923. Smith practiced a different style of blues vocal—one in which the vocal line was freed from the accompaniment. This simple difference allowed for greater expressive possibilities for the singer—and the public bought it. Twentieth-century popular music would follow Smith's line rather than Rainey's; in the innovations of the former lay the origins of scat singing, jazz, and soul.

It is worth remembering that both singers had very short careers. Ma Rainey recorded for only six years and quit music in 1933. Bessie Smith made her last recording that year and died four years later in a car crash. Rainey died, completely forgotten, in 1939. It is Smith who is remembered today, with Rainey recorded chiefly as a practitioner of a dead branch of music.[13] Ma Rainey, like Troy Maxson, is an unrecorded great, a leftover of history, a richer subject of reading.

*Ma Rainey's Black Bottom* is set in 1927, just past the peak of Ma Rainey's success. Sturdyvant and Irvin already are warning Ma of Smith's rise, and Ma recognizes this specter by denying it: "Bessie what? Ain't nobody thinking about Bessie. I taught Bessie. She ain't doing nothing but imitating me. What I care about Bessie? I don't care if she sell a million records. She got her people and I got mine. I don't care what nobody else do. Ma was the *first* and don't you forget it!" (64). Irvin and Sturdyvant are quite aware of the gap in styles and how it is hurting Ma's salability. In a variety of dishonest ways, Irvin tries to get Ma to record "Moonshine Blues," a Bessie Smith hit. When Ma refuses, he tries to get her to record "Black Bottom," not in her arrangement (with the stuttering Sylvester as tent caller) but in Levee's: "Ma, that's what the people want now. They want something they can dance to. Times are changing. Levee's arrangement gives the people what they want" (51). When Ma stands firm, Levee nevertheless insists on improvising over the tune. His clash with Ma Rainey finally names the gap over which they have been at war:

> *Ma Rainey:* Levee . . . what is that you doing? Why you playing all them notes? You play ten notes for every one you supposed to play. It don't call for that.
> *Levee:* You supposed to improvise on the theme. That's what I was doing.
> *Ma Rainey:* You supposed to play the song the way I sing it. The way everybody else play it. You ain't supposed to go off and play what you want.
> *Levee:* I was playing the song. I was playing it the way I felt it. (84)

Just as with Troy and Cory, the ulterior clash here is over whether there has or has not been a gap.

Among the many gaps and disjunctions here, two stand out. The first is the gap between an oral time, in which performance was indissolubly linked to the artist's presence, and an aural time, in which performance could be reproduced (or so claimed the supply side) via the technological innovation of recording. Few histories are less continuous, less rational than this one. Each of the formative discoveries, by Bell, Edison, Berliner, included a large number of accidents, experiments, and leaps of intuition.

More interesting than these technological changes are the shifts they occa-
sioned in the conception of performance. Irvin, Sturdyvant, and Levee are
more than comfortable in the new age—but their reading of this change is
very different, and the difference allows us to measure Levee's tragedy. Levee
stands for a new way to play but an old way to think of performance. He embraces the legitimacy of recording, yet he assumes that in recording his songs
he is extending his personality, banishing his death. This becomes clear
whenever he speaks about his songs and his band: "I'm gonna get me a band
and make me some records. I done give Mr. Sturdyvant some of my songs
I wrote and he say he's gonna let me record them when I get my band together. . . . But everybody can't play like I do. Everybody can't have their own
band" (19). Slow Drag, Cutler, and Toledo realize how things really stand:
They are work for hire, not artists, as Levee pretends, and their best chance
for survival lies in playing as they are told. As Slow Drag puts it, "When the
time comes to go up there and record them songs . . . I just wanna go up
there and do it" (17). They see Levee's assumption that "I got time coming to
me" as an obvious self-deception. As his stories about himself show, he has
been broken by his contact with the white man.

Toledo, in his elusive philosophical manner, attempts to teach Levee with
his parable of history as a stew and African Americans as "leftovers": "See,
we's the leftovers. The colored man is the leftovers. Now, what's the colored
man gonna do with himself? That's what we waiting to find out. But first we
gotta know we's the leftovers. . . . But we don't know that we been took and
made history out of" (47). Toledo's metaphor portrays history not as linear
but as a process full of waste and discontinuity. Levee, conversely, is arguing
for the continuity and perpetuity of the self. Refusing to recognize the limits
of his own talent or the social limits imposed on him, he is trying to construct a romance of a meritocracy in which he will be surely rewarded. As the
older musicians point out, this conflicts with what Levy himself knows about
his past and present—that his choices are limited and ruin is always near.

But Levee insists that recording preserves the old personal ties between
performer and audience; he forgets that recording renders each invisible and
unknown to the other. He tries to ignore Sturdyvant's viewpoint, in which
Levee's music, far from being an extended personal contract, is product that
changes hands for money, a business transaction driven by the irrational
needs of the public for music and sex. When the band finally finishes the
date, Irvin chortles, "Good! Wonderful! We have that, boys" (84). The pro-
prietary capitalism in his chosen phrase, the "having" of a recording in order

to sell it, shows how his assumptions differ from Levee's. Sturdyvant's success as a seller of records depends on the sustained anonymity of the actual performers. Sturdyvant not only assents to the establishment of their deaths through recording, he actively promotes it. Ma Rainey the person must be erased in favor of the superior selling potency of her "name"; now that Bessie Smith is on the rise, even Ma Rainey's "name" is endangered.

Ma is far less naive than Levee about the nature of recording. She places such a value on presence in performance that she considers recording to be a kind of prostitution: "They don't care nothing about me. All they want is my voice. . . . As soon as they get my voice down on them recording machines, then it's just like if I'd be some whore and they roll over and put their pants on" (64). This and other comments suggest that for Ma Rainey, live performance is more authentic than recording. The "blues" is a way of learning, a deeply personal thing that needs to be performed to be understood: "You don't sing to feel better. You sing because that's a way of understanding life" (66). It's interesting that singing is, itself, a way of reading.

Yet hers is a losing game, as all the players know. Although imperious (hilariously so) and assertive, Ma as much as admits that with each move she is aiding in her own eclipse. She has decided that, if she is a whore, she had better be well paid. In this, she is different from Troy, less insistent on the continuity of self. She is aware that by signing away her commercial rights to her records she is relinquishing control, and so she holds the moment off as long as she can. When at last she does sign the papers, she covers up for her loss of power by reversing it: "You tell Sturdyvant . . . one more mistake like that and I can make my records someplace else" (88). Though Levee is impressed by Ma's attitude ("As soon as I get my band together and make them records . . . I'm gonna be like Ma and tell the white man just what he can do" [78]), Cutler and Slow Drag know that Ma's "difficult star" act is simply a way to milk the last drop of power from a completely circumscribed situation. As Slow Drag puts it, "You let her go down to one of them white-folks' hotels and see how big she is" (78).

Ma and the older musicians are thus assenting more or less consciously to their own exploitation. This is what Levee cannot forgive them for, even as he himself does it. In selling records that bring the illusion of Ma into every buyer's home, Irvin and Sturdyvant are actually selling the fact of her absence. They will profit from that absence in every copy of "Ma Rainey's Black Bottom" they sell. In signing the release forms, Ma is establishing rather than banishing her death.

A second disjunction, even less rational than that between a time of presence as authenticity and absence as commercial product (the latter captured in the oxymoron "high-fidelity recording"), is that of the difference in styles. There is no complete account of why Ma Rainey sang with her accompaniment and Bessie Smith sang free of it. Both are the blues, and neither is "like" the other. There is no complete account of why the urban-centered "hot" style of playing that would become big-band jazz gained commercial ascendancy over the "down-home" style. (And this was no binary opposition; there were many other styles vying for the public's dollar, and nearly all of them have utterly perished.) Nor can there be a complete account of why the American record buyer endorsed the freer style—and has consistently continued to do so down to the present. (The obvious answers—that this expressed the "American spirit," that in preferring this kind of singing, record buyers were expressing their own aspirations to personal freedom—are so true that they are banal.)

Levee's destruction does not so much prefigure Ma's eclipse as it prefigures the sacrifice of all the black performers. When Sturdyvant attempts to pay him for the songs, thus making clear his death as author, Levee is left to plead for the special case of his self: "You got to hear *me* play them, Mr. Sturdyvant! You ain't heard *me* play them. . . . I'd set them down in the people's lap!" (90–91).

And that reminds us of how classical a Wilson drama really is. For what is this tragic inability to change readings other than the protagonist's *hamartia*, that error in judgment emanating from what is most admirable? Ma Rainey refuses to acknowledge that a shift has taken place in the way jazz is performed and recorded. Although she knows that other ways of singing are passing her up, Rainey maintains her demands that things be done *her* way, the way they have always been done. Troy in *Fences* refuses to allow Cory to play football, in part because he fears that his son *will be allowed to play* as he himself was not. To allow Cory to play would be to acknowledge the inadequacy of his way of reading the world. His refusal has tragic consequences for both Troy and Cory. Cory sees the missed opportunity with the recruiter as "the one chance I had" (57), which, as far as football is concerned, appears to be true. He finds his way into the army and is faced with the burden of learning not to hate his father. At the end of the play, Cory states that he will not reenlist, but, chillingly, it is 1965, the year of great changes in American society and in Indochina. What we are encouraged to see as admirable in both Ma Rainey and Troy Maxson—their insistence on their right to assert themselves in the ambit of their experience (even if that experience is mean, shabby, or poor)—also produces their blindness to the change in time. As it does for Oedipus, the failure to shift readings renders them noble and tragic.

In this respect, Wilson's drama closely follows Aristotelian precepts. Dramatic irony issues from the audience's ability to mark the historical shift that the protagonist insists on denying. We guess that Cory at least *might* get a chance to play if Troy would let him; from what Sturdyvant, Irvin, Ma, and Levee say, we know that a change in popular music threatens to end Ma's career. Troy's tragedy is that he refuses to allow his son to have a future; he insists on the past as present. Cory tells him so: "Just cause you didn't have a chance! You just scared I'm gonna be better than you, that's all" (58). Ma's tragedy is that, being obsolete, she cannot see that she is obsolete. Levee's tragedy is related but different: he has embraced the new paradigm—of a new jazz, a new way for a black man to be—but cannot be part of it himself. His is the Moses complex.

.................

## WHAT HAPPENS ELSEWHERE

Audiences are invited to compare their own readings with those of the characters onstage. That comparison registers a difference, and that difference is what tells us that history has "passed." Note that we do not directly view the change—rather, we realize that a shift *must have happened elsewhere* to enable this difference in readings to exist. Again, Wilson has set these plays at junctures of decisive change in African American history—Chicago in 1927, Pittsburgh in 1957—to sharpen the disparity between our readings and those of the characters. From our privileged perspective, we may well know that "hot" jazz took off in urban centers in the 1920s; we may well know that black athletes were beginning a great tradition in the mid-1950s. A Wilson play presents us with a gradient of readings (Troy-Rosa-Cory, Irvin-Cutler-Ma-Levee), with which we may triangulate our own readings, our own good, better, and best guesses.

I mentioned that in these plays we see not the moment itself passing but rather evidence of a shift that has occurred elsewhere. I don't wish to suggest that such shifts, in a parlance I have always found arrogant, "always occur elsewhere." In fact, they don't. A great shift in the history of American music occurred on a December night in 1939, at "a chili house on Seventh Avenue between 139th and 140th Streets." Saxophonist Charlie Parker had become increasingly "bored with the stereotyped changes" in the jazz of that period.

His frustration had arisen from being able to hear something different but not being able to play it. "That night, I was working over 'Cherokee,' and, as I did, I found that by using the higher intervals of a chord as a melody line and backing them with appropriately related changes I could play the thing I'd been hearing. I came alive."[14]

Among other things, Parker found an improvisational technique through which he could imply passing chords not actually stated by his accompaniment.[15] Parker thus discovered a novel approach to melody and harmony that made possible the creation of bebop, "cool" jazz, and late-century jazz. To be sure, despite the fact that he was there for the change, much about Parker's discovery was clearly out of his control—as he says, he "finds" a new way to play. Parker once told the guitarist Jimmy Raney that "sometimes I look at my fingers and I'm surprised that it's me playing."[16] While acknowledging what was out-of-control in Parker's discovery, we must, out of decency, find a way to acknowledge that Parker was there for the change; in part, he was the change.

For the rest of us, however, that historic change in American music did indeed happen elsewhere—and still happens, nearly every time we hear a contemporary tune. For most people, as for Wilson's tragic characters, great historic changes occur in other minds, are spoken on other lips—and they must either accept these changes or not. Ma Rainey is being left behind because people are buying and dancing to Bessie Smith's records. Cory's chances in football are better than his father's in baseball because of Kenny Washington, Hank Aaron, and Roberto Clemente. Because of the way things are, these characters are condemned to a predicament of relation in regard to the origin of change. This origin they themselves cannot know or find. If we are like Troy, Ma Rainey, and Levee, our tragedy lies in our inability to be there for the change itself. Yet that shift is our fait accompli, what we cannot change or avoid. It is precisely the *anangke* before which, according to Sophocles, "even the gods give way." Knowing is complicated by our position (the Mother of the Blues, for instance; former Negro League baseball great, for instance) and our wishes (to be treated as an authoritative figure, to be continuous and eternal).

These plays suggest that we read history for self-advantage. It is to Cory's advantage that he reads history as discontinuous, as much as it is to Troy's to read history as continuous. Ma Rainey, Levee, Cutler, Irvin, Sturdyvant—each character adopts a reading that best serves his or her wishes and position.

It would be a naive reader who assumed that, given his or her own experience, either Troy or Ma Rainey would value "political awareness" over personal survival. Neither does, and neither takes any comfort in having contributed to the new possibilities that may exist for others. Survivor's guilt is clear in both, but so are fear and resentment at having been sacrificed. The rise to prominence of the jazz singer and the black athlete do not change the facts about the future. To paraphrase Walter Benjamin, we might say that the future is an emptiness that it will take human labor and suffering to fill.

And so to the answer to our opening question. The excluded and the empowered *do* read history differently. Indeed, they cannot but do so, since so much of reading consists of position and wishes, of constructing and projecting. As Nietzsche and Foucault imply, empowerment leads to a history that assumes empowerment: a way of reading that begs the question, rationalizes what it assumes out of sheer privilege. The empowered read history as a "fullness" of time. As Wilson's art construes the question, exclusion leads to other voices, other ways of reading. The excluded often read history as an emptiness that must be filled. The highest praise Ma Rainey receives is from Toledo: "You fill it up with something the people can't be without, Ma. . . . You fill up the emptiness in a way ain't nobody ever thought of doing before" (68). History for the excluded is non-linear, non-rational. That is why, as of this writing, American culture may be the first in which so many kinds of history are being written by the losers. For more than two centuries, African American writers have helped build up an alternative model of history: not an authoritative presentation of "what really happened," but an array of readings that challenge the dominant way.

And this suggests much about African American history, which, far from being a smooth, uninterrupted progress, a "flow," has proceeded by bursts, leaps, shifts, disjunctions, tragic disagreements, the total experience of a group of peoples sharing a diaspora into various fates that have included oppression and exclusion. There have been many positions, many competing wishes (assimilation, radicalism, the Bumpies, the Black Middle Class), many good, better, and best guesses. There will be more. To see African American history as a great river running up to the present is to deny the true richness, tragedy, and achievement in that history. To read it—as Foucault suggests we read anything, and as August Wilson's powerful imagination portrays it—as a series of painful, inevitable rents in what we thought we knew, is to achieve a greater terror, a richer, purer compassion.

·················

## NOTES

1. James, *Principles of Psychology*, p. 507.

2. Neither the term nor the concept of the "specious present" was James's invention. In his essay he credits its originator, E. R. Clay. I am grateful to Ralph Slaght for his insights on this topic.

3. Mundle, "Consciousness of Time," p. 138.

4. Foucault, *Language, Counter-Memory, Practice*, p. 146.

5. Foucault, *Archaeology of Knowledge*, pp. 169–70.

6. Richards, Introduction, pp. vii, xviii.

7. James, *Principles of Psychology*, p. 574.

8. For a more detailed discussion about the vexed issue of integration in professional football, see Ocania Chalk, *Pioneers of Black Sport* (New York: Dodd, Mead, 1975).

9. Black professional baseball players referred variously to these organizations as "the Negro League(s)," "the League," and "the Negro Major Leagues" to differentiate them from the white major leagues, black minor leagues such as the Texas Negro League, and the numerous private barnstorming teams of the period. The Negro Leagues have been better represented in literary treatment than in scholarly research. Part of the problem is the scarcity of materials; few teams could afford the printed programs, team brochures, and team magazines common in the white majors. The best work on the Negro Leagues has thus been done by scholars who have interviewed players, recovered sports reports from the black press of the period, and tracked down personal memorabilia. This work includes John Holway's *Voices from the Great Black Baseball Leagues* (New York: Dodd, Mead, 1975), biographies such as William Brashler's *Josh Gibson: A Life in the Negro Leagues* (New York: Harper and Row, 1978) and Art Rust, Jr.'s *"Get That Nigger Off the Field!"* (New York: Delacourt, 1976), and the work of John Lomax. An excellent study of its kind is Janet Bruce, *The Kansas City Monarchs: Champions of Black Baseball* (Lawrence: University Press of Kansas, 1985). Information also appears in the autobiographies of Negro League greats, such as Leroy "Satchel" Paige's *Maybe I'll Pitch Forever* (Garden City, N.Y.: Doubleday, 1962) and Jackie Robinson's *I Never Had It Made* (New York: G. P. Putnam's Sons, 1972). A good, though glamorizing, early overview is A. S. "Doc" Young's *Great Negro Baseball Stars and How They Made It to the Major Leagues* (New York: A. S. Barnes, 1953). Later studies, such as Effa Manley and Leon Herbert Hardwick's *Negro Baseball . . . Before Integration* (Chicago: Adams, 1976) and Quincy Trouppe's *Twenty Years Too Soon* (Los Angeles: S & S Enterprises, 1977), focus more steadily on the social undercurrents that sustained

and eventually killed the Negro Leagues. The two best overviews, Robert Peterson's *Only the Ball Was White* (Englewood Cliffs, N.J.: Prentice-Hall, 1970) and Donn Rogosin's *Invisible Men: Life in Baseball's Negro Leagues* (New York: Atheneum, 1983), are (perhaps unavoidably) anecdotal in nature, and, while both are furnished with statistics and players lists, neither has a bibliography.

It is worth noting that the "death" of the Negro Leagues was a relative matter. The most prestigious of the Negro Leagues, the Negro National League, was in operation, on and off, between 1920 and 1948. Jackie Robinson's signing prompted many Negro League players to sign minor league contracts with the white major leagues. The National Negro League's prestige plummeted, attendance and gate earnings declined drastically and almost immediately, and the league was dead within two years. (It is interesting also to note that some teams unsuccessfully petitioned the white major leagues to be accepted into the minors.) The Negro American League, however, was in continuous operation between 1937 and 1960; after Robinson's signing, it too was promptly drained of its best players. As the play makes clear, Troy Maxson was already past his prime by 1947, and although many black players (notably Luke Easter and Satchel Paige) lied about their age to protect their marketability, players were not even recruited unless they were standouts and willing to accept ill treatment from fans and management. This last "requirement" is surely lacking in Troy's case.

10. Foucault, *Archaeology of Knowledge*, p. 210.

11. Neft and Cohen, *Sports Encyclopedia*, pp. 309, 312.

12. The blues is one of the most thoroughly documented of American cultural inventions. On Ma Rainey herself, the best scholarly study is Sandra R. Lieb, *Mother of the Blues: A Study of Ma Rainey* (Amherst: University of Massachusetts Press, 1981); on the place of women in the history of the blues, see Chris Albertson, *Bessie* (New York: Stein and Day, 1972); Daphne Duval Harrison, *Black Pearls: Blues Queens of the 1920s* (New Brunswick, N.J.: Rutgers University Press, 1988); and Hettie Jones, *Big Star Fallin' Mama: Five Women in Black Music* (New York: Viking, 1974). Interesting comparisons of the style of the early female blues singers appear in Paul Oliver, *Blues Fell This Morning* (Cambridge: Cambridge University Press, 1990). An important study of the "down-home" style of blues is Jeff Titon, *Early Downhome Blues: A Musical and Cultural Analysis* (Urbana: University of Illinois Press, 1977). Many good studies now exist of the myriad regional blues styles. These include Bruce Bastin, *Red River Blues: The Blues Tradition in the Southeast* (Urbana: University of Illinois Press, 1986) and William P. Ferris, *Blues from the Delta* (New York: Da Capo, 1984). One of the best overviews of blues history is Robert Palmer, *Deep Blues* (Harmondsworth: Penguin, 1981). Two more are Paul

Oliver, *The Blues Tradition* (New York: Oak Publications, 1970) and *The Story of the Blues* (Philadelphia: Chilton, 1973). Two good discographies are John Godrich and Robert Dixon, *Blues and Gospel Records 1902–1942* (London: Storyville, 1969), and Paul Oliver, ed., *The Blackwell Guide to Blues Records* (Oxford: Blackwell, 1989). An excellent bibliography is Mary L. Hart, Brenda M. Eagles, and Lisa N. Howorth, *The Blues: A Bibliographical Guide* (New York: Garland, 1989), and the standard biographical reference is Sheldon Harris, *Blues Who's Who* (New Rochelle, New York: Arlington House, 1979). Important readings include Houston Baker, *Blues, Ideology, and Afro-American Literature: A Vernacular Theory* (Chicago: University of Chicago Press, 1984); Samuel Barclay Charters, *The Roots of the Blues: An African Search* (Boston: M. Boyars, 1981); and Mary Ellison, *Extensions of the Blues* (New York: Riverrun, 1989).

13. The transitional nature of Ma Rainey's career bears some note. She began as a traveling tent show singer with her husband's group, the Rabbit Foot Minstrels. Thus she did not, in fact, grow up in the blues tradition at all, being seduced to it only after hearing a "strange and poignant" [her words] blues song sung by a young girl in 1904. In 1910, the Rabbit Foot Minstrels took on young Bessie Smith for a while; Smith was later to disclaim having been influenced by the elder singer. Rainey was probably bisexual (Oliver, *Blues Fell This Morning*, p. 100); she had a reputation for avid pursuit of young men and women alike. This sheds some interesting light on the reference to Dussie Mae as "Ma's girl." Finally, Rainey's retirement from recording was not caused solely by the rise of Bessie Smith. In fact, Rainey retired in order to stay at home and tend sick family members. It is clear, however, that the triumph of Smith's style was a decisive one.

14. Shapiro and Hentoff, *Hear Me Talking to Ya*, p. 354.

15. Harrison, *Charlie Parker*, pp. 31–32.

16. Reisner, *Bird*, pp. 190–91.

..................

## WORKS CITED

Foucault, Michel. *Archaeology of Knowledge.* Translated by A. M. Sheridan Smith. New York: Pantheon, 1972.

———. *Language, Counter-Memory, Practice.* Edited by Donald F. Bouchard. Translated by Donald F. Bouchard and Sherry Simon. Ithaca: Cornell University Press, 1977.

Harrison, Max. *Charlie Parker.* New York: A. S. Barnes, 1961.

James, William. *Principles of Psychology.* Edited by Frederick H. Burkhardt. Vol. 1. Cambridge: Harvard University Press, 1981.

Mundle, C. W. K. "Time, Consciousness of." *Encyclopedia of Philosophy*. Edited by
    Paul Edwards. Vol. 8. New York: Macmillan, 1967.
Neft, David S., and Richard M. Cohen. *The Sports Encyclopedia: Baseball*. New
    York: St. Martin's Press, 1989.
Reisner, Robert G. *Bird: The Legend of Charlie Parker*. New York: Da Capo, 1975.
Richards, Lloyd. Introduction to *Fences*, by August Wilson, pp. vii–viii. New York:
    New American Library, Plume, 1986.
Shapiro, Nat, and Nat Hentoff. *Hear Me Talking to Ya*. New York: Dover, 1955.
Wilson, August. *Fences*. New York: New American Library, Plume, 1986.
———. *Three Plays*. Pittsburgh: University of Pittsburgh Press, 1991.

ALAN NADEL

# Boundaries, Logistics, and Identity: The Property of Metaphor in *Fences* and *Joe Turner's Come and Gone*

··························································································

The idea of a fence is inextricable from the idea of property. To construct a fence is to delimit, to divide up property, to separate the proper from the improper. The act of naming is fence-building; it is giving propriety to the named, marking it off as proper.

One could argue, furthermore, that this act of naming is the source of all rights. For if we apply a Western theological standard—by invoking some version of natural law—then we can trace these laws from the originary act of naming that separated order out of chaos, and that classified the order through God's agency and Adam's surrogacy, to the naming of a chosen people who would accept the restrictions and thus the inherent freedoms in God's law. If we reject theology in favor of a socially constructed understanding of rights, then naming is the act that creates the parties consenting to any social or personal contract. To put it simply, the unnamed have no properties and therefore cannot claim rights, for the claim to rights, regardless of how one constructs the source of those rights, is the claim that one belongs to the class—either general or particular—to which those rights accrue. The right to life, liberty, or the pursuit of happiness, for example, cannot be claimed for a car axle or a baseball bat; they do not have the necessary properties.

As this example suggests, one significant name that distinguishes a large body of rights is the name "human"; to be named human is to have claim to human rights. For the human race, as for the American Express card, membership has its privileges. (Even the term "human race" suggests the possibility of racial traits that are non-human.) In America, one of the privileges of being human is that one cannot be treated as property; another privilege is that one has property rights, i.e., the right to treat that which is named non-human as property. Property has no rights; property rights, like human rights, are the property of humans. In one case, they are rights that protect the human, and in the other they protect the human's ownership. Property can never be the damaged party or claim rights on its own behalf; the claims are made by the owner, and the damages accrue to him or her. The property itself is mute and neutral.[1]

A fence, then, is a sign of property rights. It thus implies an owner who is human and is manifesting his or her rightful claim. If a literal fence, by being part of a delimited property, represents *metonymically* the presence of property rights, the general concept of a fence or boundary *metaphorically* represents the necessary condition for the abstract accumulation of human rights. Just as the literal fence separates the owner's property from his or her non-property, the metaphoric fence separates human properties from non-human ones.

In antebellum America, race or skin color was just such a fence. It served to separate blacks from humans, denying blacks the properties of humans and giving to humans property rights over blacks. About part of antebellum America, at least, we can say this with certainty. In the South, legal scripture and social precedent affirmed without flinching the distinction between blacks and humans, a distinction made fuzzy but not eliminated by the presence of Southern free blacks or even Southern black slaveholders.[2] In the North, on the average, the boundaries were less clear, the fences less sturdy, although their power to separate was indeed bolstered by the Dred Scott decision and the Fugitive Slave Law.

The Dred Scott decision and the Fugitive Slave Law arbitrated between human rights and property rights by deciding that property rights were universal and human rights were local. The Fugitive Slave Law, passed as part of the Compromise of 1850, made it illegal, even in the North, to help runaway slaves or to refuse to assist in catching them. The Dred Scott decision, in 1857, went so far as to declare the Missouri Compromise, which created the Mason-Dixon line, unconstitutional because it violated the Fifth Amendment by depriving slaveholders of their property without due process of law. To put it another way, these laws and decisions mandated that the humanity of blacks be treated as a metaphor, while their non-humanity—their condition as property—be treated as literal. The fact of their existence, implicitly, was that they had the properties of property, while the circumstances of their logistics might allow them to be treated *as if* they were human, so long as no one could claim that that treatment abrogated his or her property rights. In black American antebellum experience, to consider oneself human was to privilege a metaphoric representation of oneself over the literal "facts" of American culture. Within the codes of the dominant discourse, black humanity existed only as representation, only as its own simulacrum.

For black Americans, then, their humanity lay on the other side of the fence; it was not essential but contingent, a function not of experience but of imagination, situated not geographically but geopolitically. For black Americans, in other words, to consider oneself human was to hold that the truth was not literal but figurative. On some sites, holding to this figurative truth was prohibited by law; on others, it was not. The fence that divided these sites was the Mason-Dixon line. For the slave, that line represented the fence on the other side of which his or her humanity ceased to be figurative. So long as he or she believed that crossing it made one's humanity literal, the line itself was a literal division—a real fence across which lay the name of real humanity. If the Fugitive Slave Law and the Dred Scott decision mitigated that understanding, the failure of the Civil War and of Reconstruction, by eliminating the line but not the distinctions it represented, universalized it. The Mason-Dixon line, no longer literal, became the universal metaphoric fence that marked the properties of race as criteria for inhuman treatment.

The truth of the Mason-Dixon line, like the truth of black humanity, required privileging the figurative over the literal. With the failure of Reconstruction—what Ralph Ellison has called the American counterrevolution of 1876—the metaphoric truth of the Mason-Dixon line became endemic to black American experience, that is, it became a constant awareness that the construction of a site where black humanity became literal was always a personal feat, a function of knowing where the local Mason-Dixon fence lay and staying on the right side of it. This is a humanity constructed tactically and logistically against the larger strategic constructions working to create what de Certeau calls an "institution of the real."[3]

.................

My thesis in this essay is that August Wilson's drama investigates the implications of this condition by creating conflicts whose resolution requires inverting the traditional designations of "literal" and "figurative," and by situating those resolutions within the context of white American historical narrative in such a way as to reveal what Michel de Certeau and Hayden White have demonstrated is the figurative nature of all historical discourse. Both de Certeau and White, each influenced by Michel Foucault, explain how, in historiography, as in all institutionalized discourse, "facts" are the product of discourse, not its foundation.

In historiography, then, the figurative does not substitute for the literal, but rather it makes literal representation possible. From this perspective, the analysis of history becomes not the search for facts but the attempt to discover the privileged metaphors and the consequences of that privilege. Wilson's historicizing, I believe, impels such an examination of American history's representation of race. These traits, I think, typify all of Wilson's drama and, as well, his general attempt to construct a decade-by-decade chronicle of twentieth-century black American experience. *Ma Rainey's Black Bottom*, for example, puts in conflict the literal and figurative value of Ma Rainey's music, as construed by black and white audiences or situated in black or white histories, and our understanding of the motivation for the brutal stabbing at the end depends on our privileging the figurative value of Levee's shoes. In *The Piano Lesson*, again the figurative value of music, this time inextricably connected to the instrument on which it is produced, makes literal the ghosts who haunt the play. *Fences* and *Joe Turner's Come and Gone*, more than the others, however, emphasize the importance of the relationship between logistics and identity. Viewed in juxtaposition, moreover, they illustrate Wilson's interest in the historical context of this relationship.

In *Fences*, August Wilson examines the effects of having to internalize that metaphoric Mason-Dixon line, as he describes Troy Maxson's struggle to build a fence around his property and thus create a site in which his properties can be considered human. A fifty-three-year-old garbageman who owns a small house in a run-down section of Pittsburgh, in 1957, Troy during the course of the play works at building a small fence around his meager back yard. At the same time, he works constantly to delineate his rights and responsibilities, as husband, brother, worker, friend, and father. His name, Maxson, suggests a shortened "Mason-Dixon,"[4] a personalized version of the national division over the properties of blackness. His character similarly embodies the personal divisions that come from living in a world where the Mason-Dixon line exists as the ubiquitous circumscription of black American claims to human rights.

Troy lives in a house with Rose, his wife of eighteen years, and their seventeen-year-old son, Cory. The down payment for the house came from the

$3,000 his brother Gabriel received in compensation for a World War II head wound that left him a virtual half-wit, harboring the belief "with every fiber of his being that he is the Archangel Gabriel" (23). Troy takes pride at having housed and cared for Gabriel since the injury, and at the same time expresses shame at having had to rely on Gabriel's misfortune to provide the down payment he could never have acquired through years of honest labor. Having run away from a cruel and abusive father when he was a teenager, he found his way to the city, where he married and supported his family through theft until he was convicted of assault and armed robbery and sent to jail for fifteen years. There he learned to play baseball and give up robbery. By the time he was released, his wife having left him, he met Rose, remarried, and after playing baseball in the Negro Leagues, became a garbageman.

The central conflicts in the play arise from his refusal to let his son play football or accept a football scholarship to college, and from his having fathered a daughter through an extramarital affair. But these are framed by conflicts with the father he fled, the major leagues that wouldn't let him play baseball, and Death himself, with whom Troy had once wrestled. Whatever else he loses, he vigilantly maintains his property and his property rights, demanding his authority within its confines, eventually building a fence around his yard and guarding the entrance with all of his human power against the force of Death, whose representation in human form is generally perceived to be metaphoric.

It is on these grounds—and on his home ground—that Troy chooses to be sized up. For in all other locales he is a large man who has been underestimated. As a baseball player and even as a garbageman, the world has not taken his measure. To "take the measure of a man" is to make a metaphor derived from a set of primary physical traits. "To measure up" means to fulfill a role in the same way one fills out a suit of clothes; "to take measure of oneself" means to assess one's ability to fill a specific role in the same way that one selects that suit of clothes. Implicit in all these metaphors is a set of objective physical standards—what Locke called primary characteristics—against which such intangibles as character, courage, loyalty, skill, or talent can be determined.

In the logistics of *Fences*, however, these standards form the variables measured against the standard of Troy Maxson's largeness. From the outset of the play, his size is a given: "Troy is fifty-three years old, a large man with thick heavy hands; it is this largeness that he strives to fill out and make an accommodation with. Together with his blackness, his largeness informs his sensibilities and the choices he has made in life" (1). And after his death, as Rose explains to Cory, "When I first met your daddy, . . . I thought here is a man you can open yourself up to and be filled to bursting. Here is a man that can fill all them empty spaces you been tipping around the edges of. . . . When your daddy walked through the house, he filled it up" (93). Cory perceived Troy as "a shadow that followed you everywhere. It weighed on you and sunk in your flesh. It would wrap around you and lay there until you couldn't tell which one was you any more" (93), but Rose argues that Cory is just like his father:

> That shadow wasn't nothing but you growing into yourself. You either got to grow into it or cut it down to fit you. But that's all you got to make life with. That's all you got to measure yourself against that world out there. Your daddy wanted you to be everything he wasn't . . . and at the same time he tried to make you into everything he was. (93)

In addition to establishing Troy's size as the standard, both negative and positive, Rose is setting that standard against the standards asserted by the dominant white culture. Cory, in other words, is being urged not to measure himself against Troy but to use Troy's size as a defense against the other, implicitly figurative, norms of "that world out there."

In so doing, Rose is asking him, in fact, to continue his father's quest. For the problem of the play can be seen as Troy's attempt to take measure of himself in a world that has denied him the external referents. His struggle is to act in the literal world in such a way as to become not just the literal but the figurative father, brother, husband, man he desires to be. The role of father is the most complex because he is the father of three children from three different women. The children, precisely seventeen years apart, represent Troy's paternal responsibilities to three successive generations of black children. As each of these children makes demands on him, he must measure up to his responsibilities, and for each generation he measures up differently.

When his older son, Lyons, a would-be musician, for example, regularly borrows money from him, Troy puts Lyons through a ritual of humiliation constructed out of the process of differentiating Lyons from himself: "I done learned my mistake and learned to do what's right by it. You still trying to get something for nothing. Life don't owe you nothing. You owe it to yourself." At issue here is not only Troy's sense of himself as role model but also his sense of himself as negative example. He is both the father to emulate and the father not to emulate: Lyons should be like Troy by not making Troy's mistake. This lesson has a double edge, though, because the earlier, error-ridden life that Troy has learned to reject included not only his criminal acts but also his marriage to Lyons's mother and his fathering of Lyons. At that point in his life, we later learn, he felt he was not ready to be a father or to accept the responsibilities of fatherhood. For Lyons to recognize Troy's mistakes, then, is for him to acknowledge the inappropriateness of his own existence.

Troy deals with his younger son, Cory, in the same way. Like Troy, Cory is a talented athlete. A superstar in the Negro baseball leagues, Troy was never given an opportunity to play in the white leagues. Believing that white America would never allow a black to be successful in professional sports, he refuses to allow his son to go to college on a football scholarship. Once again, he becomes what he sees as a positive example for his son by virtue of his ability to reject himself. In a completely self-contained economy, he becomes both the model of error and the model of correction.

In regard to sports, particularly, he does this by constructing a division between personal history and American history. An extraordinary baseball player whose talents are compared with those of Babe Ruth and Josh Gibson, Troy was unfortunately over forty years old when professional baseball was first integrated. Within the time frame of American history, as his friend Bono says, "Troy just come along too early" (9). Troy rejects Bono's opinion with a triple negative: "There ought not never have been no time called too early" (9). "I'm talking about," he explains, "if you could play ball then they ought to have let you play. Don't care what color you were. Come telling me I come along too early. If you could play, then they ought to have let you play" (9).

In his critique of Bono's historical analysis, Troy is exposing its figurative nature and, by implication, what Hayden White has identified as the tropic nature of all history. Whereas Bono privileges the events of American professional sports integration as the given fact, Troy privileges the athletic requirements of the sport, not the political requirements surrounding it, as the context that determines meaning. To suggest that there was a right time to meet the requirements of a sport is to reveal that the requirements are figurative, just as suggesting that one can meet those requirements too early is to reveal that the time frame is figurative. At stake again is the dominant discourse—the one echoed by Bono—that takes the time frame of segregation as a fact in light of which a black player's physical ability can be seen as metaphoric.

For Troy to assert that his physical ability can be valorized only within a time frame that is racially determined is to impose the Mason-Dixon line onto his body. And if, as I have suggested, the name "Maxson" suggests this imposition from outside, the name "Troy" suggests the creation of a defensive wall, the internal resistance against alien assaults, with each assault being the precursor of Death. After the death in childbirth of his girlfriend, therefore, Troy issues his challenge to Death in terms of the wall he is constructing between himself and it:

> I'm gonna build me a fence around what belongs to me. And I want you to stay on the other side. See? You stay over there until you're ready for me. Then you come on. Bring your army. Bring your sickle. Bring your wrestling clothes. I ain't gonna fall down on my vigilance this time. You ain't gonna sneak up on me no more. When you ready for me . . . that's when you come around here. . . . Then we gonna find out what manner of man you are. . . . You stay on the other side of that fence until you ready for me.

This is the metaphoric fence constructed to complement the literal fence Rose had been requesting from the outset. When Death accepts Troy's challenge, he confirms Troy's mastery over the literal, his power to turn his property into the visible recognition of his human properties, such that his responsibilities to his family, his athletic prowess, and his physical presence confirm his ability to confront Death—and hence to construct his life—on his own terms. In his terms, as he stated earlier in the play, "Death ain't nothing but a fastball on the outside corner" (10). Rose's description of Troy's death confirms that terminology: "He was out there swinging that bat and then he just fell over. Seem like he swung it and stood there with this grin on his face . . . and then he just fell over" (91). The inference is not only that he had protected his family by striking a final blow at Death but, more significantly, that he was able to do so because Troy made Death come to him on Troy's terms. Although Troy's challenge may be seen as figurative, Death's accepting it makes it literal, and thus the man-to-man battle between Troy and Death becomes a literal fight and simultaneously affirms Troy's power to create a site—however small—in which the figurative becomes literal. The conversion not only reduces Death to a man but also affirms Troy's status as one.

Within the context of the play, moreover, Wilson affirms the literal status of that conversion by having Gabriel perform a similar feat. Released from the mental hospital in order to attend Troy's funeral, Gabriel arrives carrying his trumpet. Although it has no mouthpiece, he uses it to "tell St. Peter to open the gates" (99). After three attempts, with no sound coming from the trumpet, "he begins to dance. A slow, strange dance, eerie and life-giving. A dance of atavistic signature and ritual. He begins to howl at what is an attempt at song, or perhaps a song turning back into itself in an attempt at speech. He finishes his song and the gates of heaven stand open as wide as God's closet" (100).

Gabriel's ability to invert the literal and the figurative thus confirms our understanding of Troy's death, at the same time that it revises our understanding of Gabriel's marginality or "madness." For we can read his wound as a function of attributing literal power to such figurative institutions as nation and warfare. As a soldier in World War II, he invested his primary literal claim to human rights—his human life—in support of a figurative structure—the United States—that on the very site of his investment, the segregated armed forces, denied the status of that life as human. One can only assume that the part of his brain blown away in the war contained the beliefs and conceptions that allowed him to accept the figurative status of his own humanity. Lacking that part of his brain, he is not functional within the dominant white culture, as is evidenced by his numerous arrests as well as his institutionalizations.

The Mason-Dixon line, marking off the site where he may consider himself literally human, has become for Gabriel the walls of the mental institution. By the end of the play—providing a virtual survey of the institutionalized power critiqued by Michel Foucault—all the Maxsons are disciplined within figurative Mason-Dixon lines. With Gabriel in the mental hospital, Cory in the armed services, Lyons in prison (we could conceivably even add Rose's recent involvement with the church), they find only this moment of relief within the boundary of the fence that Troy built. In the play's final pronouncement, with Gabriel speaking now as prophet and miracle worker rather than as marginalized madman, he asserts and demonstrates that the order of things—the relationship of figurative to literal—should be reversed: "And that's the way that go!" (100).

This is a tactical victory, a method of subverting and resisting the strategic power of the dominant culture. For that culture has urged the black American man to flight with the implication that his humanity was the function of logistics; confined by sites that denied literal confirmation of that humanity, the culture has offered the promise of an elsewhere, a site where the literal and figurative reconfigure. To pursue that promise, to seek that site, often meant sacrificing familial responsibilities. Instead of pursuing that site at the expense of his family, Troy created it in order to protect them. As Rose, referring to the fence, noted to Cory, "Oh, that's been up there ever since Raynell wasn't but a wee little bitty old thing. Your daddy finally got around to putting that up to keep her in the yard" (91).

In this way, Troy fought not only Death, but also history. For the normative discourse of white American history, in 1957, was one of progress and assimilation. Textbooks promoted the idea of the melting pot and of upward mobility; historical films and dramas reinscribed the myth of the nuclear family; and despite the continued presence of Jim Crow laws, segregated schools and facilities, rampant denial of voter rights, and extensive discrimination in housing and employment, American history and, more important, its popularizations represented the United States as a land of equal opportunity, with liberty and justice for all. Those whose personal narratives failed to confirm this hegemonic discourse became invisible; as Ralph Ellison so dramatically illustrated in *Invisible Man*, they fell outside of history. Despairing of the possibility of altering dominant historical discourse, Troy devotes himself to reconfiguring the paternal patterns that compose his personal history.

In thus making himself both the positive and the negative model for his sons, he also makes his father a positive and a negative model. For unlike many men of his generation—Bono's father, for example—Troy's father refused to leave the family, however much he detested it. As Troy points out, "He felt a responsibility toward us. May be he ain't treated us the way I felt he should have, but without that responsibility he could have walked off and left us, made his own way" (49). In contrast, as Bono points out, "Back in those days what you talking about, niggers used to travel all over. They get up one day and see where the day ain't sitting right with them and they walk out their front door and just take on down one road or another and keep on walking. . . . Just walk on till you come to something else. Ain't you never heard of nobody having the walking blues?" (50–51).

The "back in those days" to which Bono refers is the period in which *Joe Turner's Come and Gone* is set. And the play, we could say, is very much about exactly those "walking blues" that Troy's father rejected. Set in a Pittsburgh boardinghouse, perhaps not far from the site that would eventually become the Maxson home, it becomes the intersection at which we meet numerous characters like Bono's father, each with his or her own form of walking blues. The characters, in other words, have literalized the idea signified by the

Mason-Dixon line—that a site exists where they become human. For each of the characters, that quest for humanity is for a form of completeness which their circumstances, and history, has denied them. It may be economic security or fair employment practices, or a mate, or a family. The haunting specter of this quest comes in the form of Herald Loomis, a man traveling with his eleven-year-old daughter, searching for his estranged wife, from whom he had become separated during his seven years of forced labor on a Southern chain gang.

In numerous ways, this experience, all too typical for Southern blacks, indicates the ways in which the Emancipation effected by the Civil War was only figurative. Loomis, first of all, was forced into a slave-labor situation. Nearly half a century after Emancipation, he still could be denied his human rights and treated as property. After seven years, when he is freed from the chain gang, he experiences the situations of a newly freed slave. Rent of his roots, without family, home, or job, he is in an environment that still fails to recognize his human rights. Although he is looking to start anew, everywhere around him his circumstances replicate the past. Under such conditions, many came to assume that the future lay elsewhere. They looked for their human rights—i.e., the legal and social confirmation of their status as human—in a place, just as their antebellum ancestors had, rather than in time, as their parents had. In this sense, especially in light of the exacerbated violence against blacks in the turn-of-the-century South, the characters with the walking blues in *Joe Turner* can be seen as walking on a historical treadmill, arriving at neither a time nor a place at which their humanity was construed as literal. Instead they replicate infinitely the quest for freedom, for the site, in other words, where they are construed as having the properties of humans.

The play thus equates these walkers to newly freed slaves. In the preface, for example, Wilson writes:

> From the deep and the near South the sons and daughters of newly freed African slaves wander into the city. Isolated, cut off from memory, having forgotten the names of the gods and only guessing at their faces, they arrive dazed and stunned, their heart kicking in their chest with a song worth singing. They arrive carrying Bibles and guitars, their pockets lined with dust and fresh hope, marked men and women seeking to scrape from the narrow, crooked cobbles and the fiery blasts of the coke furnace a way of bludgeoning and shaping the malleable parts of themselves into a new identity as free men of definite and sincere worth.[5]

Only the words "sons and daughters" differentiate those described here from the newly freed. Because the generational shift, in other words, has produced no concomitant shift in status or identity, these migrants imply that a shift in locale will.

Seth Holly, the Northern-born black owner of the boardinghouse, questions their goals, but he does not dispute their status as newly freed slaves:

> Ever since slavery got over, there ain't been nothing but foolish-acting niggers. Word get out that they need men to work in the mill and put in these roads . . . and niggers drop everything and head North looking for freedom. They don't know the white fellows looking too. White fellows coming from all over the world. White fellow come over and in six month got more than what I got. But these niggers keep on coming. Walking. . . riding . . . carrying their Bibles. . . . Niggers coming up here from the backwoods . . . looking for freedom. They got a rude awakening. (6)

Like Troy Maxson, Holly underscores the difference between the narrative history of white America—one that incorporates personal narratives of effort, achievement, and reward into a coherent national narrative of progress—and the narrative history of black Americans who, again like Ellison's invisible man, continue to run like an escaping slave toward an ever-receding horizon. Within the dominant discourse, Holly sees the black emigrants as still—vainly—trying to escape slavery.

To put it another way, he is recognizing the figurative power of the Fugitive Slave Law, the power to deny blacks their human properties, regardless of their locale. That power, Wilson makes clear, is economic and applies as much to Holly himself as it does to the tenants who pass through his house. For Holly too is a man whose labor is being exploited. As he himself acknowledges, even a property owner like himself was quickly surpassed economically by white emigrants. But Holly is also a tradesman, making pots with the raw materials furnished by a white pedlar named Rutherford Selig. Although Holly ought to be able to capitalize on his skills, because he is dependent upon Selig for both materials and distribution, he cannot amass enough capital to set up a shop of his own and hire other workers in the community. Instead of returning to the community, the surplus value of his labor becomes the profit of the white community. Nor will that community finance Holly's attempts to capitalize his labor with a loan unless he puts his property up as collateral. Holly had inherited his property from his father, who was a freeman; for Holly, therefore, as for Troy, the property signifies the site on which he has human properties, the site on which he is the *subject with* property rights, not the *object of* property rights. Refusing therefore to jeopardize his property, he nevertheless becomes the virtual property of Selig, with the fruits of his labor circumscribed completely by Selig's allowance and demand.

The connection between this relationship and slavery is underscored in several ways. First, Selig enters immediately after Holly announces that the blacks looking for freedom have "a rude awakening." More significantly, Selig is also known as the People Finder, a name he gets because his door-to-door and town-to-town travels enable him to locate people for a fee, in much the way that a slave catcher did. This connection is later made by Selig himself, who identifies his current practices as deriving from his family's historical connection with the slave trade:

> My great-granddaddy used to bring Nigras across the ocean on ships. . . . it set him well in pay and he settled in this new land and found him a wife of good Christian charity and with a mind for kids and the like and well . . . here I am, Rutherford Selig. . . . Me and my daddy have found plenty Nigras. My daddy, rest his soul, used to find runaway slaves for the plantation bosses. He was the best there was at it. . . . After Abraham Lincoln give all you Nigras your freedom papers and with you all looking all over for each other . . . we started finding Nigras for Nigras. Of course, it don't pay as much. But the People Finding business ain't so bad. (41)

This speech is significant for several reasons. The first is its anachronistic quality that suggests Selig worked with his father as a slave catcher, and that he started tracking blacks for blacks immediately after the Civil War. Since Selig is in his early fifties, however, he was under ten years old in 1865. This conflating of time does not seem to me so much an error as a recognition of continuum, a recognition of the ways in which Selig's role is no more a significant break with that of his slave-selling and slave-catching ancestors than Loomis's is with that of slaves.

The speech also validates Holly's (and Maxson's) sense of dual histories. As Selig acknowledges, slavery enabled the slave merchants to establish coherent families with histories, traditions, extended lineage, while it left the slaves "all looking all over for each other." White America, the speech indicates, historically rewarded the practice of slave trade—with both money and respect— while it historically punished the victims of that practice. This is "historical" discrimination in that it created a continuum—an institutionalized repetition of practices that, despite some differences (e.g., level of profit, abolition of some laws in some areas), compose a coherent pattern of discipline and exploitation transcending the alleged historical rupture of the Civil War. While the principles fought for in and established by that war—most notably, that the United States would not be a slave-holding nation—cannot, I think, be underestimated, the failure of the nation to address adequately the implications of Emancipation and to institutionalize the human rights of black Americans, gives the Civil War a different position and significance in black American history than in the dominant historical narratives of white America.

The failure of those historical narratives to acknowledge black American history, then, becomes another form of historical discrimination. It is not just the history of denying blacks their human rights but also the practice of denying the story of that denial—or at least the significance of that story—in the dominant discourse named "American" history.

In this context, even attempts to bind the rifts created by the practice of slavery become another source of profit for the former slave catchers. If the black's body is no longer the property of the slave catcher, his or her name, identity, location are. His profit comes from controlling the economy in which these properties are exchanged for money, in just the same way that he controls the economy in which Holly's labor is traded.

Selig's control over this human exchange, however, is even more extensive in that he represents the institutions and practices that have initially reduced blacks to the property whose properties he trades upon. As Holly's wife, Bertha, points out,

> You can call him a People Finder if you want to. I know Rutherford Selig carries people away too. He done carried a whole bunch of them away from here. Folks plan on leaving by Selig's timing. They wait till he get ready to go, then they hitch a ride on his wagon. Then he charge folks a dollar to tell them where he took them. Now that's the truth of Rutherford Selig. This People Finding business is for the birds. He ain't never found nobody he ain't took away.

This characterization draws direct parallels between Selig and the mythic Joe Turner. Joe Turner is the name, immortalized by a blues song, of the man who caught blacks to work on his chain gang. In catching Loomis, he broke up Loomis's family. Unable to work the land herself, his wife, Martha, was thrown off her tenant farm, and after five years of waiting for Loomis to return she presumed him dead and went North, leaving their daughter in the care of her mother. When Loomis was released by Joe Turner, he set out for the North in search of his wife. At the same time, however, explains Martha, who had returned for her daughter, "I wasn't but two months behind you when you went to my mama's and got Zonia. I been looking for you ever since" (89).

Just like the newly freed slaves that Selig described, in other words, Loomis and Martha were "all looking all over for each other." When Loomis gives Selig the dollar to find Martha, he is paying Selig to find somebody whom Joe Turner took away. This creates a parallel between Loomis and Holly, both black Americans living in the aftermath of captivity and delimited by the economy created by that aftermath. That economy is constructed out of a dual historical perspective that marginalized the victims of slavery while it valorized the practitioners; it is an economy in which black labor becomes the property that allows white society to deny blacks their human rights. In transcending time, this economy denies blacks their participation in the American historical narrative, and this motivates Wilson's call for an alternative historical project, suggesting that in the performing arts—those inscribed in what de Certeau has called the practices of everyday life—can be found the site of black American history: the traces of its African origins, the scars of bondage, the economy of otherness, the encoded language of ghettoization, the arts and customs forged by the conditions of a double diaspora. As much criticism has noted, black American literature needs to be read through an awareness of such practices as storytelling (and the folkloric), the blues, black vernacular, folk art, and the "dozens."[6]

Wilson thus privileges music as the source of a reality that transcends logistics, making it in all of his plays the link between humanity and history. As Bynum points out to Loomis, Joe Turner's ability to exercise his property rights over Loomis's body was an attempt to steal not merely Loomis's labor but also his claim to human rights. In describing his captivity by Joe Turner, he implicitly raises this issue:

> I asked one of them fellows one time why he catch niggers. Asked him what I got he want? . . . He told me I was worthless. Worthless is something you throw away. Something you don't bother with. I ain't seen him throw me away. . . . I ain't tried to catch him when he going down the road. So I must got something he want. What I got?

At stake here is the contradiction implicit in enslavement. To treat a person as property is to deny his or her human worth, while to steal and guard that person is to ascribe some inherent value to him or her. Holly's explanation— "He just want you to work for him. That's all"—Loomis finds inadequate: "I can look at him and see where he big and strong enough to do his own work. So it can't be that. He must want something he ain't got." To Holly's literal explanation, in other words, Loomis gives a literal response, thus pointing out that a person's desire to have someone do his or her work and the formulation of that desire into a master-slave relationship cannot be attributed simply to the need to get work done. To accept this literal formulation, Loomis must allow that his only properties are *qua* property, that he does not have human rights which are being stolen along with his labor. So Loomis returns to that which he has or is, beyond the tangible property of producing labor or of being a machine. Since acknowledging his worth simply as machine legitimizes Joe Turner's use of him, he instead points out that such a need is an inadequate explanation. This turns him to the figurative construction of his worth, but he makes the turn in the form of a question, the answer to which Bynum supplies:

> That ain't hard to figure out. What he wanted was your song. He wanted to have that song to be his. He thought by catching you he could learn that song. Every nigger he catch he's looking for the one he can learn that song from. Now he's got you bound up to where you can't sing your own song. Couldn't sing it them seven years 'cause you was afraid he would snatch it from under you. But you still got it. You just forgot how to sing it. ·

In this response, Bynum not only answers Loomis's question but also explains why Loomis himself doesn't know the answer. Since the song, as Wilson represents it, is one of the sites of black American history, it is the authority upon which rests Loomis's claim to human rights. To steal that song is thus to deprive Loomis of the claim and thereby to legitimize the treatment of him as property. At the same time, Loomis's attempt to protect his song, in the way he was unable to protect his body, has forced him to suppress that song in the same way that Berniece in *The Piano Lesson* forced herself not to play the piano. In denying Joe Turner access to the source of his claim to human rights, he has also had to deprive himself of that access. In consequence, now that Joe Turner has come and gone, Herald Loomis doesn't know whether he is coming or going. The figurative source of his claim to human rights, his song, has turned into a literal search for logistics, the walkin' blues. Hence he searches for his lost wife not to recapture her—which would replicate Joe Turner's enslavement—but rather to recapture the history he lost when he suppressed his song. As he points out, he wants to find Martha so that he can start again:

> That's the only thing I know to do. I just want to see her face so I can get me a starting place in the world. The world got to start somewhere. That's what I been looking for. I been wandering a long time in somebody else's world. When I find my wife that be the making of my own.

The temporal and the geographic are inextricably connected in Loomis's speech. He is looking for a starting *place*, a site from which to initiate his entrance into *time*, into history. That entrance into history, in turn, is figured as the creation of a place, a world of his own. He is estranged from that place, however, not by distance but by time: "wandering for a long time in somebody else's world." In thus refiguring Moses' experience of being a stranger in a strange land, Wilson exposes the ways that black Americans have lived outside of the governing metanarratives of white Western culture. Although he is the slave who has wandered for years and arrived at the destination north of the Mason-Dixon line, it provides no promised land, i.e., no property on which his claims to human rights are literal; and although he seeks to return to his origins, unlike Odysseus, he has no homeland to claim, i.e., no property on which his claims to human rights once were literal. Loomis, in other words, seeks a figurative place with literal power, and Wilson provides it by imbuing it, like Troy Maxson's fence and Gabriel's identity, with superiority over its literal representation.

The song becomes a truer form of history than white historical discourse, and being bound to his song allows Loomis a historical identity as a human being that no geographical site allows. Troy Maxson is similarly bound to a song about his dog Blue. And his son, like Loomis, finds a starting place when he sings Blue's song and thus binds himself to his father's blues. The song is an elegy for a hunting dog. "Blue laid down and died like a man," the song tells us. "Now he's treeing possums in the Promised Land" (98). In Blue's song, as in the blues, the dog crosses the true Mason-Dixon line to the Promised Land, the land, in other words, that promises conversion from beast to man, servitude to freedom—the figurative land on which one acquires human properties instead of being the property of humans. This is indeed Troy Maxson's song, and when his son and daughter sing it together, Gabriel can arrive to prove that the song's claim, which has become theirs, is real.

If reality is authorized for black Americans by performance and for white America by text, Wilson's plays, as both text and performance, mediate between the site of dominant discourse and the practices of black American life. In this regard, we can view his project to create a decade-by-decade cycle of plays as an attempt to make history, that is, an attempt both to construct an event and to construct the story in which it figures. This is figurative history, but as we have seen, in the context of American history, to privilege the figurative, to invert its relationship to the literal, has been a means to construct a claim for the human rights of black Americans.

········

## NOTES

1. Property is the silent other to all litigants who speak on its behalf. If Michel de Certeau is correct that all discourse speaks for the silent body that nourishes it (see, for example, in *The Writing of History*, "The Discourse of Separation: Writing," pp. 2–6, or *Heterologies*, pp. 199–221), then we can see how speaking for the Other is always paradigmatically treating that Other as property—i.e., designating it with the property of silence. For de Certeau this constitutes colonialization, for Jean-François Lyotard, terrorism.

2. Ira Berlin, in *Slaves without Masters*, clearly demonstrates the dehumanizing racial caste system that prevailed in the antebellum South, independent of manumission.

3. *Heterologies*, p. 200; see also de Certeau's distinctions between strategic and tactical in the General Introduction to *The Practice of Everyday Life*.

4. In *Ma Rainey's Black Bottom*, in fact, Levee refers to it as the "Maxon-Dixon line" (82).

5. Wilson, *Joe Turner's Come and Gone*.

6. See, for example, Baraka, *Blues People*; Baker, *Blues, Ideology, and Afro-American Literature*; Byerman, *Fingering the Jagged Grain*; Callahan, *In the African-American Grain*; Ellison, *Shadow and Act*; and Gates, *Signifying Monkey*.

········

## WORKS CITED

Baker, Houston A., Jr. *Blues, Ideology, and Afro-American Literature: A Vernacular Theory*. Chicago: University of Chicago Press, 1984.

Baraka, Amiri (LeRoi Jones). *Blues People: Negro Music in White America*. New York: Murrow, 1963.

Berlin, Ira. *Slaves without Masters.* New York: Pantheon, 1974.

Byerman, Keith. *Fingering the Jagged Grain: Tradition and Form in Recent Black Fiction.* Athens: University of Georgia Press, 1985.

Callahan, John. *In the African-American Grain.* Urbana: University of Illinois Press, 1988.

de Certeau, Michel. *Heterologies. Discourse on the Other.* Translated by Brian Massumi. Minneapolis: University of Minnesota Press, 1986.

———. *The Practice of Everyday Life.* Translated by Steven Rendall. Berkeley: University of California Press, 1984.

———. *The Writing of History.* Translated by Tom Conley. New York: Columbia University Press, 1988.

Ellison, Ralph. *Shadow and Act.* New York: New American Library, 1966.

Gates, Henry Louis. *The Signifying Monkey: A Theory of Afro-American Literary Criticism.* Oxford: Oxford University Press, 1988.

Lyotard, Jean-François. *The Postmodern Condition: A Report on Knowledge.* Translated by Geoff Bennington and Brian Massumi. Minneapolis: University of Minnesota Press, 1984.

White, Hayden. *The Content of Form: Narrative Discourse and Historical Representation.* Baltimore: Johns Hopkins University Press, 1987.

———. *Tropics of Discourse: Essays in Cultural Criticism.* Baltimore: Johns Hopkins University Press, 1978.

Wilson, August. *Fences.* New York: New American Library, Plume, 1986.

———. *Joe Turner's Come and Gone.* New York: New American Library, Plume, 1988.

———. *Ma Rainey's Black Bottom.* New York: New American Library, Plume, 1985.

**MICHAEL MORALES**

# Ghosts on the Piano: August Wilson and the Representation of Black American History

· · · · · · · · · · · · · · · · · · · · · · · · · · · · · · · · · · · · · · · · · · · · · · ·

In a *New York Times* interview coinciding with the Broadway opening of *The Piano Lesson*, August Wilson described how Romare Bearden's painting *Piano Lesson* originally inspired the play, and he explained what the piano initially meant to him: "It provided a link to the past, to Africa, to who these people are. And then the question became, what do you do with your legacy? How do you best put it to use?"[1] In this essay, I would like to take that same question and apply it to Wilson's project of writing a play for every decade of this century, in order to begin considering whether a specific "philosophy of history" is emerging from the expanding body of his dramatic work. Although Wilson's larger project is still a "work in progress," since he has completed five major works we can begin to look critically at some of the ideas he "proposes" about history and the assumptions upon which those ideas are based, as well as the larger historical, social, and ontological implications.

Wilson's task, one shared by many black American writers, is a simultaneously reactive/reconstructive engagement with the representation of blacks and the representation of history by the dominant culture. As Wilson has explained, he is "more and more concerned with pointing out the differences between blacks and whites, as opposed to pointing out similarities. We're a different people. We do things differently."[2] This statement necessarily leads us to the question, though, of what is the basis upon which cultural difference is explained? What are the assumptions behind a shared identity? Considering Wilson's overall project, one might assume that the basis would always be historical. Yet that assumption seems to waver in respect to the strong mystical content of both *The Piano Lesson* and *Joe Turner* and forces the question of why history is being represented in such terms.

In *Joe Turner's Come and Gone* and *The Piano Lesson*, August Wilson's historical project moves into a world of ancestral visitations, visions, and ghosts, that even includes an onstage self-crucifixion as well as an exorcism. The mystical elements intertwine closely with Wilson's historical project in what might be characterized as an experiment in African American historiography. In these two plays Wilson predicates the relationship of the past to the present for black Americans on an active lineage kinship bond between the living and their ancestors. In this sense, the transmission of history becomes a binding ritual through which his characters obtain an empowering self-knowledge, a tangible sense of their own self-worth and identity, that gives them the strength to manage the future on their own terms. Like Herald Loomis, they are able to find their own songs. In *Joe Turner's Come and Gone* the ancestor's visitations grant visions of the middle passage to Bynum and Herald Loomis in order that they may discover themselves; in *The Piano Lesson*, the spirits of the ancestors are called upon for protection from Sutter's ghost, and through their protection they resolve the internecine struggle between Boy Willie and Berniece, subsequently preserving that kinship bond and, presumably, opening a world of self-realization to Berniece. In both plays meaningful progress toward the future and self-realization are achieved only by establishing connections to the past—connections represented as the power of the ancestors.

Using *The Piano Lesson* as the example, both the literal and the metaphoric functions of the piano serve to elucidate Wilson's framing of black American history as an active relation (kinship bond) between the living and the dead. The piano provides the key links to the past in what I argue are its interrelated, dual ritual functions. First, it functions as a mnemonic device for the transmission of oral history; and second, it functions as a sacred ancestral altar, bridging the world of the living to that of the dead.

The piano parallels similar devices used to preserve the oral history of several African civilizations, such as the memory boards (*lukasa*) of the Luba and the brass plaques of Benin. While controversy still exists about the precise representational intention of many of the brass plaques of Benin, accounts of nineteenth-century visitors to the kingdom attest to their historiographic function.[3] These plaques, which covered the supporting pillars of the royal palace, represented in relief major events of the Benin kingdom, the daily court life, and the lineage of rulers.[4] Even though art historians may disagree as to whether some of the representations are of individual kings or of more general signifiers of a royal line, it is clear that the plaques served as a pictorial repository of lineage history and provided a stable mechanism to maintain the narrative of origin and cultural assumptions upon which the ruling class justified itself. In many respects, the carvings on the piano in *The Piano Lesson*, though no longer serving a sacral kingship and a royal order, function similarly to this Benin tradition by pictorially preserving important events of the family's history as well as the images of the ancestors themselves. While the example of Luba traditions are not specifically pictorial, as are the carvings on the piano, they are especially close to the historiographic function of the piano because they preserve history through the integration of the narrative with the plastic arts and music.[5] The communal oral historians of the Luba, known as the *men of memory*, sculpture concave boards (*lukasa*) implanted with a design of cowries and beads to help them accurately retain the lineage history and recall major historical events.[6] The design of the cowries, although not writing per se, contains specific patterns that help the historians to replicate the lineage history. The correct retention of history from generation to generation is further assured by the tonal and rhythmic patterns of the narrative itself, which can be played on the two-tone slit gong or the signal drum.[7] While the actual narrative may change according to the individual performance and situation, the rhythms of the music and the patterns of the boards help maintain the historical continuity upon which the social order depends. In *The Piano Lesson*, Doaker plays a similar role to the *men of memory* as he recalls three generations of his own lineage history in order to explain to Lymon why Berniece will not sell the piano. Boy Willie also assumes this role when he begins to recount the history of the piano carvings to Maretha in order to give her a sense of pride, and he explains to Berniece that with knowledge of the piano Maretha "could walk around here with her head held high" (91). The piano is both the slit gong and the memory board, contained in one site in the family living room, and the music played on that piano, from Boy Willie's improvised boogie-woogie to Wining Boy's "Rambling Gambling Man," reach, like the style of the carvings, across the middle passage back to Africa—to the original ancestors and their gods. The images carved on the piano preserve a narrative-generating, visual memory that connects the family to their own ancestors who brought those rhythms and styles from Africa and transformed them in the context of slave life.

While this function of the piano may seem to be purely historical, the connections established between the past and present through the piano are represented in metaphysical dimensions. Within the imaginative world of the play, the piano also serves as a site of direct mystical connections with the ancestors, functioning similarly to sacred ancestral shrines or altars in many traditional African cultures. In the terms of Yoruba cosmography it is an *orita meta*, a crossroad between the world of the living and that of the dead. For the Yoruba, ancestral shrines are key links between the two worlds, where descendants may contact their ancestors for protection, support, and guidance.[8] Of all the characters in the play, Berniece is closest to fully realizing this aspect of the piano, even though concurrently she distances herself from the piano more than any other character does:

> I used to think those pictures came alive and walked through the house. Sometimes late at night I could hear my mama talking to them. I said that wasn't going to happen to me. I don't play that piano because I don't want to wake them spirits. They never be walking around in this house. (70)

Berniece believes in the mystical power of the piano, recognizing it as the site of connection to her ancestral spirits, but at the same time she denies those spirits access to her life.

The blood sacrifices made over the piano intensify its sacral properties and parallel similar African practices of pouring blood, meal, and urine over sacred representations of the ancestors or gods in order to feed them and maintain their spiritual existence. The piano initially becomes family property with the human sacrifice of Boy Willie's and Berniece's father, who is burned alive in the Yellow Dog railway car. Subsequently, as Berniece recounts, Mama Ola, her mother, makes daily sacrifice at the altar of the piano:

> You ain't taking that piano out of my house. Look at this piano. Look at it. Mama Ola polished this piano with her tears for seventeen years. For seventeen years she rubbed on it till her hands bled. Then she rubbed the blood in . . . mixed it up with the rest of the blood on it. Every day that God breathed life into her body she rubbed and cleaned and polished and prayed over it. "Play something for me, Berniece. Play something for me, Berniece." Every day. "I cleaned it up for you, play something for me, Berniece." (52)

For Mama Ola the piano becomes a shrine to her murdered husband, where she pours the libations of her own blood and tears. It is a cleansing ritual that is consummated daily with music, and the piano becomes the prayer site where Mama Ola connects with her deceased husband and tragic past. But upon her death and with the eventual transference of the piano to Pittsburgh, the next generation loses this sacral connection to the piano and it becomes the source of internecine conflict.

Berniece shuts the piano in order to forget her past, and the family shrine becomes moribund except for the childish tinkering of Maretha and the occasional bursts of life that come with Wining Boy's visits. While it is easy to sympathize with Berniece's desire to forget her painful memories, if we draw the parallel between the piano and African ritual practice, the spiritual and physical consequences of forgetting her past and not using the piano are very serious. In the parallel context of most African ancestral worship, neglect of the ancestors and the ancestral altars results in loss of their protection and threatens the destruction of the entire community.[9] As a Yoruba diviner explains: "If a person neglects his or her shrine (by not offering prayers or gifts) the spirits will leave . . . all you are seeing is the images . . . the person has relegated the deities to mere idols, ordinary images" (parenthesis added).[10] Ritual neglect of the ancestors not only results in the loss of ancestral protection from forces destructive to living members of the lineage, but it also threatens the very existence of the ancestors who require the food of sacrifice to maintain their existence in the realm of the dead.[11] The kinship between the living and the dead is a symbiotic relation—mutually beneficial or self-destructive—and it must be carried on in order to guarantee the continuation of the lineage. The ancestors are still members of the lineage, an active part of the clan, and after a period of time most of the ancestors will reenter the world of the living by reincarnation back into the lineage, thus completing a cycle of life and death that ensures the continuity and survival of their own kinship line.[12] Any break in this cycle has potentially catastrophic effects.

Within the play, a lack of sacral connection to the piano eventually threatens fratricide when Boy Willie attempts to remove the piano from Doaker's home against Berniece's will. This loss of ritual connection also allows the invasion of Doaker's home by Sutter's ghost, who begins to play his *own* songs on the piano. Doaker and Berniece ask Avery to perform a Christian exorcism of the ghost, but that only seems to feed Sutter's power rather than diminish it. Boy Willie, the consummate materialist, then tries to fight the ghost physically. But it is only when Berniece calls upon the protective spirits of her ancestors that the family finally can exorcise Sutter from their house:

*(It is in this moment, from somewhere old, that* Berniece *realizes what she must do. She crosses to the piano. She begins to play. The song is found*

*piece by piece. It is an old urge to song that is both a commandment and a
plea. With each repetition it gains strength. It is intended as an exorcism
and a dressing for battle. A rustle of wind blowing across two continents.)*

Berniece: *(Singing.)*
    I want you to help me
    I want you to help me
    I want you to help me . . .
    Mama Berniece
    I want you to help me
    Mama Esther
    I want you to help me
    Papa boy Charles
    I want you to help me
    Mama Ola
    I want you to help me . . .
    *(The sound of the train approaching is heard. The noise upstairs subsides.)*
(107)

It is important to note that this was not Berniece's song in the original productions or in the play's first publication in *Theater*. By the time the play
reached Broadway and was published in soft cover, Wilson changed the song
and the ending. Berniece's original song was "Oh, Lord I want you to help
me," repeated fourteen times in succession, and the play ended with Boy
Willie chasing Sutter's ghost up the stairs.[13] The change in song from a call to
God to an appeal to the ancestors strengthens the African ritual properties of
the play and simultaneously distances Berniece from a Christian context.
The success of this appeal in defeating Sutter and Boy Willie's final warning
further emphasize the piano's ritual power and the necessity of keeping the
ancestors alive with the food of music. As he leaves, Boy Willie threatens,
"Hey Berniece . . . if you and Maretha don't keep playing that piano . . . ain't
no telling . . . me and Sutter both liable to be back" (108).

    The battle against Sutter transforms the conflict that threatens fratricide
and the destruction of the kinship group into a conflict against a mutual
enemy that only the combined action of the kinship group can resist—with
Boy Willie fighting the ghost physically and Berniece invoking the ancestors'
protection. This deus-ex-piano ending reveals the mutual interests of the kinship group by demarcating what is truly Other to the group itself. It is a moment of self-definition, defining the boundary of kinship (the family of the

play) against the Other of the kinship group (the ghost of Sutter). On the literal level of the play, the strict lineage kinship group is the immediate family who are linked by bloodlines and a shared history. When we move from the literal level to the level of metaphor, however, it is easy to imagine a number of possible correlatives to the situation of the family, especially in regard to black American cultural identity vis-à-vis the dominant culture of the United States. The lineage kinship bond, which is literal within the world of the play, becomes a metaphor for the historical connection between black Americans and their past, and "kinship" in general becomes a metaphor for the historical connection among all black Americans. The ghost of Sutter becomes the disembodied embodiment of the slaveholder's historical perspective (and perhaps even the dominant culture's control of history). This perspective is expelled from the community with the reestablishment of the kinship bond (the historical connection). In this respect, the expulsion of Sutter is a metaphor of historical self-definition for blacks in America. Inasmuch as this self-definition occurs through expelling the dominant culture's historical perspective, it is also an appeal for a separate history and separate historical institutions, necessitated by a cultural difference based upon a distinct narrative of origin and historical perspective.

This distinct narrative of origin for blacks in America is also framed within the idiom of lineage kinship in *Joe Turner's Come and Gone*, where both Bynum and Herald Loomis connect with their history through visions guided by their ancestors. If the expulsion of Sutter in *The Piano Lesson* can be characterized as defining the kinship group through a cleansing exclusion, both Bynum's and Loomis's visions can be characterized as defining the kinship group through a historical inclusion. The visions of both characters appear to be identical or very similar to one another when Bynum is able to anticipate the esoteric content of Loomis's vision (54). In addition, both characters express the ineffable quality of their individual visions with the identical phrase: "ain't got no words to tell you" (10, 53). Although each character experiences his vision separately, the visions are deeply interconnected. Loomis's vision itself—where the bones rise out of the ocean, becoming the people that he must follow—is clearly the middle passage. This personal revelation, which is the shared historical past of most people of African descent in the Americas, becomes the renewed kinship bond that was broken in the middle passage. Historically it is a moment of rupture from the widely differing kinship systems of various African civilizations; yet simultaneously, in bringing together different peoples from the African continent, it is the shared historical experience that creates a new kinship. Because they share an interconnected vision, Herald and Bynum are inextricably bound by the realization of a common kinship (the bond of a consciously realized, shared history), even though each character's vision is individually self-affirming and provides him with his *own* song. They are able to affirm themselves individually by the realization of a larger kinship made possible through a union with the past. And this new American kinship, like traditional African kinship, is possible only through the maintenance and continuity of a historical consciousness, of that narrative of origin that unites the diverse interests of the kinship group.

If we interpret both plays as establishing kinship bonds through the realization of historical connections, the metaphysical aspects of the plays become historical, at least on the level of metaphor. This does not suggest, however, that the mystical elements of the plays can be "desupernaturalized" through an interpretive maneuver nor that they are subordinate to the historical ideas. Since the historical connections in both plays are represented as mystical encounters with ancestors who still have power to intervene in the world of the living, the interconnection of the mystical and the historical cannot be brushed aside.

For the sake of the analysis above, I separated the historiographic parallels between the piano and African practice from the sacred ancestral parallels; within most traditional African frameworks of lineage kinship, however, the dichotomy between historical and metaphysical does not exist. In the cycle of life, death, ancestral existence and rebirth, the historical is always metaphysical and the metaphysical is always historical.[14] Historical memory is a metaphysical act extending from the gods and the cosmological origins of the kinship line, to the realm of the deceased ancestors, and back again to the world of living humans. To separate the historical from the metaphysical, or to read the African elements of the plays simply as metaphors, loses key elements of Wilson's use of African traditions. Wilson uses his "ancestral legacy" to differentiate his own historical tradition as well as to emphasize the "cultural retentions" of his characters. By drawing upon this connection between the historical and the metaphysical in African cosmologies, Wilson frames history in his plays from a perspective antithetical to the secular views of history in the West, especially positivist conceptions of history that presume historical objectivity and a scientific method. Wilson's championing of this African worldview implicitly critiques the ecumenical claims of a Western, historical perspective that systematically has represented Africa, Africans, and peoples of the diaspora as the uncivilized, history-less, human Other to a rational and objectively "civilized" humanity. In addition to the value in the retention of African mystical beliefs as an alternative historical perspective, Wilson considers it to be an important element of cultural difference. As he stated in a 1984 interview following the initial productions of *Joe Turner*:

> I set the play in 1911 to take advantage of some of the African retentions of the characters. The mysticism is a very large part of their world. My idea is that somewhere, sometime in the course of the play, the audience will discover these are African people. They're Black Americans, they speak English, but their world view is African. The mystical elements—the Binder, the ghosts—are a very real part, particularly in the early 20th century, of the Black American experience. There was an attempt to capture the "African-ness" of the characters.[15]

While the mystical elements may operate on several levels of meaning and express different historical ideas, they are also just what they seem to be: mystical encounters. For Wilson, this retention of a cosmological perspective is equally important as historical experience in accounting for cultural difference, and we find a merging of the two within the world of these plays. It is important to recognize that Wilson conceives of this African retention not as a fixed cultural trait but as a worldview always subject to transformative processes. His emphasis on mysticism in the early twentieth century indicates his own concern with how this perspective is changing over time, and it will be interesting to see if this manifests itself in new forms in his plays about the late twentieth century.

....................

## NOTES

1. Rothstein, "Round Five," p. 8.
2. Ibid.
3. Ben-Amos, "History and Art," pp. 13–14.
4. Ibid., p. 14; Blackmun, "Wall Plaque," p. 84.
5. Reefe, *The Rainbow and the Kings*, pp. 10, 40.
6. Ibid., p. 39.
7. Ibid., p. 10.
8. Drewel, *Yoruba*, p. 15.

9. Sharevskaya, *Religious Traditions of Tropical Africa*, p. 54.

10. Drewel, *Yoruba*, p. 26.

11. Sharevskaya, *Religious Traditions of Tropical Africa*, p. 54.

12. Ibid.; Drewel, *Yoruba*, p. 15.

13. Wilson, "The Piano Lesson," *Theater*, p. 68.

14. The historical is always metaphysically contingent because the ancestors still exist in another realm where they intervene in history, and the metaphysical is always historically contingent because the survival of the ancestors depends upon the preservation of the lineage history and proper ritual practice.

15. Powers, "Interview," p. 52.

······

## WORKS CITED

Ben-Amos, Paula. "History and Art in Benin," In *The Art of Power/The Power of Art: Studies in Benin Iconography*, edited by Paula Ben-Amos and Arnold Rubin. Los Angeles: Museum of Cultural History at UCLA, 1983.

Blackmun, Barbara Winston. "Wall Plaque of a Junior Titleholder Carrying an *Ekpokin.*" In *The Art of Power/The Power of Art: Studies in Benin Iconography*, edited by Paula Ben-Amos and Arnold Rubin. Los Angeles: Museum of Cultural History at UCLA, 1983.

Drewal, Henry John, and John Pemberton III, with Rowland Abiodeen. Edited by Allen Wardell. *Yoruba: Nine Centuries of African Art and Thought.* New York: Center for African Art, 1989.

Hall, Stuart. "Cultural Identity and Cinematic Representation." In *Exiles: Essays on Caribbean Cinema*, edited by Mbye Cham. Trenton, N.J.: Africa World Press, 1992.

Mudimbe, V. Y. The Invention of Africa: Gnosis, Philosophy, and the Order of Knowledge. Bloomington: Indiana University Press, 1988.

Powers, Kim. "An Interview with August Wilson." *Theater* 16, no. 1 (1984): 50–55.

Reefe, Thomas Q. *The Rainbow and the Kings: A History of the Luba Empire to 1891.* Berkeley: University of California Press, 1981.

Rothstein, Mervyn. "Round Five for a Theatrical Heavyweight." *New York Times*, 15 April 1990.

Sharevskaya, B. J. *The Religious Traditions of Tropical Africa in Contemporary Focus.* Budapest: Center for Afro-Asian Research of the Hungarian Academy of Sciences, 1973.

Wilson, August. *Joe Turner's Come and Gone.* New York: New American Library, Plume, 1988.

———. *Ma Rainey's Black Bottom.* In *Totem Voices: New Plays from the Black World Repertory*, edited by Paul Carter Harrison. New York: Grove Press, 1989.

———. "The Piano Lesson." *Theater* 19, no. 3 (1988).

———. *The Piano Lesson.* New York: New American Library, Plume, 1990.

MARK WILLIAM ROCHA

# American History as "Loud Talking" in *Two Trains Running*

•••••••••••••••••••••••••••••••••••••••••••••••••••••

*Well, I wasn't signifying at her, but like I always say,
if the shoe fits, wear it.*

In a staged performance of *Two Trains Running*, Holloway, the community elder and oral historian, most often speaks while seated in his regular booth in Memphis's restaurant. This booth is upstage right and places Holloway closest to the audience, which he faces when speaking. For this character's longest speech about the black man's historical relationship to America's capitalist economy, director Lloyd Richards has blocked the action onstage so that Holloway rises from his booth, walks to the exact middle of the stage, and in Brechtian fashion faces the audience, whom he appears to address directly.[1]

> It's simple mathematics. Ain't no money in niggers working. Look out there on the street. If there was some money in it, if the white man could figure out a way to make some money by putting niggers to work, we'd all be working. He ain't building no more railroads. He got them. He ain't building no more highways. Somebody already stuck the telephone poles in the ground. That's been done already. The white man ain't stacking no more niggers. You know what I'm talking about stacking niggers, don't you? (66)

The blocking of the stage action makes explicit the usually implicit theatrical premise that there are two addressees of Holloway's speeches, the other black characters in Memphis's restaurant and the mostly white audiences of August Wilson's play. This establishes the triadic relationship that is essential to what in the black vernacular is referred to as "loud-talking," one of the ritual performances that Henry Louis Gates classifies as an example of signi-fyin(g). According to Gates:

> One successfully loud-talks by speaking to a second person remarks in fact directed to a third person, at a level just audible to the third person. A sign of the success of this practice is an indignant "What?" from the third per-son, to which the speaker replies, "I wasn't talking to you." Of course, the speaker was, yet simultaneously was not.[2]

With recourse to Gates and Claudia Mitchell-Kernan, upon whose de-scription of signifyin(g) and loud-talking Gates relies, I want to propose loud-talking as the paradigmatic metaphor for the African American theater in general and for August Wilson's history plays in particular. In the above ex-ample from *Two Trains Running*, Holloway—or, one should properly say, the actor playing Holloway—is consciously loud-talking on the audience, osten-sibly addressing in this case the character of Memphis, played by a fellow black actor, but really intending to elicit a response from a "third person"— the members of the audience—that will establish an audience's relationship to the represented experience onstage. This is the purpose of Holloway's overtly historical question which alludes to the middle passage, "You know what I'm talking about stacking niggers, don't you?" One's response to this question largely determines the historical "message" one takes from the play. If, for example, one essentially defends oneself against the implied indictment of Holloway's narrative by offering genuine sympathy and expressing thanks that things aren't that way anymore, the loud-talker has succeeded in exposing one's refusal of history and can then observe archly, "If the shoe fits, wear it."

In other words, loud-talking is the way August Wilson is *doing* American history in his plays, and especially in *Two Trains Running*, in which loud-talking becomes the vehicle for the play's primary historical theme that much of Wilson's white audience still is unable to locate themselves in the repre-sented stage experience. To put it in the vernacular, "white folks just don't get it." The historical point of *Two Trains Running* is not merely to offer a salu-tary addition or correction to an already existing American history. Instead the play offers its audience the opportunity to *do* American history by in-cluding them as participants in a ritual of signifyin(g) through which they can become self-conscious about their odd disconnectedness to a black expe-rience around which, as W. E. B. Du Bois put it, "the history of the land has centered for thrice a hundred years."[3]

The loud-talking of Wilson's play "tricks" members of the audience into demonstrating their ignorance of the African sensibility that produced the play and shaped the basic assumptions of black culture, especially that of signifyin(g), which Gates describes as that fundamentally black rhetorical practice that "turns upon forms of figuration rather than intent or content."[4] This ignorance is the cause of what may be termed a *refusal of history*, a failure, inadvertent or not, to set the American past into a living and therefore paradoxical relationship to the present. The central historical point of Wilson's historical cycle of plays is that American history itself could be narrated as a record of our refusals of our paradoxical past. Whether or not one refuses *Two Trains Running as* history, the play itself *is* history because it provides the means of performing an idea of an America always already informed by the refusal of its own history. To put it another way, refusing history is a historical act that *Two Trains Running* enables us to perform.

Loud-talking is thus the means through which Wilson *does* American history. In Gates's schema, Wilson himself would be the trickster who puts his characters up to loud-talking on the audience, thus offering it an opportunity to become self-conscious about one's historical relationship to Wilson's black community—which is to say, it is an opportunity to find one's self in America's past.

## "TWO TRAINS RUNNING": A TEXTBOOK OF SIGNIFYIN(G)

By now, with Wilson's five plays before us, it should be clear that signifyin(g) as Gates proposes it in *The Signifying Monkey* (1988) is *the* sociolinguistic performance that defines Wilson's black vernacular telling community. One could even characterize Wilson's cycle, and especially *Two Trains Running*, as the textbook of black signifyin(g) as this rhetorical practice was first described by Claudia Mitchell-Kernan in 1971 in *Language Behavior in a Black Urban Community* and then developed by Gates into an encompassing theory of African American literary criticism and history.

Let us first clearly establish *Two Trains* as a signifyin(g) textbook. Mitchell-Kernan states: "A precondition for the application of the term signifying to some speech act is the assumption that the meaning decoded was consciously and purposely formulated at the encoding stage."[5] Wilson has been remarkably explicit in stating his agenda to present "the field of manners and ritual of intercourse that sustain a man once he's left his father's house."[6] But even if Wilson had never acknowledged his aim to preserve and teach the culture of his black vernacular telling community, his intention is clearly manifest in *Two Trains Running*, a play that is permeated with such displays of signifyin(g) as "sounding" (getting on someone's case, as Wolf does at the beginning of the play when he asks Memphis, "You hear from your old lady, Memphis?"); "rapping" (using the vernacular with great dexterity); sweet-talking (as Sterling does with Risa); marking (mimicking the words of others, as Holloway and the others do when they tell a story); and of course, loud-talking. According to H. Rap Brown, signifyin(g) at its best "can be heard when brothers are exchanging tales,"[7] and of course *Two Trains Running* may be suitably described as an exchange of tales. Gates notes, "It is this sense of storytelling, repeated and often shared (almost communal canonical stories, or on-the-spot recountings of current events) in which Signifyin(g) as a rhetorical strategy can most clearly be seen."[8] The emphasis on storytelling as the mode that subsumes most methods of signifyin(g) also serves to detach signifyin(g) from its too common negative association with the "cut-fight" of the dozens, something that never appears in *Two Trains*.

In *Two Trains Running* Wilson incorporates two types of third-party signifyin(g), or loud-talking. I shall term the first type Allegorical Loud-talking, following Mitchell-Kernan's explanation of allegorical signifyin(g), in which the audience, or at least large parts of it, does not realize at the time that it is being signified at. I shall term the second type "In-Your-Face" Loud-talking, in part to invoke the primal black vs. white showdown which Kimberly Benston describes as a unifying topos of the African American literary tradition. In "In-Your-Face" Loud-talking, the audience *does* realize it is being signified at.

Wilson's intent in Allegorical Loud-talking is, in Mitchell-Kernan's words, to teach his audience how "to understand and appreciate implications,"[9] with the analogy being that of black parents raising up their children in the tales of the Signifying Monkey. On the other hand, Wilson's intent is more aggressive in "In-Your-Face" Loud-talking: to bring an indictment against the theatrical audience with the expectation that public exposure to the third party of the characters onstage will force the audience to accept rather than dismiss the charges.

In Allegorical Loud-talking Wilson is doing what black people call "schooling" his audience in signifyin(g). An anecdote offered by Mitchell-Kernan is worth quoting at length because it establishes a point-to-point allegory for Wilson's relationship to his audience. In Mitchell-Kernan's story, the adult "schooler" Mr. Waters may stand for Wilson, and the young Mitchell-Kernan represents Wilson's audience:

> At the age of seven or eight I encountered what I believe is a version of the tale of the "Signifying Monkey." In this story a monkey reports to a lion that an elephant has been maligning the lion and his family. This stirs the lion into attempting to impose sanctions against the elephant. A battle ensues in which the elephant is victor and the lion returns extremely chafed at the monkey. In this instance, the recounting of the story is a case of signifying for directive purposes. I was sitting on the stoop of a neighbor who was telling me about his adventures as a big game hunter in Africa, a favorite tall-tale topic, unrecognized by me as a tall-tale at the time. A neighboring woman called to me from her porch and asked me to go to the store for her. I refused, saying that my mother had told me not to, a lie which Mr. Waters recognized and asked me about. Rather than simply saying I wanted to listen to his stories, I replied that I refused to go because I hated the woman. Being pressured for a reason for my dislike, and sensing Mr. Waters' disapproval, I countered with another lie, "I hate her because she say you were lazy," attempting, I suppose, to regain his favor by arousing ire toward someone else. Although I heard someone say that he was lazy, it had not been this woman. He explained to me that he was not lazy and that he didn't work because he had been laid-off from his job and couldn't find work elsewhere, and that if the lady had said what I reported, she had not done so out of meanness but because she didn't understand. Guilt-ridden, I went to fetch the can of Milnot milk. Upon returning, the tale of the "Signifying Monkey" was told to me, a censored prose version in which the monkey is rather brutally beaten by the lion after having suffered a similar fate at the hands of the elephant. I liked the story very much and righteously approved of its ending, not realizing at the time that he was *signifying* at me. Mr. Waters reacted to my response with a great deal of amusement. It was several days later in the context of retelling the tale to another child that I understood its timely telling. My apology and admission of lying were met by affectionate humor, and I was told that I was finally getting to the age where I could "hold a conversation," i.e., understand and appreciate implications.[10]

Holloway's "stacking niggers" speech in act 2, scene 3, cited above at the outset, is an example of Wilson's historical signifyin(g) at his audience, who, like the young Mitchell-Kernan, may not realize until later that the story is directed at *them*. An audience may be unaware of Wilson's/Holloway's signifyin(g) for two reasons. First, getting the point of Holloway's speech depends upon acquisition of a field of reference that includes, among other things, the middle passage, the date Eli Whitney invented the cotton gin (1793) and the way this invention served to institutionalize slavery, and the use of chain gangs to build the nation's infrastructure—a field of reference unfamiliar to many whites, for whom Holloway's speech is a string of empty signifiers, which in the aggregate signify only something like "things that happened a long time ago." The second reason for the audience's inability to discern that Wilson/Holloway is signifyin(g) is that it has to do with historical distance. Holloway's allusions are to a past seemingly so distant that when he concludes the speech, "Now that they got to pay you they can't find you [work]," the audience is quite able to disconnect "they," the white people of the past, from themselves, the white people of the present in the audience. And of course this is precisely the historical point of the speech and the play, that whites today have managed to profoundly disconnect themselves from America's past. It is this point that Wilson wants the audience eventually to "get," much as Mr. Waters wanted the young Mitchell-Kernan to get the point of the Signifying Monkey tale. Furthermore, the theater is the literary generic site that is best suited to help the audience get this point because as a member of the audience, one is made to be conscious of one's response *in relation to others.* That is, even if Holloway's speech goes over one's head (which in the four performances I have seen is usually indicated by laughter, as if Holloway is joking), one shares the room with others who are *not* laughing, some of whom perhaps are black. This may lead to a realization similar to that of the young Mitchell-Kernan, that the joke is really on them.

Another "schooling" by Wilson/Holloway is the "nigger and a gun" speech in act 2, scene 2. This speech provides an excellent example of how the historical context *outside* the theater building may affect whether the audience becomes aware of whether Wilson is signifyin(g) at them. First, the speech:

You can't even use the word nigger and gun in the same sentence. You say the word gun in the same sentence with the word nigger and you in trouble. The white man panic. Unless, "The policeman shot the nigger with his gun" . . . then that be alright. Other than that he panic. He ain't had nothing but guns for the last 500 years . . . got the atomic bomb and everything. But you say the word nigger and gun in the same sentence and they'll try to arrest you. Accuse you of sabotage, disturbing the peace, inciting a riot, plotting to overthrow the government and anything else they can think of. You think I'm lying? You stand in front of the number two police station and say "The niggers is tired of this mistreatment, they gonna get some guns," and see if they don't arrest you. (64)

When I saw the play at the Old Globe Theater in San Diego on 26 March 1991, it was at the height of the controversy generated by the videotaped beating of Rodney King by the Los Angeles Police Department on 3 March 1991. An uncomfortable hush fell over the audience on this night that indicated that they took Holloway to be signifyin(g) at them, an instance of "In-Your-Face" Loud-talking which was interpreted as a direct indictment of the LAPD. A year later when I saw the play again in Los Angeles on 27 February 1992, the audience laughed almost raucously, as if the popular moral outrage at the Rodney King incident allowed them to be in on Holloway's stinging barb.[11] Whatever one's response, the point is that one cannot *avoid* a response to Holloway which measures the degree to which one feels responsible for the treatment of blacks by police. Such a response is unavoidable, largely because of the signal Wilsonian rhetorical device of the direct question "You think I'm lying?" This kind of direct question, which also appears in Holloway's "stacking niggers" speech, helps to achieve the fundamental aim of loud-talking, which is to expose a third party in front of others.

Normally, the triadic relationship of direct "In-Your-Face" Loud-talking comprises a speaker, an addressee, and an audience which the speaker makes sure can overhear him. There are many purposes for loud-talking, such as to accuse, censure, or persuade, but the one that seems most relevant to *Two Trains* is "to expose the failure of the addressee to fulfill some obligation."[12] A typical example from Mitchell-Kernan:

Larry reported that he had loaned several dollars to a young man he did not know well at the request of a mutual friend. On the occasion that he next saw the fellow, several months later, he requested payment. There was a rather large audience present, including several young girls who were accompanying the debtor. Larry apparently made no attempt to be circumspect saying, "When you gon give me my money, man?" This accusation of being beholden in the context served to raise Larry's status at the expense of loss of face on his addressee's part.[13]

This example is quite similar to the one in *Fences* in which Troy Maxson loud-talks his son Levee about the ten dollars he lends him every week. But there is another example in *Two Trains* whose importance to the play cannot be overstated, and this is Hambone's loud-talking "facing" of Lutz, which was the central theatrical event and ritual on the Hill—the neighborhood where Memphis's restaurant is located—for the entire decade of the 1960s. There can be no doubt that Hambone is deliberately loud-talking Lutz in order "to shame Lutz into giving him his ham," as Holloway explains it, for in performance Hambone's mantra, "I want my ham," is literally bellowed by the actor Sullivan Walker, a behemoth of a man.[14] But I also want to propose Hambone's loud-talking on Lutz within the play as the unmistakable allegory for Wilson's own loud-talking on his audience. This allegorical relationship may be graphed as follows:

| Speaker | Addressee | The "Overhearing" Audience |
|---|---|---|
| Hambone | Lutz | Holloway and the black community |
| Wilson (through character speeches) | White theater audience | The black community of characters/actors on stage |

The meta-dramatic scene that illustrates this allegorical relationship is the "play within a play" that opens act 1, scene 2. Here the theater audience is observing Wolf and Memphis observing another "play" that is taking place out on the street:

> *The lights come up on the restaurant.* Wolf *is looking out the window of the door.* Memphis *is at the end of the counter. . . .*
> *Wolf:* Here he come now. Lutz coming down the street. Hambone standing there.
> (Memphis *comes around the corner of the counter and walks to the door. Looks out.*)
> *Memphis:* What's Holloway doing?
> *Wolf:* He watching him. He just standing there. He wanna hear what they say. Look at him. . . . Look at him. Look at Hambone.
> *Risa: (Enters from back.)* What you all looking at?

*Wolf:* We watching Hambone. We want to see what he say to Lutz.
   Holloway went over there to stand on the corner. Hambone talking
   to Lutz now.
*Memphis:* That's the damndest thing I ever seen. (49)

Wilson's intentional foregrounding in this scene that it's a black audience witnessing Hambone's facing of Lutz establishes an important analogy: Just as the black audience of the characters onstage serves as the witnesses to Hambone's facing of Lutz, this same black audience serves as the third party for Wilson's/Holloway's loud-talking on the theater audience. The identification of the *theatrical audience* as the direct addressee of Wilson's characters is crucial for the loud-talking to achieve its end of exposing the failure of the theatrical audience to fulfill an implied historical obligation. In other words, through his characters Wilson is "facing" his audience in an effort to compel its agreement and tacitly admit its failure of social responsibility because of the presence of blacks onstage. This is what occurs in Memphis's speech about a boy who had been killed by the police:

They had that boy, Begaboo. The police walked up to him and shot him in the head and them same niggers [who organize rallies] went down there to see the mayor. Raised all kinds of hell. Trying to get the cop charged with murder. They raised hell for three weeks. After that it was business as usual. . . . Didn't even bother to transfer the cop to another precinct. (63)

In bringing this charge directly to his audience, Wilson may calculate that the presence of the black audience onstage will cause the audience to accept quietly Memphis's story and deplore the crime committed by the police. The basic trick of Wilson as loud-talker is to engineer his addressee, the theater audience, into a position before a group of blacks in which a charge can be brought that otherwise would be rejected as being deliberately confrontational. But whether or not the charge Wilson brings goes over one's head at the moment of performance, one's subsequent realization that Wilson is indeed loud-talking helps to reveal the aggressive, if not overtly hostile, subtext of *Two Trains.* Mitchell-Kernan notes:

To loud-talk is to assume an antagonistic posture toward the addressee. When it is used to censure, it reveals not only that the loud-talker has been aggrieved in some way, it also indicates, by virtue of making the delict public, that the speaker is not concerned about the possibility of permanently antagonizing his addressee. It is therefore revealing of the speaker's attitude toward the addressee. Although such a breach is not irreversible, one would ordinarily not loud-talk an individual one liked. Whether it occurs as a provocation or a sanction, it frequently serves to sever friendly relations if they were held heretofore.[15]

This is an apt description of Wilson's relationship to his audience, one that gives the tiger back his claws and brings him closer to Baraka, the black writer Wilson has explicitly acknowledged as his most important literary influence. It is therefore all the more ironic that reviewers have characterized Wilson in general, and *Two Trains* in particular, as *benign*.[16] Quite the contrary, Wilson's loud-talking attitude toward his audience might better be termed one of disdain and pity for a historical aphasia so profound that the audience can encounter a play like *Two Trains* which directly loud-talks on white folk *no less than twenty-seven times* and *still* fail to address how they might be historically represented in the play.

It is very nearly a miracle of virtuoso tricksterism by Wilson as the Signifying Monkey that reviewers and audiences can fail to find themselves in the play despite the palpable presence of so many white characters. To name but a few: Hartzberger, the furniture store owner who in *Fences* denies blacks credit and in *Two Trains* is mentioned by Memphis as owning most of the buildings on the Hill; Zanelli, the jukebox operator who has promised but failed to bring Memphis a replacement for his broken jukebox; Lutz, of course; Mellon, the renowned Pittsburgh banker who set Prophet Samuel up in the religion business; Stovall, the man who appropriated Memphis's farm and ran him out of Jackson; Hendricks, the businessman who did not keep the promise of a job to Sterling; Joseph Bartoromo, the second lawyer Memphis retains to represent his case at city hall; Mason, the retired cop, notorious for shooting so many blacks, hired by West to guard his funeral home; the Alberts, who run the numbers game and cut Sterling's number; Meyer, whose drugstore is destroyed in a fire that Holloway asserts will result in walking away with "200 thousand dollars and somebody going to jail for three years." And these are only the ten white offstage characters who are specifically *named*. "White folk" in general are referred to at least another seventeen times.

The historical question of the play then becomes, How could a largely white audience *not* see itself as historically connected to the events of *Two Trains Running*? The answer is that such a failure to see oneself in the play must be a product of either a willful refusal of American history or an unintentional ignorance of what American history really is. Wilson seeks to expose the former and rescue the latter. For the historical fact of the matter is that far more Americans should be able to locate themselves in *Two Trains* than in the conventional historical narratives of the 1960s that leave the mistaken impression that most Americans were connected in some significant way to the Civil Rights Movement and the Vietnam War protests that are constantly invoked as characteristic of the decade.

In the final analysis, American history as loud-talking is a process, a *way* of doing something together, and what *Two Trains* enables us to do is to keep open the problem of American history. Suffice it to say that Du Bois's prophetic announcement "The problem of the Twentieth Century is the problem of the color-line"[17] resonates throughout *Two Trains*, which takes Du Bois to mean that the solution for this problem would be to get whites rather than blacks to cross the color line. This is why the signifyin(g) in *Two Trains* as that "fundamentally black" exercise "in which the play is the thing—not specifically what is said, but how" is so important:[18] It enables and empowers its audience to cross the color line and become "black" by becoming schooled in signifyin(g). To cross the color line into Wilson's black community is to enter a figurative domain. There one becomes a communicant in the perpetual rituals of telling and interpreting, acts that in themselves form the ground of a community.

Taking *Two Trains* as a signifyin(g) textbook has two further advantages. First, it disposes of the judgment of the play as "talky." *Talk* is the very point of the play and the soul of the African sensibility that wrote it. Second, it enables us to see the play as challenging rather than accepting the assumptions of the naturalistic theater.

As to the first advantage, Wilson makes himself clear:

> The talk is the whole point because I'm dealing with a culture that has an oral tradition. You want talky, go read Chekhov. These stories mean something different to these people [in *Two Trains*]. They're not just passing the time or entertaining themselves, they're creating and preserving themselves. In the oral tradition, stories are the way history gets passed down, so they better be told right. By "right" I mean in a way that's memorable. Africans judge a storyteller by how long he can hold an audience.
>
> If a character repeats something, it's because he *needs* to repeat it. I've heard it said that the reason a line is so often repeated in most blues lyrics is that originally singers repeated themselves until they could think of

something new to say. That's ridiculous. There's a point being made in the song and you need to *listen.*[19]

As to the play's seemingly conventional naturalism, Wilson's signifyin(g) in effect breaks the fourth wall of the proscenium stage, since the theatrical audience is directly addressed through loud-talking in an effort to welcome or pressure the audience into becoming part of the black community. Such anti-naturalistic technique has of course been familiar in Western drama since Brecht and his epic theater, which tried for an "alienation effect" by showing familiar experience in the unfamiliar light of historical distance, thus forcing an audience to think critically about assumptions it has taken as natural. What is special about August Wilson and perhaps the reason for the astonishing visceral response to his cycle is the understanding that Wilson supplies the American theater with something it has never had: an American history that is the product of an African rather than a European sensibility. As Wole Soyinka points out, the African sensibility in drama will be found not merely in the level of noise from the audience at any given performance but in a ritualistic sense of space. Soyinka seems to explain Wilson's dramaturgy well:

Ritual theater, let it be recalled, establishes the spatial medium not merely as a physical area for simulated events but as a manageable contraction of the cosmic envelope within which man—no matter how deeply buried such a consciousness has latterly become—fearfully exists. And this attempt to manage the immensity of his spatial awareness makes every manifestation in ritual theater a paradigm for the cosmic human condition.[20]

Within his "cosmic envelope" Wilson includes everyone, even "West," who may one day return to Aunt Ester's to get his soul washed and this time throw his twenty dollars into the Monongahela River.

.................
## WILSON AS TRICKSTER:
## EXPOSING OUR REFUSAL OF HISTORY

*Two Trains Running* is indeed a tricky play because what looks at first glance like a fairly conventional dramatization of a slice of black life is actually a clever signifyin(g) by Wilson upon his audience for the purpose of exposing its refusal of American history.

It's 1969 in a diner in the black neighborhood of Pittsburgh known as "the Hill." The putative theme of *Two Trains Running*—Gates would call it the less important "content" of the play—concerns the fundamental injustice of an American economic system in which the black man has never been paid a fair price for his contributions. To employ the metaphor of the numbers game, which extends throughout the play, the fix is always in against the black man. This point seems inarguable, and it therefore seems unlikely that Wilson's primary goal for this fifth play in the cycle would be to reprise such an obvious message. For what it is worth, however, considerable sympathy is engendered for the two male characters who are fighting to get their fair price: Memphis, who insists that city hall pay him his price for his restaurant, and Hambone, who insists that the white grocery store owner Lutz pay the ham he promised him for painting a fence.

These two external black vs. white conflicts may be taken as a pretext for the more compelling internal conflicts that all the members of this community feel over their status as displaced persons. Memphis, for example, tells of coming north to Pittsburgh from Mississippi after being kicked off his land by whites. Holloway, the elder of the community who acts as oral historian by keeping and interpreting the experiences of others, also dreams of a return to the South he left in 1927 and he invests the realization of the communal quest for a home in an offstage character, Aunt Ester, the 322-year-old conjure woman to whom Holloway refers all for healing. Aunt Ester is to be taken as the original African American, as old as the black experience in America. She is in part the home that lies in the past, the home in the South before the migration to the northern cities severed blacks from their vital relationship to the land.

The allegorically named "West" is, appropriately, the only member of this diverse telling community who overtly refuses faith in Aunt Ester. A wealthy black entrepreneur, West shows little concern for the black community from which he has reaped great profit. West tries to buy out Memphis for the sake of a quick profit, and he forces the ex-con Sterling to beg him for a job. Sterling's name is also an allegorical measure of value, for this orphan grown up into a bank robber is the one who places most faith in Aunt Ester, with the result that he finds love and new life with Risa, a waitress who has mutilated herself by slashing her legs so that men like the numbers runner Wolf would no longer look on her as a sexual object.

Memphis does win his fight with city hall by getting $35,000 for his restaurant,[21] but this victory is undercut by its similarity to Sterling's hit on the number 781, a matter of luck that has no effect on the system under which the game will continue to be played. In any case, Memphis's announcement of the payout at the end of the play is far less important than his announcement that he has visited Aunt Ester, who has given him the resolve to return to Jackson to confront Stovall, the first white man to cheat him. If Memphis survives his confrontation with Stovall, he will return to the Hill and invest his $35,000 in a grand new entrepreneurial dream, "a big restaurant right down there on Centre Avenue" that will employ "two or three cooks and seven or eight waitresses." When Memphis finally arrives at this plan, two differing versions of black entrepreneurship, represented by Memphis and West, have been fully articulated in the play.

But the heart and soul of this play, and in whose name the play ends, is Hambone and his tragic quest to get his due. In the character description in the text, Wilson writes, "He is self-contained and in a world of his own. His mental condition has deteriorated to such a point that he can only say two phrases and he repeats them idiotically over and over" (47). For nearly ten years Hambone has refused to accept a chicken instead of the ham Lutz promised him. When Hambone dies without his ham, everyone in the community invests in Hambone's death by identifying with his quest. *Two Trains Running* therefore becomes a play about the community's canonization of Hambone as a primal creation myth of black identity. As Wilson puts it, "Hambone shows us that a new black man was created in the 1960's who would not accept a chicken."[22]

*Two Trains Running* certainly shares much with Wilson's previous four plays in the cycle, and yet as a history play it stands at a much different relationship to its audience because it deals with the era of the 1960s which still seems fresh in our minds and which we mistakenly think we know well. Like all of Wilson's plays, *Two Trains* poses a problem that invites us to reconsider what we know of American history. During the play's two-year tour of the United States in advance of its Broadway opening on 13 April 1992,[23] perplexed newspaper critics noted this historical problem, but they often chose to explain it away as a flaw rather than to consider it as the very point of the play itself. Sylvie Drake's review in the *Los Angeles Times* serves as a representative example:

> *Two Trains* is still waters—a less eventful, deceptively mundane, talky play that, [when it appeared last year] in San Diego, had seemed like an overextended vignette. Not so now. Experiencing it anew some nine

months later, the piece proves much more compelling than before, a symphonic composition with a rich lode of humanity running through it.

That it happens to be African-American humanity means it relates to a specific history and experience. That it is set in 1969, at the height of the Vietnam war and the civil rights movement, yet feels more like a 1930's play, remains a problem. We find ourselves thrown in with a group of regulars in Memphis Lee's dingy Pittsburgh cafe whose references or direct connections to the time of their lives are too few and too casual.[24]

Could it be that the "problem" of historical disconnection that worries Drake is the very point of the play? I put this question to Wilson himself, showing him Drake's review. Wilson responded:

> You see, she's talking about what *white* folks think of as the 1960's. But the point of the play is that by 1969 nothing has changed for the black man. You talk about King and Malcolm, but by 1969, as it says in the play, both are dead. The reality is that Sterling is just out of the penitentiary and someone like Holloway, who is sixty-five, has been struggling his whole life and still has nothing to show for it.

Wilson continued:

> Some critics have said, "Well, nothing *happens* in the play." That's because they can't *see* anything happening because they don't understand the specifics of black culture. Something *does* happen. There are important transformations occurring in these black people. Sterling is sour on life at the beginning, can't find a job, doesn't want to bring children into this world, but at the end he's with Risa and wants a family. He's going to raise up new life. There's always new life. There's always the next generation in my plays, Raynell in *Fences*, Zonia in *Joe Turner*, Maretha in *The Piano Lesson*. . . . And there's a transformation in Memphis. His story is that he's been run out of Jackson and of course that's not something you'd want to reveal to others. But eventually he does tell his story. That's a big change in this man and it leads him back to Jackson. Memphis learns that lost territory can be regained.

Thus critics who fail to detect such transformations reveal more about themselves than about the play before them. This is *precisely* the purpose of loud-talking, to trick a third-party addressee into displaying what the trickster believes to be a shortcoming or ignorance.

Wilson's plays will also fully accommodate an application of the intertextual component of Gates's theory of signifyin(g) which arranges the African American literary tradition around such primal figures as the African god Esu, on whom is inscribed the search of the black subject for a textual voice. In *Two Trains* Esu can be refigured as Aunt Ester, the 322-year-old conjure woman who heals by getting her visitors to tell their life stories. The figure of Aunt Ester as the embodiment of black experience as a healing maternal presence might then lead to a reading of Wilson's historical cycle about the black experience in America for each decade of the twentieth century as a signifyin(g) upon Langston Hughes's poem *Ask Your Mama*, which Gates notes amounts to a twelve-section history of Afro-America. It will bear rich fruit indeed to explore how *Two Trains Running* signifies upon antecedent texts in both the black and the white traditions, especially the 1960s plays of Amiri Baraka and Ed Bullins, both of whom Wilson has acknowledged as influences. But here one raises the issue of intertextuality primarily to reinforce the premise that Wilson's plays taken together represent an extended signifyin(g) upon the text of American history for the purpose of subsuming that text under the name of African American experience and in the name of African American experience.

..................

## NOTES

1. This is the way it was staged in each of four performances I attended: 19 April 1990, at the Yale Repertory Theater in New Haven; 26 March 1991, at the Old Globe Theater in San Diego; 21 January 1990 and 27 February 1990, at the James A. Doolittle Theater in Los Angeles.

2. Gates, *Signifying Monkey*, p. 82. I shall follow the "arbitrary and idiosyncratic convention" of Gates by inscribing the word as "signifyin(g)."

3. Du Bois, *Souls of Black Folk*, pp. 214–15.

4. Gates, *Signifying Monkey*, p. 74.

5. Mitchell-Kernan, *Language Behavior*, p. 95.

6. A phrase from James Baldwin that Wilson has often cited in interviews.

7. Quoted in Gates, *Signifying Monkey*, p. 74.

8. Ibid.

9. Mitchell-Kernan, *Language Behavior*, p. 113.

10. Ibid., pp. 111–13; also quoted in Gates, *Signifying Monkey*, p. 84.

11. Note that this was *before* the not-guilty verdicts in the King trial were issued

on 29 April 1992 and the subsequent devastation in Los Angeles. Wilson's play seems extraordinarily prescient, which is to say historical.

12. Mitchell-Kernan, *Language Behavior*, pp. 134–35.

13. Ibid., p. 135.

14. Walker originated the role and is the only one to have played it to date.

15. Mitchell-Kernan, *Language Behavior*, p. 134.

16. For one example, see the laudatory review in *Daily Variety*, 19 March 1991, p. 14. The reviewer writes, "*Trains* is surprisingly mellow . . . this group radiates a feeling of warmth and bonding, and matters conclude on a more optimistic note than is usual for Wilson."

17. Du Bois, *Souls of Black Folk*, p. 1.

18. Gates, *Signifying Monkey*, p. 70.

19. Wilson, Interview with author, *Diversity* 1, no. 1 (Fall 1992): 24–42.

20. Soyinka, *Myth, Literature, and the African World*, p. 41.

21. In the original version published in *Theater*, this payout was $25,000.

22. Author's interview with August Wilson, 24 January 1992. Unless noted otherwise, all quotations are from this interview.

23. The play premiered at the Yale Repertory Theater, New Haven, on 27 March 1990.

24. Drake, *Los Angeles Times*, 17 January 1992, sec. F, p. 1.

..................

## WORKS CITED

Drake, Sylvie. *Los Angeles Times*, 17 January 1992, sec. F, p. 1.

Du Bois, W. E. B. *The Souls of Black Folk*, 1903. Reprint. New York: Penguin, 1989.

Gates, Henry Louis, Jr. *The Signifying Monkey: A Theory of Afro-American Literary Criticism*. New York: Oxford University Press, 1988.

Mitchell-Kernan, Claudia. *Language Behavior in a Black Urban Community*. Monographs of the Language Behavior Research Laboratory, University of California, no. 2 (February 1971).

Soyinka, Wole. *Myth, Literature, and the African World*. Cambridge: Cambridge University Press, 1976.

Wilson, August. "Two Trains Running." *Theater* 22, no. 1 (Winter 1990–91): 41–72.

JOAN FISHMAN

# Romare Bearden, August Wilson, and the Traditions of African Performance

..................................................

A painter and a playwright. Romare Bearden and August Wilson. Perhaps with nothing in common. Romare Bearden grew up among the elite, acquainted with Duke Ellington and Eleanor Roosevelt. August Wilson grew up on the street. Bearden is schooled. Wilson is self-taught, a high school dropout. When Bearden began his work, he had studied classical forms and painting history for years. When Wilson began, he had not read Shakespeare, or Molière, or Williams, or O'Neill.

And yet, as if they stood side by side peering through the same window on life, Romare Bearden and August Wilson created art that similarly presents the human condition: art that simultaneously captures the energy of the African American experience and releases it back into the world, art that speaks clearly to African Americans and is heard clearly by all audiences, and art that speaks for a generation and to a generation.

What brings these two artists together is the incorporation into their art of the elements that define traditional African performance forms. In the selection of their themes and the portrayals of their characters, they incorporate the true-to-life and the familiar into ritualistic drama recognizable and influential to their audiences. They present a rainbow of the life cycle incorporating the past and the present, the dead and the yet-to-be-born, offering images and inspirations intended to heal the community. They offer conflict and struggle not within what Wole Soyinka identifies as the traditional Western context, which sees "human anguish as viable only within strictly temporal capsules," but rather within the African context, "whose tragic understanding transcends the causes of individual disjunction and recognizes them as reflections of a far greater disharmony in the communal psyche."[1] Wilson and

Bearden searched for and found the ritualistic roots that reward their work with universal application. In these efforts and results Bearden's paintings and Wilson's plays share many qualities.

Romare Bearden's painting career spanned fifty years and included experimentation and mastery of social realism, abstract design, figurative painting, and the photographic and textural collages for which he is perhaps most well known. Bearden was fifty-five when he left his civil service job to paint full time. Still, in his lifetime, he had ten solo exhibitions, including shows at the Corcoran Gallery in Washington, D.C., and the Museum of Modern Art in New York. In 1966, he was elected to the American Academy of Arts and Letters and the National Institute of Arts and Letters. In 1987, the year before his death, Bearden was awarded the President's National Medal of Arts.

When Wilson discusses the history of his playwriting, he notes a very specific moment of inspiration: "I discovered the art of Romare Bearden."

> My friend Claude Purdy had purchased a copy of *The Prevalence of Ritual*, and one night in the fall of 1977, after dinner and much talk, he laid it open on the table before me. "Look at this," he said. "Look at this." The book lay open on the table. I looked. What for me had been so difficult, Bearden made seem so simple, so easy. What I saw was black life presented on its own terms, on a grand and epic scale, with all its richness and fullness, in a language that was vibrant and which, made attendant to everyday life, ennobled it, affirmed its value, and exalted its presence. It was the art of a large and generous spirit that defined not only the character of black American life, but also its conscience. I don't recall what I said as I looked at it. My response was visceral. I was looking at myself in ways I hadn't thought of before and have never ceased to think of since.
>
> In Bearden I found my artistic mentor and sought, and still aspire, to make my plays the equal of his canvasses.[2]

Two of Bearden's còllage/paintings directly inspired Wilson plays. Wilson first saw Bearden's 1978 work *Millhand's Lunch Bucket* in a magazine. This Bearden work came from his series of paintings titled *The Twenties* and was one of his Pittsburgh memories—works which came from the childhood years Bearden spent at his maternal grandmother's boardinghouse in Pittsburgh.

*Millhand's Lunch Bucket* fascinated Wilson, who was particularly drawn to the man sitting at the table, "the haunting and brooding figure at its center."[3] When Wilson first saw the painting, he was working on a series of poems

*Romare Bearden.* Millhand's Lunch Bucket. *1978. Collage on board. Private collection. Photo by Richard Herrington.*

titled "Restoring the House," which followed the search of a freed slave for his wife, who had been sold to another plantation owner five years before Emancipation. Wilson translated the action of his poetry into a play of the same title, and from the dark and mysterious figure at the center of Bearden's work, Wilson created Herald Loomis, a man who has been separated from his wife because of his involuntary servitude to the legendary Joe Turner, based on the real Joe Turner, who was the infamous brother of the governor of Tennessee. Turner captured young black men, chained them, and forced them to work his land for seven years.

Wilson set his play in 1911, about ten or twelve years earlier than the time in which the painting is set in order to incorporate the historical figure of Joe Turner and draw the characters closer to the continuing impact of slavery. The earlier time frame made the industrial setting of Bearden's painting impossible, and thus the men in Wilson's boardinghouse work on a road instead of in the steel mills suggested by Bearden's painting. But both activities evoke images of the African American emigration to the North. The first draft of the play, in fact, had the same title as the painting, but by the third draft Wilson had changed the title to *Joe Turner's Come and Gone.*

Aspects of Bearden's life, as well as his painting, find their way into *Joe Turner's Come and Gone.* For example, the physical set for Wilson's play closely resembles the sketches Bearden made of his grandmother's boardinghouse in Pittsburgh. And Wilson goes so far as to create a young character he names Ruben who is a representation of Bearden himself as a boy at this boardinghouse.

Bearden lived in this house in the mid-1920s. It was here that he met Eugene, a sickly child who taught him to draw. Bearden's grandmother was pleased with her grandson's interest until she discovered that the bulk of the artwork was drawings of the nearby brothel where Eugene lived and his mother was employed. Bearden's grandmother immediately moved Eugene into her home, and he brought with him his collection of pigeons and doves, which Eugene made Bearden promise to free when Eugene died. This occurred one year later.

Wilson alludes directly to this event in *Joe Turner's Come and Gone* when young Ruben explains to his new friend Zonia Loomis, that the pigeons he keeps were left to him by his friend, Eugene, who recently died. Ruben was supposed to have let the pigeons go free. But he hasn't had the heart to give the birds up. Finally, late in the play, when he dreams he is visited by a ghost, Ruben comes to believe that Eugene is waiting for the birds and he can't "get the door to the coop open fast enough" (80).

Wilson took elements of one real life, Bearden's, and combined them with elements of other real lives, and he created a drama. This formation of art out of life is a creative effort like that which produces traditional African performance. Traditional African performance rises out of the community. As Soyinka points out, in African performance, "we encounter human beings whose occupation and environment are elemental and visceral. Flood and ebb affect their daily existence, their language, their spectrum of perception."[4] The performances themselves are often reenactments of real life event or simulation of real life events.

Such reenactments of real life events—for example, scenes of cooking and eating—weave through Wilson's work as they do through Bearden's. Berniece is preparing to bathe in *Piano Lesson,* as is the woman in Bearden's

*Grey Cat. Fences'* Rose hangs clothes on the line, as does the woman in Bearden's *Farewell to Lulu.*

This attention to quotidien, shared by Bearden and Wilson, connects them firmly with an African art tradition where closeness to the work often engenders participation on the part of the audience. During performance of Zulu traditional poetry, for example, the audience frequently makes comments on portions of the poems being presented. The performance of Ghambian folktales is also heavily dependent on the interaction between audience and storyteller, and the listeners interrupt to add, to correct, or to create an accompanying rhythm. In performances of the Kwagh-Hir Theatre, members of the audience sometimes rush into the performance, participating physically in the show. The works rise from the community and continue to exist, during performance, as part of the community.

In keeping with this tradition, the works of Bearden and Wilson encourage audience response. The activity within Bearden's collages, as exemplified by the characters in *The Street*, invites his viewers to respond to the artwork. Bearden's people seem to address their audience directly and ask for participation in their lives.

Wilson tells a story of one performance of *Fences.* At the end of the play, the character of Gabriel, who suffers from delusions of sainthood, is preparing to blow his trumpet so that the gates of heaven will open to welcome his dead brother, Troy. "You ready, Troy?" he asks. A woman in the audience stands up and yells to the stage, "You don't need to blow that trumpet, cause he's going straight to hell!"

The extreme recognizability of Wilson and Bearden's work, and the innumerable connections between their work, can be attributed to a similar method of creation, one which again bears resemblance to the creation of traditional performance. As a community or its key members prepare a performance, bits and pieces of their life and culture, such as a recurring event, a traditional costume, a familiar song, are brought together to create a whole.

In the collage form for which he is perhaps best known, Bearden used a variety of found objects, assembling a relationship between them. He thought of his work as play—not child's play but "a kind of divine play": "Collage is almost by definition an improvisational medium, in that it allows the artist to combine found objects from the everyday world—pieces of wood, fragments of photographs from old catalogues, fabrics—and literally play with them until they form a coherent composition."[5]

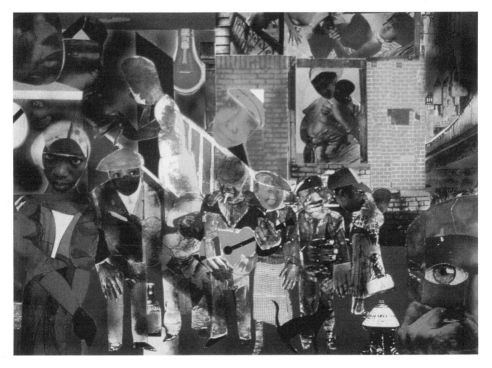

*Romare Bearden.* The Street. *1975. Collage on board.*
*Sheldon Ross Gallery, Birmingham, Michigan. Photo by Richard Herrington.*

Not unlike Bearden, Wilson builds his plays from small pieces, in a collagist style. Wilson does not study the historical periods about which he writes; rather he allows bits of the history he remembers to float into his mind and he places these into his larger artistic agenda. In the creative processes of both artists, disparate elements are brought together to form a whole—which Wilson believes is "the key to the vitality of black culture."[6]

As they create their work, both Bearden and Wilson are guided by the characters who appear in their paintings and plays. When Bearden creates a collage, he says, "people start coming into my work, like opening a door."[7] "One day, these people came walking into my work and seemed to know just where to go within the painting."[8] This is similar to the way Wilson describes his process of writing. In discussing the play he is currently writing, *Moon Going Down*, Wilson tells this story: He is writing about several men. Suddenly a woman opens the door. She enters and encourages Wilson to create a place for her in the play.

Of the common images that weave through the two artists' works, trains are perhaps the most important. They recur in many of Bearden's works, appearing either centrally (*The Train*) or in the background (*Southern Limited*). As Bearden explains, "Trains are so much a part of Negro life. Negroes lived near the tracks, worked on the railroads and trains carried them North during the migration."[9]

Wilson's most recent play, *Two Trains Running*, also recognizes that centrality. The title comes from a blues song whose lines are "two trains runnin', neither one going my way." In *Two Trains*, the character Memphis speaks about returning to his home in the South. But knowing "what they do to a nigger they see driving a Cadillac" Memphis plans on taking the train: "They got two trains running everyday" (40).

Bearden's painting *Watching the Trains Go By* (1964), moreover, could easily have been the influence for the early Wilson work *The Homecoming*, although this Wilson play was written before his discovery of Bearden. The play is set in a small train station, where the local men await delivery of the body of a friend. During the course of the play, they take revenge for his death.

The guitar held by one of the characters in *The Homecoming* is another important image for both Wilson and Bearden. This instrument, which appears in Bearden's *Blues at the Crossroads, The Street,* and *The Guitar Player*, to name a few examples, also figures in Wilson's plays. In *Joe Turner's Come and Gone*, the character of Jeremy has brought only his guitar with him from the South, and it becomes the instrument of a profitable livelihood.

Guitar players also become central in the homage of both artists to the contribution by African Americans to the music industry: Bearden's *Of the Blues* series of paintings and Wilson's *Ma Rainey's Black Bottom*. While Bearden's work tends to be more celebratory, *Ma Rainey* explores the trials of survival of African American artists in the entertainment industry in the 1920s.

Music is a way of approaching life. And the blues stands as a vital source of inspiration for both Bearden and Wilson. Wilson describes his discovery of the blues: "It was a watershed event in my life. It gave me a history. It provided me with a cultural response to the world. . . . The blues gave me a firm and secure ground. It became, and remains, the wellspring of my art."[10]

Bearden was schooled in music; Wilson was not. Bearden knew many musicians; he understood the structure and methods of music and was himself a composer. Wilson describes himself as a "good listener." Still, both men understood the integration between African American music and daily life—music not as performance but as an extension of African storytelling, a tradition which represents the continual search for roots by African Americans in a white-dominated environment. Bearden writes:

> Music has always been important for me the way it has been important for many blacks. Blacks have made their own sound, their own musical language like jazz. It is theirs and they identify with it. In a world of constantly changing identities, certain forms of music represent a solid identity for blacks.[11]

Music finds its way into the work of both artists not only as subject but also as technique. For both artists, the process of creation has an improvisatory quality, with experimental variations on a theme. Listening to Wilson's dialogue, one hears the soulfulness of the blues in the long speeches of the characters and the repartee of jazz in carefully orchestrated quick dialogue exchanges. Wilson sees "Bearden's use of the collage . . . [as] the visual equivalent of rapping and blues—music that you sort of have to piece together as it jumps from one thing to the next."[12]

The use of music as technique has its roots in traditional African performance, where music is certainly a fundamental element. Most frequently a creation of rhythm, with which movement often becomes synonymous, inspires a ritualistic element. Consistent drumming, singing, and chanting are common characteristics. The music is directly related to the drama, as exemplified in the traditional Ethiopian *asmari*, whose talent is to engage and challenge the audience by telling a story, often poetic or philosophical, accompanied by an instrument. The singing/storytelling element is central to traditional forms.

Music is therefore a natural focus for Bearden and Wilson because they are both storytellers. Many of Bearden's friends remember him to be a wonderful storyteller as he shared the varied experiences of his life with them. Certainly his paintings fulfill the same end in pictures rather than in words. Bearden's *The Block* tells the story of the whole neighborhood, alive with the action in the street and enriched by details of the lives of those within the buildings, revealed through the windows Bearden leaves open in the work. Bearden's characters tell long stories about their lives through his intricate assemblage of their faces and their surroundings.

Wilson also creates characters who are master storytellers. These characters, along with Wilson, understand that "there's an oral tradition of black culture in which the verbal agility is very highly prized among blacks."[13] The nonlinear structure of Wilson's plays, particularly his first and latest works, speaks to the African storytelling mode.

Music is a way of approaching life, and because of its ritualistic, primal nature, music offers cohesion to the community. Traditional performance affirms the unity and traditional values of the group. Images of community and themes of community life are central to both Wilson's and Bearden's work.

And at the heart of the community, for Wilson and Bearden, are women. Here, too, their work reflects traditional matriarchal theories of creation and existence central to many traditional performances. The fullness of Wilson and Bearden's female characters results from the depth of human understanding shared by these two artists. Bearden scholar Mary Schmidt Campbell notes: "No one could doubt the reality of the women in Romare Bearden's art . . . he has penetrated their reality and found something profound, basic."[14] Wilson's women embody love and laughter, strength and pathos; the character Bynum describes them in *Joe Turner* as "a whole way of life kicking up under your hand" (45).

The women in Bearden's paintings, like those in Wilson's plays, are mothers and seductresses, teachers and lovers, musicians and magicians. Both Bearden and Wilson have an admiration for women which stems from their understanding of women as the holders of true power through the gift of sustenance that they offer. The images of life-givers and the themes of sustenance that weave through traditional African arts are often cyclical and present a pattern of repeating events and a continuation of life. Life and death are included in the plays as part of an ongoing process; often they are the focus of comedy to remind the audience to maintain their perspective on these unavoidable natural events.

The work of both Wilson and Bearden illuminates life's cycle. The image of the grown man with the small baby in Bearden's *Continuities* is very similar to the image of Troy holding his tiny daughter in Wilson's *Fences*. Bearden places a funeral in *The Block*, and Wilson has one offstage in *Two Trains Running*. Neither is the central action, but each serves as a reminder by the artist of the facts of life.

Any examination of the cycle of life necessarily leads to issues of expanded community, that is, the relationship of the living with their communal ancestors. The characters in many African plays exist not only in relationship with their direct physical counterparts but also in relation to those who have come before them; the presence of ancestors is a common characteristic of African drama. In this way, the extended community is united. The physical and spiritual worlds are often connected through the ritual aspects of the performance. Often there is a reenactment within a performance of a recognizable activity which becomes ritualistic in its repetition; e.g., in Ghanian dance/drama, the reenactment of wheat thrashing is performed over and over again until its significance moves beyond an everyday context.

Similarly, Bearden and Wilson choose to portray the repeated rituals of everyday life. Both artists take ordinary people and endow their everyday activities—bathing, train watching or guitar playing—with ritualistic significance, again connecting the physical and spiritual worlds.

The two Wilson plays directly influenced by Bearden, *Joe Turner's Come and Gone* and *The Piano Lesson*, are his most spiritual plays, having moved away from traditional Western forms and including non-naturalistic elements. In Bearden's most innovative collages, the artist finds a place for African spiritualism; for example, the presence of the conjure woman in the several paintings which bear this title.

In these spiritual elements combined with the everyday ritualistic actions of their characters, Wilson and Bearden capture a strong sense of continuity which speaks to the mysterious connection between the past and present. And, in order to emphasize the linkage between generations, both Bearden and Wilson bring traditional African elements into contemporary African American culture. Bearden combines African masks with African American faces cut out from magazines; Wilson's characters in *Joe Turner* perform the African juba dance after Sunday dinner.

Common to African performance is an exploration of the reconciliation of old and new ways. Traditional values vs. modern methods is a recurring theme. Many works carry the same clear message: For life to continue, each of the traditional and modern ways must moderate itself in the face of the other.

Wilson and Bearden similarly portray African Americans trying to find their place in time, to meld past and future. This requires an acceptance of what African culture provides to all African Americans and a reconciliation of this with their contemporary culture. "In a world dominated by white culture," Wilson explains, "the black must be strong enough not only to survive but to re-establish his own identity and heritage which flows unbroken from an African fountainhead."[15]

The issues of baggage or treasure from the past and their integration into contemporary life are the backbone of Wilson's fourth play, *The Piano Lesson*,

*Romare Bearden.* The Piano Lesson. *1984. Silk screen.*
*Private collection. Photo by Richard Herrington.*

inspired by Bearden's painting of the same name. When Wilson saw Bearden's painting in an art gallery, he turned to a friend and said, "This is my next play."[16]

*The Piano Lesson* focuses on a struggle between brother, Boy Willie, and sister, Berniece, over whether to sell an heirloom piano. The piano was previously owned by the Sutter family, who held Boy Willie and Berniece's family enslaved. The slaveowner acquired the piano in a trade—he traded Berniece and Boy Willie's grandmother and their father for it. Berniece and Boy Willie's grandfather carved portraits of his family into the piano legs in memory of the loss of his wife and son.

Boy Willie wants to sell the piano to buy a piece of the property where his family served as slaves. His eye is only to the future. Berniece refuses to part with the instrument. She is unable to play the piano that she insists on retaining because she fears that to do so is to raise the spirits embodied within it. Berniece cannot reconcile her past with her present. At the end of *The Piano Lesson*, however, when Boy Willie is struggling for life against Sutter's ghost, Berniece finally understands that the only way to save him is to call upon her heritage, thereby empowering herself with its strength. Her Christian faith alone is not enough; Berniece plays the piano and in a ritual chant calling on her ancestors, defeats the evil spirit.

In *Joe Turner's Come and Gone*, Wilson has brought to life another Bearden creation in the character of Bertha (*Miss Bertha and Mr. Seth*, 1978). In contrast to Berniece, Bertha serves as a positive example of reconciling old and new. She brings with her the remedies of the past and combines them with a practical approach to the future.

When her husband, Seth, bothers Bertha about her daily activities, about "all that heebie-jeebie stuff . . . sprinkling salt all over the place . . . pennies lined up across the threshold," Bertha responds, "It don't hurt none. I can't say if it help . . . but it don't hurt none" (2). For Bertha, there is no contradiction between attending church and maintaining the more ritualistic traditions of the past.

This theme of conflict between cultures is still strong in contemporary African performance. For example, in the Ethiopian play *The Coffin Dealer and the Grave Digger*, the central character has a comical nightmare which inverts Christian ideals of heaven and hell as they have been unsuccessfully laid onto African culture. The juxtaposition of African and Western ideas about death appears in many plays.

Both Wilson and Bearden address the juxtaposition between African and Christian religious tradition, revealing parallels and contrasts. Bearden weaves together aligned cultural rituals. His *Baptism* is linked to John the Baptist, which leads back to ancient purification rites in Africa. Bearden says, "I feel this continuation of ritual gives a dimension to the works so that the works are something other than mere designs."[17] Bearden's painting titled *The Prevalence of Ritual: Conjur Woman* also connects two worlds.

Wilson's and Bearden's works serve the same function as the traditional performers. As Soyinka notes, the principal function of these performers "is to reinforce by observances, rituals, and mytho-historical recitals the existing consciousness or cosmic entanglement in the community, and to arbitrate in the sometimes difficult application of such truths to domestic and community undertakings."[18]

Traditional African performance shares many characteristics with traditional forms of other cultures. Thus, Wilson's and Bearden's use of these elements promotes a universal applicability of their art. Wilson and Bearden have addressed what Wole Soyinka describes as the "deep-seated need of creative man to recover this archetypal consciousness," and their art, which shares many characteristics, shares most of all its ability to speak across racial and cultural lines.

Wilson and Bearden thus understand a theory which underlies the tragedy in traditional performance in which the sickness of one individual, according to Soyinka, "is a sign of, or may portend, the sickness of the world around him. Something has occurred to disrupt the natural rhythms and the cosmic balances of the total community."[19]

In African performances history is thus often repeated for moral or educational purposes. Both Wilson and Bearden understand the power of revisiting the past and undertake the African view of art as what Soyinka calls "retrieval vehicles for, or assertive links with a lost sense of origin."[20]

Bearden's paintings therefore speak through centuries of history, and, as Campbell writes, "what makes Bearden's art particularly difficult to grasp . . . is that even as his art points to the future, it also wholeheartedly embraces the past."[21]

Wilson intends to write a play for every decade of this century. He, like Bearden, has brought to contemporary audiences a powerful chronicle of African American history. And yet, neither Wilson's nor Bearden's works stand merely as historical reflections. Rather they carry great relevance to

*Romare Bearden.* The Prevalence of Ritual: Conjur Woman. *1964. Collage on board. Collection of Sheldon and Phyllis Ross, Birmingham, Michigan. Photo by Richard Herrington.*

contemporary life, and they promote promise for tomorrow. Wilson says, "Without knowing your past, you don't know your present—and you certainly can't plot your future."[22]

Improving prospects for the future is at the center of traditional performances whose goal is the harmonious resolution of issues and an improvement in the well-being of the community. Wilson's characters are examples meant to help heal. Wilson hopes his work may "indicate some directions toward which we might possibly move."[23] He speaks to all people when he addresses our need to make a connection with the past as we move toward the future. In *Two Trains Running*, Memphis is advised by Aunt Ester: "If you drop the ball you got to go back and pick it up. Ain't no need in keeping running cause if you get to the end zone, it ain't gonna be a touchdown" (146).

Wilson's plays and Bearden's paintings, like traditional performances, rarely guide toward external solution. Instead, they focus on the greatest magic, the magic of the individual to become part of the community and thus to heal himself and the community. African performance doesn't offer resolution; the final outcome will be determined by the learning the performance has hopefully inspired in its audience. The performances rise out of their communities, reflect social and political upheaval within their communities, and they hold the potential for harmonious resolution not within the confines of the actual drama but within the workings of the community.

..................

August Wilson and Romare Bearden challenge women and men to respect and believe in who they are on their own and as part of a larger population. They challenge every heart to search for truth and every individual to sing his own song loudly for survival, strength, and growth. It is a powerful and valuable message.

Wilson offered to send a limousine to bring Bearden to a performance of his play *Fences*. Bearden chose instead to travel by bus with a senior citizens group. In the end, he decided not to make the trip at all. Later Bearden was scheduled to attend the opening of Wilson's *Joe Turner's Come and Gone* but sadly died two weeks before the event.

Wilson writes:

> I never had the privilege of meeting Romare Bearden. Once I stood outside 357 Canal Street [New York] in silent homage, daring myself to knock on his door. I am sorry I didn't, for I have never looked back from that moment when I first encountered his art.

I have often thought of what I would have said to him that day if I had knocked on his door and he had answered. I probably would just have looked at him. I would have looked, and if I were wearing a hat, I would have taken it off in tribute.[24]

Romare Bearden never saw an August Wilson play performed, the men never met, and they never spoke. But these two artists drank from the same well and carry to contemporary audiences art created from age-old elements.

On their separate roads, these two artists offer images of a people, indeed of all people, in defeat and triumph, joy and despair. In the smallest details of day-to-day existence, Wilson and Bearden find the energy of life, and through their art, they send it out to each of us.

..................

## NOTES

1. Soyinka, *Myth, Literature, and the African World*, p. 46.

2. Schwartzman, *Romare Bearden*, p. 8.

3. Ibid., p. 9.

4. Soyinka, *Myth, Literature, and the African World*, p. 50.

5. Schwartzman, *Romare Bearden*, p. 217.

6. Weiss, "Playwright Pays Homage," p. 7.

7. Patton, "Memory and Metaphor," p. 38.

8. Schwartzman, *Romare Bearden*, p. 24.

9. Tomkins, "Putting Something over Something Else," p. 60.

10. Schwartzman, *Romare Bearden*, p. 8.

11. Patton, "Memory and Metaphor," p. 65.

12. Weiss, "Playwright Pays Homage," p. 7.

13. Shafer, "Interview," p. 162.

14. Campbell, "History and the Art of Romare Bearden," p. 67.

15. Nelson, "August Arrives," p. 5.

16. Weiss, "Playwright Pays Homage," p. 7.

17. Campbell, "History and the Art of Romare Bearden," p. 9.

18. Soyinka, *Myth, Literature, and the African World*, p. 54.

19. Ibid., p. 50.

20. Ibid., p. 54.

21. Campbell, "History and the Art of Romare Bearden," p. 11.

22. DeVries, "Song in Search of Itself," p. 25.

23. Wilson, "How to Write a Play," p. 1.

24. Schwartzman, *Romare Bearden*, p. 9.

..................

## WORKS CITED

Campbell, Mary Schmidt. "History and the Art of Romare Bearden." In *Memory and Metaphor: The Art of Romare Bearden, 1940–1987*, pp. 7–17. The Studio Museum in Harlem. New York: Oxford University Press, 1991.

DeVries, Hilary. "A Song in Search of Itself." *American Theater*, January 1987, pp. 22–25.

Nelson, Don. "August Arrives," *Daily News*, 6 March 1988, p. 5.

Patton, Sharon. "Memory and Metaphor: The Art of Romare Bearden, 1940–1987." In *Memory and Metaphor, The Art of Romare Bearden, 1940–1987*, pp. 18–70. The Studio Museum in Harlem. New York: Oxford University Press, 1991.

Schwartzman, Myron. *Romare Bearden: His Life and Art*. New York: Harry Abrams, 1990.

Shafer, Yvonne. "An Interview with August Wilson." *Journal of Dramatic Theory and Criticism* (Fall 1989): 161–73.

Soyinka, Wole. *Myth, Literature, and the African World*. Cambridge: Cambridge University Press, 1976.

Tomkins, Calvin. "Putting Something over Something Else," *New Yorker*, 28 November 1977, pp. 53–61.

Weiss, Hedy. "A Playwright Pays Homage to a Painter." *Chicago Sun Times*, 22 September 1991, sec. E, p. 7.

Wilson, August. Introduction to *Romare Bearden: His Life and Art*, by Myron Schwartzman. New York: Harry Abrams, 1990.

———. "Fences." *Theater* (Summer/Fall 1985).

———. "How to Write a Play like August Wilson," *New York Times*, 10 March 1991, Arts and Leisure sec., pp. 1 and 17.

———. *Joe Turner's Come and Gone*. New York: New American Library, Plume, 1988.

———. *Ma Rainey's Black Bottom*. New York: New American Library, Plume, 1985.

———. *The Piano Lesson*. New York: New American Library, Plume, 1990.

———. *Two Trains Running*. Unpublished. Property of Yale Repertory Theater, 1990.

SANDRA G. SHANNON

# The Ground on Which I Stand: August Wilson's Perspective on African American Women

· · · · · · · · · · · · · · · · · · · · · · · · · · · · · · · · · · · · · · · · · · · · · · · · · · · · · · · · · · · · · · · · ·

In 1979 August Wilson wrote *Jitney!*, a play about a black-owned transportation service located in a section of Pittsburgh slated for demolition. Set in 1971, this work not only enjoys the distinction of being the first of the playwright's ongoing chronicles of the black experience in America, but it also began a so-far-uninterrupted pattern of works that revolve exclusively around black men. Two women—one named Rena, another simply Woman—make brief appearances, but their importance to the play is made obvious by the respective labels given them: "Youngblood's woman" and "Booster's woman."[1] Wilson is forthright in acknowledging his intentional focus upon the motivations of black men in this particular play: "I simply wanted to show how the station worked, how these guys created jobs for themselves and how it was organized. . . . The important thing was for me to show these five guys working and creating something out of nothing."[2]

In fact, Wilson seems neither apologetic nor actually concerned about his tendency toward stocking *Jitney!* (1979), *Ma Rainey's Black Bottom* (1984), *Fences* (1986), *Joe Turner's Come and Gone* (1988), *The Piano Lesson* (1988), and *Two Trains Running* (1990) with a healthy supply of black men who have plenty to talk about. Although he acknowledges that the women in his plays are neither as visible nor as vocal as his men, he does not feel compelled to make any changes. He explains,

I doubt seriously if I would make a woman the focus of my work simply because of the fact that I am a man, and I guess because of the ground on which I stand and the viewpoint from which I perceive the world. I can't do that although I try to be honest in the instances in which I do have women. I try to portray them from their own viewpoint as opposed to my viewpoint. I try to—to the extent that I am able—to step around on the other side of the table, if you will, and try to look at things from their viewpoint and have been satisfied that I have been able to do that to some extent.

The ground on which August Wilson stands has yielded a number of intriguing male characters, from the reluctant murderer Levee to the talkative tyrant Troy Maxson to the raging vagrant Herald Loomis. Yet this very same ground has produced the African American woman—the manifestation of a playwright whose sensibilities are admittedly and understandably masculine. Despite Wilson's grounding in a decidedly male frame of reference, his portrayals of African American women cover as wide a range as do those of his men. Although individually his feminine portrayals tend to slip into comfort zones of what seem to be male-fantasized roles, collectively they show Wilson coming to grips with the depth and diversity of African American womanhood. It is important to note that Daisy Wilson, the playwright's mother, is the model on which he bases the majority of his women: "My mother's a very strong, principled woman. My female characters like Rose come in large part from my mother."[3] Thus they regularly reflect some degree of his mother's indomitable spirit, her maternal warmth, and her fierce independence.

In each of the five chronicles following *Jitney!*, Wilson continues to focus on male protagonists, but another pattern also emerges. In each play a singular African American woman manages to wrestle free from prevailing social restraints or domestic concerns to, in some way, affirm a separate identity. Although their motives are not always made clear and each of their victories amounts to a compromise, in Gertrude "Ma" Rainey (*Ma Rainey's Black Bottom*), Rose Maxson (*Fences*), Martha Pentecost Loomis (*Joe Turner's Come and Gone*), Berniece Charles (*The Piano Lesson*), and Risa (*Two Trains Running*), Wilson has created an array of powerful African American women.

Gertrude "Ma" Rainey, the title character in *Ma Rainey's Black Bottom*, seems most unlike the fond images Wilson retains of his late mother. On the surface she appears capable of taking on (or taking out) any man—black or white—who dares to take advantage of her because of her gender. Far from a paragon of virtue and femininity, Ma Rainey is a sassy-talking, demanding prima donna who disrupts a planned rehearsal session to remind her subordinates that she is "Madame" Rainey, not just some black woman who can sing. Her court includes a pair of hangers-on: Sylvester (her stuttering nephew) and Dussie Mae (her young lesbian associate). Despite the implications of her nickname, Ma Rainey is the antithesis of the traditional homemaker. Essentially a transient because of her profession, she spends little time in what may be called home.

In addition to her attention-getting antics and her nomadic lifestyle, Ma Rainey's physical appearance and dress further place her in a category of one. Various photographs of her and accounts from some of her contemporaries reveal that she was "a short, heavy, dark-skinned woman with luminous eyes, wild wiry hair, and a large mouth filled with gold teeth."[4] *Current Biography* describes her as "a massive bejeweled and befeathered regal figure,"[5] and August Wilson's stage directions call for a "heavy woman . . . dressed in a full-length fur coat with matching hat, an emerald green dress and several strands of pearls of varying lengths" (48). Onstage her repertoire, which consisted of double entendres about sex and dance, soothed and amused the weary Southerner fresh from the clod hills of some rural town.

Although this powerful presence may suggest that Ma Rainey is in control of her career, she knows full well that whites, such as her record promoters Sturdyvant and Irvin, ultimately determine her longevity in the business. Thus any sense of victory Ma may enjoy is usually tempered by an awareness of how very expendable she is. She explains,

> They don't care nothing about me. All they want is my voice. Well, I done learned that, and they gonna treat me like I want to be treated no matter how much it hurt them. They back there now calling me all kinds of names . . . calling me everything but a child of god. (79)

Despite her acknowledged degradation, Ma's victory seems to be in maintaining her dignity in the face of the apparent "prostitution" of her talents and in exercising as much control as possible over the rights to her music. As a result, her skin has toughened over the years to survive the frequent backlash directed, first, against an African American and second, against a woman—especially one who dares to thrive in a white-controlled industry.

This unsinkable blues-singing woman in this 1984 play establishes a challenging precedent for subsequent portrayals of African American women. Although Gertrude Rainey brings new meaning to the term "Ma," Wilson does not represent her as totally antithetical to her maternal label. The fictitious Ma Rainey, like subsequent feminine portrayals, approximates a human mixture of inner strength, defiance, and fierce independence on the one hand and warmth and compassion on the other. Out of the tension between these traits, her character and much of the conflict in the play is forged. While first impressions of Ma Rainey cast her as a whirlwind of antagonism, as the play progresses, she reveals a tender—even nurturing—side.

Ma is most insular during quiet moments when the rehearsal session recesses. While away from the cause of her agitation, she reveals her true motivation—singing the blues. She tells the leader of her band, "The blues help you get out of bed in the morning. You get up knowing you ain't alone. There's something else in the world. Something's been added by that song. This be an empty world without the blues. I take that emptiness and try to fill it up with something" (83). During these quiet times, Ma is able to reveal that she is just as vulnerable as any African American woman of her day who dares to step outside her traditional role and confront head-on the forces of racism and oppression.

In her relationship with her nephew Sylvester, Ma reveals a maternal side of her character. She apparently informally adopts her sister's son and makes it her business to teach him a profession and to force him to overcome his severe speech impediment. Against the better judgment of her band and her promoters, she insists that he be allowed to introduce her on the group's new recording. While others grow more and more anxious to complete the recording session, Ma is ever so patient in coaxing her nephew so that he can master this seemingly impossible task. To do this she steps outside the tough character reserved for her strictly business persona and into the nurturing role of a gentle instructor: "Come on, Sylvester. You just stand here and hold you hands like I told you. Just remember the words and say them. . . . That's all there is to it. Don't worry about messing up. If you mess up, we'll do it again" (75).

Sylvester also brings out of Ma a certain maternal fussiness over his appearance and behavior. She scolds him just as a loving mother might: "Sylvester, tuck your clothes in. Straighten them up and look nice. Look like a gentleman" and "Sylvester, take your hat off inside. Act like your mama taught you something. I know she taught you better than that." Ma also counsels her nephew on appropriate behavior toward his own mother, telling him, "When you get your money, you gonna send some of it home to your mama. Let her know you doing all right. Make her feel good to know you doing all right in the world" (61).

Ma's young lover Dussie Mae exemplifies the singer's flagrant disregard for the social restraints of her day and her apparent need for intimacy. Gertrude Rainey, the real-life legend on which the play is based, frequently made known her affections for younger men, yet she was just as frequently rejected and humiliated by their rude comments about her stark physical features. Thus she sought intimacy with members of her chorus as well as with rival blues singer Bessie Smith.[6]

She is neither a saint nor the kind of hopelessly dependent creature the image of which often stigmatized women of her day. In fact, Ma belongs to an exclusive group of female blues singers, such as Ida Cox, Clara Smith, Ethel Waters, and Bessie Smith, who endured racism and sexism on a daily basis. Those who survived and flourished learned to repress their femininity and become shrewd businesswomen. Making such concessions becomes second nature to Ma for her survival. The role of "Ma" as public image masks the (ma)ternal, nurturing role necessary to hold a band together and create a private life.

This conflict between public and private is not an issue for the chief agent of nurturing in *Fences*. Rose Maxson is a woman who chooses to direct her energies toward being a wife, a mother, and a homemaker. She is the Maxson family's peace negotiator, soothing the friction between her domineering husband, Troy, and her strong-willed son, Cory, while keeping her stepson, Lyons, and Troy on good terms with each other. In addition to cooking, cleaning, and providing for her immediate family, she watches over her mentally impaired brother-in-law Gabriel. Married eighteen years to a hardworking garbage collector, she has had to sacrifice and make do on his meager wages. Apparently she does not require material goods to keep her happy—she needs just the knowledge that her family is well fed, loved, and reasonably complacent.

Confined to the private sphere, Rose perhaps best exemplifies the ambivalence exhibited in Wilson's African American women between the innate desire to nurture and the concomitant need to maintain self-respect and a sense of self. Apparently Rose finds a happy medium between these seemingly incompatible forces within her. When her husband, Troy, delivers devastating news that he not only is having an affair with a "big-legged Florida gal" but also that he is "gonna be somebody's daddy" (66), her response to the situation appears somewhat unorthodox although extremely compassionate. When the infant's mother dies in delivery, leaving Troy with no other alternative than to ask Rose to be its surrogate mother, she accepts. However, Rose's agreeing to raise Troy and Alberta's daughter comes with her strictest stipulation: "From right now . . . this child got a mother. But you a womanless man" (79).

In her heroic decision to rescue the infant from a life of instability, Rose becomes susceptible to the too freely used term "victim." However, her strong sense of what is morally right allows her to nurture the helpless infant without feeling that she is in any way sanctioning Troy's extramarital affair with Alberta. Instead she has found a way both to salvage some dignity in the wake of her crumbling marriage and to exercise her desire to nurture. Though obviously daunted by Troy's affair, she rises to a level of human consciousness that allows her to attend to the needs of a motherless child while in no uncertain terms letting her husband feel the full extent of her fury. Thus Rose initiates her own brand of female consciousness that allows her to remain in control throughout the play. She also comes to some conclusions about what constitutes victimization—conclusions shared by feminist Dale Spender: "We women find ourselves in the position of being the nurturing sex in an exploitative society; our nurturance is taken and used by men. We must confront the problem of how to make ourselves nurturantly unavailable for exploitation—an oppression—without repudiating nurturing itself."[7]

The initial action of *Fences* takes place in the waning years of the 1950s, a decade which saw women's roles still very much defined by men. Education was neither a particularly popular nor a financially feasible alternative for most African American women, and marriage was, for many, considered their best investment in long-term security. But the play's 1957 setting also stands on the brink of a decade of social and political revolutions in the wider arena of women's rights. As symbolized by the "burning bra" of the 1970s, many women went from conforming to traditional domestic roles to affirming their rights to individual preferences.

Rose Maxson's dynamic character traces such a revolution. During the course of *Fences*, she evolves from a long-suffering heroine to a fiercely independent woman—this, despite first impressions given by Wilson's description of her:

> She is ten years younger than Troy, her devotion to him stems from her recognition of the possibilities of her life without him: a succession of abusive men and their babies, a life of partying and running the streets, the Church, or aloneness with its attendant pain and frustration. She recognizes Troy's spirit as a fine and illuminating one and she either ignores or forgives his faults, only some of which she recognizes. (5)

Because of her consuming love for Troy, Rose willingly puts any ambitions that she has in storage and lives vicariously through and for him. This blind devotion soon changes, however, as she realizes that her raison d'être has added infidelity to his list of other vices.

Rose's conversion from passive homemaker to an enraged woman is swift and riveting. After Troy stuns her with admissions of his infidelity and impending fatherhood, her character transforms instantaneously. In a matter of moments she steps out of her predictable character to deliver a salvo of pent-up emotions:

> I been standing with you! I been right here with you, Troy. I got a life too. I gave eighteen years of my life to stand in the same spot with you. Don't you think I ever wanted things? Don't you think I had dreams and hopes? You not the only one who's got wants and needs. (70–71)

Despite her feelings of anger, hurt, and betrayal, Rose's diatribe serves to purge her of years of self-imposed repression and stagnation. Ironically, it also marks the beginning of a new and more self-serving, less altruistic Rose, but at the price of the marriage she so desired. When Rose chooses to nurture Alberta's child, she not only makes Troy a womanless man but also makes herself a husbandless woman. Wilson thus represents the disintegration of the African American family as Rose's having to choose between nurturing the father or the child.

In *Joe Turner's Come and Gone* Wilson again examines factors leading to the disintegration of the African American family structure by presenting a collage of African American women widely varied in the way they nurture. Beneath these fictional portrayals are very real personalities of women who, along with a majority of black men, actually migrated north to Pittsburgh during the early 1900s. Thus, for many, the role of nurturer was temporarily suspended until they could situate themselves in this new land. For others— especially those who brought children along on this harrowing journey— their ability to provide food, shelter, and adequate care decreased significantly once they arrived. Poverty and squalor often awaited such women in an already heavily populated steel town. One study reports, "One woman with three children left her husband in Georgia during World War I to come to Pittsburgh. She ended up living in one damp room, using an outdoor water supply, trying to nurse her sick children back to health while she took in washing to earn money."[8]

Molly Cunningham, Mattie Campbell, and Martha Loomis are survivors. Each has withstood the perils of traveling alone, yet each carries with her a different story of survival. Their separate journeys lead them to Bertha and Seth Holly's Pittsburgh boardinghouse, and along the way they are also led to an awareness of just how important being wives and mothers is to their continued survival. In this respect, Molly Cunningham is the most liberated of the three. Young, attractive, and wise beyond her years, she rejects the roles of home-maker, childbearer, and potential victim of men. Her disinterest in domesticity is forthright. She tells Seth, "I ain't gonna be here long. I ain't looking for no home or nothing. I'd be in Cincinnati if I hadn't missed my train" (47).

Unlike Molly, Mattie Campbell is so obsessed with being a wife and mother that she has lost all sense of self and has dedicated her life to locating a husband who has abandoned her after the deaths of two of their children. She internalizes blame for the double deaths and becomes her own worst enemy. Nurturing is Mattie's raison d'être, and it cannot resume unless only Jack Carper is again its focus. Despite the conjurer Bynum Walker's advice to "let him go find where he's suppose to be in the world" (23), Mattie welcomes continued victimization while pursuing this singular mission.

The boardinghouse mistress, Bertha Holly, has not known the hard lives that her female tenants have endured. A Northerner by birth, she can only imagine the experiences these women faced en route to her Pittsburgh estab-lishment. Although the play includes no mention of children born to Bertha and her husband, Seth, she exudes the same maternal warmth of an actual mother as she busies herself attending to her customers' needs. In the absence of children of her own, Bertha directs her nurturing toward the tenants in her charge. She seems genuinely concerned about their well-being and frequently offers motherly advice to those who turn to her for help. In addition to ad-vice, Bertha dishes up three meals a day, provides a weekly change of sheets, lovingly keeps her "ornery" husband in line, and promotes an overall harmo-nious atmosphere. She is the ideal surrogate mother for the dispossessed group, claiming, "I get along with everybody" (50).

Martha Pentecost is initially complacent in her role as nurturer and—but for a forced separation from her husband—would have perhaps continued to be so. But in *Joe Turner* Martha chooses a life apart from her home, her hus-band, and, for several years, her daughter. Hence, the journey north prompts both a religious and a personal conversion in her, for although she eventually reclaims her daughter, the new Martha apparently decides that time has warped her capacity to love and nurture an estranged husband. Depriving Loomis of her affection was not an easy decision for Martha. As is the case in *Fences*, one pivotal African American woman in *Joe Turner* bears the largest responsibility in determining whether the family continues to exist as a unit or, out of necessity, disbands. Martha Pentecost best exemplifies this burden of choice which other such women often carry.

At the opening of *Joe Turner's Come and Gone*, seven years have lapsed since Herald Loomis was kidnapped and separated from his wife, Martha, and his daughter, Zonia. During his absence Martha and her infant daughter are evicted from their home by their white landlord and forced to find shelter at her mother's home. In the interim, Martha also becomes a devout Christian and latches onto the church as a means of support. When her church comes under attack by Southern white vigilantes, she decides to leave her young daughter with her mother while she travels to the North, where her church is more likely to be spared such retaliations.

When Martha, who has adopted the name Pentecost, finally comes to Seth and Bertha Holly's boardinghouse, where her estranged husband Herald Loomis awaits her arrival (she is lured there by Rutherford Selig, the so-called People Finder), she offers him a passionate account of her life without him. As she talks, she also reveals that, like Rose Maxson, she defined her world according to the likes and dislikes of her husband. But also, like Rose Maxson, Martha Pentecost has the strength to deal squarely with her fate and make necessary choices to assure her own mental and physical stability:

> I stayed and waited there for five years before I woke up one morning and decided that you was dead. Even if you weren't, you was dead to me. I wasn't gonna carry you with me no more. So I killed you in my heart. I buried you. I mourned you. And then I picked up what was left and went on to make life without you. I was a young woman with life at my beckon. I couldn't drag you behind me like a sack of cotton. (90)

Martha Pentecost makes the tough decision to abandon a marriage that exists in name only for seven years.[9] She also decides that rather than risk her daughter's safety, she would leave her in her own mother's care. What is most telling, however, is that perhaps her most personally rewarding decision—to seek spiritual edification for herself—comes at the expense of nurturing her child. Homeless, moneyless, husbandless, and childless, she reasons that the best way to heal these wounds is to attend to her spiritual and psychological self. Thus after being "washed in the blood of the lamb" (93), she returns to reclaim her daughter and resume their life together.

But when she comes back to claim Zonia, she is not as successful in piecing together the original family unit. Apparently a chain of uncontrollable, centuries-old forces conspires to keep this family apart. From the ravages of the slave trade to the slow trickle of former farm hands into Northern cities, the African American family has been split asunder. The dissolution of the

Loomis family represents the very human cost of so many years of fragmentation. While the newly released Herald Loomis struggles to regain a sense of place in the world, he has grown explosive and bitter. While Martha Pentecost's spiritual retreat gives her a fresh perspective, she can no longer tolerate a heathen for a husband. The play ends in a virtual standoff: Martha Pentecost launches into a sermon on her husband's ungodliness, and Herald Loomis mocks her invitation to Christian discipleship by slashing his chest and smearing his face in his own blood.

Like *Fences* and *Joe Turner's Come and Gone*, *The Piano Lesson* prominently features an African American woman at the center of a heated domestic controversy; like Rose Maxson and Martha Pentecost, Berniece Charles makes unpopular decisions yet remains unfaltering against all odds.

As its title suggests, the center of controversy in *The Piano Lesson* is a piano. But this is not just any piano. The pictorial history carved into its surface by the enslaved great-grandfather of embattled siblings Berniece and Boy Willie elevates both its monetary and its sentimental worth. Berniece reveres the piano to the point of paranoia and refuses to let her brother turn it into a down payment for land. Her obsession, however, does not dissuade Boy Willie from what is, to him, a sensible investment in his future; he maintains that he can reap more practical good from an otherwise useless object by using it to stake him in life and thus afford him an opportunity that was denied his sharecropper father. With impeccable logic, he argues against his sister's stubborn regard for the family heirloom.

Boy Willie is not alone in his designs on the piano. Also apparently bent on retrieving the controversial object is the ghost of the piano's former white owner, Robert Sutter. This spirit is the direct descendant of the slave-owning Sutter family, who acquired the piano from a poor white farmer in a barter for Berniece and Boy Willie's paternal great-grandparents. This spirit, who still lays claim to the piano, tinkles its keys from time to time and terrorizes both Berniece and her daughter with several intrusions into their home. Exasperated over the ghost's claim to the piano, Boy Willie finally exorcises it in a climactic wrestling match, followed by Berniece's decision to play the until-then-untouched piano and Boy Willie's decision to dismiss his designs on it and return to his home on the next train.

Berniece Charles is a woman whose identity is linked to several never-to-be-recovered images from her past. Her present life is thus filled with self-denial and frustration as she plays warden over a two-hundred-year-old piano, dodges marriage proposals from a love-stricken minister, and perpetually grieves for her murdered husband and murdered father. The conflict in her life extends beyond marital concerns, however. In fact, Berniece carries the weight of several generations of her family on her shoulders, as symbolized by her attempts to preserve and idolize an old piano anointed by the spirits of her slave ancestors.

Berniece is a complex and potentially misunderstood woman. Because she harbors deep emotional scars from her own past, outwardly she appears bitter and unreasonable. Her husband, Crawley, was shot and killed in a wood-hauling venture with Boy Willie and Lymon, which, according to Berniece, was no more than a poorly executed robbery. When they invited Crawley to join them, their operation was discovered by the sheriff, shots were exchanged, and Crawley was fatally wounded in the crossfire. Although it was Crawley who initiated the shooting, Berniece blames Boy Willie for her husband's murder: "You killed Crawley just as sure as if you pulled the trigger," she explodes (52). For three years this misdirected blame fuels Berniece's anger at her brother and stands in the way of any possible reconciliation between them.

All men seem to tolerate Berniece out of respect, yet they all apparently concur that she would be less vocal, less troublesome, and less of a threat to their domain if she remarried. There is certainly no lack of male wisdom in the play concerning the way Berniece should handle her life. Doaker secretly wishes that his niece would settle down with the respectable, financially promising minister, Avery. In confidence, Doaker discusses his niece's prospects with his brother, Wining Boy:

> She doing alright. She still got Crawley on her mind. He been dead three years but she still holding on to him. She need to go out here and let one of these fellows grab a whole handful of whatever she got. She act like it done got precious. . . . She stuck up on it. She think it's better than she is. I believe she messing around with Avery. They got something going. He a preacher now. (29)

In addition to her uncle Doaker's unwelcomed wisdom, her boyfriend, Avery, also has a prescription for what ails her.

*Avery:* You too young a woman to close up, Berniece.
*Berniece:* I ain't said nothing about closing up. I got a lot of woman left in me.
*Avery:* Where's it at? When's the last time you looked at it? (66)

Even her brother's accomplice, Lymon, in an offhanded remark, gives his assessment: "How come you ain't married? It seem like to me you would be married" (78).

To be sure, Berniece's ideas about men, marriage, and her independence seem anachronistic when one considers the 1930s setting of *The Piano Lesson*. But to some extent each of the African American women examined in this study so far do not conform to the limited roles that their societies dictate for their gender. They seem decades ahead of Wilson's men in terms of envisioning new roles for themselves—roles which still involve being wives, mothers, or nurturers but which also involve freedom and independence.

August Wilson's sole black female character in *Two Trains Running* presents a baffling portrayal of a woman who resorts to self-mutilation to deflect lustful attention from men. Risa—whom director Lloyd Richards portrays as a slow-walking, slow-talking riddle—takes a razor blade to her legs as a symbolic though questionable gesture to "force everybody to look at her and see what kind of personality she is" (50). In addition to having the distinction of being the only woman in the play, Risa is its most enigmatic character.[10]

Like the black women in the other plays discussed so far, the nurturing motif prompted by the sole black woman in *Two Trains* is manifest in a very personalized manner. In the waitress Risa, Wilson continues to demonstrate that the black woman's capacity to nurture is not limited to certain members of her family, nor is it confined to a domestic setting. Like Bertha Holly, who clearly regards her boardinghouse customers as her family, or Ma Rainey, who transfers her mothering instinct to her nephew Sylvester, Risa has singled out from a variety of regular patrons one mentally impaired black man as the recipient of her compassion.

Risa's unexplained allegiance to Hambone, as he is called, leaves room for much conjecture. Her strong commitment to him seems based upon some prior common experience they apparently shared during another time and at another place. This possibly atavistic bond is underscored by Risa's exceptionally protective regard for Hambone. When it becomes necessary, she speaks for him, feeds him, and defends him, especially when his constant cry "He gonna give me my ham!" becomes a distraction in Memphis's restaurant. Her maternal concern for this mentally unstable man casts her as the epitome of altruism. Knowing that her routine kind gestures toward Hambone stand to anger the restaurant's owner, she continues to give him coffee, a warm bowl of beans, or a wrap to shelter his body from the cold. She frequently intercedes on Hambone's behalf to ward off any attacks with "He ain't bothering nobody" (54). When Hambone is found dead of multiple stab wounds, it is Risa who frowns upon the traditional welfare burial that awaits him, preferring—in spite of a $700 price tag—to "lay him out in a gold casket" (67).

Risa's unexplained nurturing of Hambone may also be a result of the respective physical and emotional scars that seem to forge a common bond between them. Risa inflicts multiple cuts on her legs, and Hambone's body is subjected to multiple wounds that lead to his death. While Risa intentionally flaunts her victimization via her scars, Hambone becomes the victim of a suspicious homicide; after he has been missing for several days, his body is found.

Hambone, like Risa, is a victim of an emotional scar. While Risa demonstrates her disgust with men who lust after her body, Hambone bears the scar of denial that comes with Lutz's nine-year refusal to give him a ham for a paint job he completed in 1959. Unfortunately, Hambone's mental retardation gives him one more scar than his guardian, Risa, has. Both he and Risa live on the fringes of society, and seemingly out of their roughly similar circumstances, they gravitate toward each other for mutual support. Thus, Risa and Hambone obviously connect on a level that transcends the specifics of *Two Trains Running*.

Over the last decade, the ground on which August Wilson has stood as an African American writer who happens to be a man has justified a steady procession of African American men with pressing stories of their pasts. They are the talkers, the dreamers, and the self-proclaimed prophets. In contrast, African American women have been placed in the more conservative roles traditionally prescribed for them by these men. But upon closer examination of how Wilson depicts women, one discovers that, rather than complementing the men around them, they actually attempt to break free of male definition, although their voices are outnumbered in each of the plays.

Fortunately, this breaking free does not carry with it a total abandonment of these women's inclinations to nurture. In a variety of ways, the nurturing capacity has been sustained in black women from slavery through the Great Migration to the North. Although too many were forced, by separation, to find other avenues for their nurturing, their compassion somehow remained constant. In some cases the maternal instinct has been modified to suit the changing circumstances of these now-industrialized women; in other cases this same critical compassion from black women continues to be the bedrock of black culture in America.

## NOTES

1. Descriptions for Rena and Woman appear under the heading "Characters" in Wilson's predominantly male *Jitney!: A Play in Two Acts*. This currently unpublished play was written in 1979 and produced in 1982.

2. Wilson, Personal interview, 9 November 1991. Other quotes without attribution also come from this interview.

3. Moyers, *World of Ideas*, p. 175.

4. Lieb, *Mother of the Blues*, p. 8.

5. "August Wilson," *Current Biography*, p. 54.

6. Lieb, *Mother of the Blues*, pp. 17–18.

7. Spender, *Women of Ideas*, p. 454.

8. Gottlieb, *Making Their Own Way*, p. 47.

9. Martha Pentecost—a woman whose loyalties are divided between the church and her marriage—might be modeled on Wilson's first wife, Brenda Burton. "My first wife was a member of the Nation of Islam. The break-up of our marriage was over religious discrepancies, over the fact that I did not want to join, even though I was sympathetic. But I always had a tremendous amount of respect for [Elijah Muhammad]. There was a time after the break-up of my marriage when I went and joined the Nation of Islam in an attempt to save my marriage, which didn't work."

10. August Wilson himself provides few clues to the root cause of Risa's masochism: "Well, I wish I could talk more about her than I can. For me the scarring of her legs was an attempt to define herself in her own terms rather than being defined by men. . . . basically for me it was her standing up and refusing to accept those definitions and make her self definition."

## WORKS CITED

Gottlieb, Peter. *Making Their Own Way: Southern Blacks' Migration to Pittsburgh, 1916–1930*. Champaign: University of Illinois Press, 1987.

Lieb, Sandra. *Mother of the Blues: A Study of Ma Rainey*. Amherst: University of Massachusetts Press, 1981.

Moyers, Bill. *A World of Ideas*. New York: Doubleday, 1989.

Rich, Frank. "August Wilson Reaches the 60s with Witnesses from a Distance." *New York Times*, 14 April 1992, sec. C, pp. 13, 17.

Spender, Dale. *Women of Ideas and What Men Have Done to Them*. London: Routledge and Kegan, 1982.

"Wilson, August." *Current Biography* 48 (August 1987): 54.

Wilson, August. Personal inverview. 9 November 1991.

———. *Fences*. New York: New American Library, Plume, 1986.

———. *Jitney!: A Play in Two Acts*. Written in 1979; produced in 1982; currently unpublished.

———. *Joe Turner's Come and Gone*. New York: New American Library, Plume, 1988.

———. *Ma Rainey's Black Bottom*. New York: New American Library, Plume, 1985.

———. *The Piano Lesson*. New York: New American Library, Plume, 1990.

———. "Two Trains Running." *Theater* 22 (1991): 40–72.

**HARRY J. ELAM, JR.**

# August Wilson's Women

· · · · · · · · · · · · · · · · · · · · · · · · · · · · · · · · · · · · · · · · · · · · · · · · · · · · · ·

The significance of August Wilson in contemporary American theatrical practice and African American cultural discourse is unparalleled. In
his dramatic cycle, Wilson has reexamined American history, foregrounding
black experience and moving it into the subject position. Wilson perceives
history not as a fixed point but rather as a site for inquiry, reexamination, and
even revision. He challenges and critiques the past choices blacks have made
as his black male protagonists press the limits of prejudice, poverty, and racial
oppression.

Wilson's black female characters also challenge orthodoxy and press against
historical limitations, recognizing and confronting the additional burdens
placed upon them by gender. Limited by their subordinate position within
the patriarchy, the women in Wilson's dramas attempt to establish relationships with men on their own terms. Black women in Wilson's dramaturgy,
however, function largely in secondary roles and act often in reaction to men.
Even in *Ma Rainey's Black Bottom*, Ma Rainey, the female title character, is
not the focus. The representation of black women by August Wilson, thus,
offers a complex and intriguing dialectic. He presents independent women
who assert feminist positions, but who, either through their own volition or
as the result of external social pressures, ultimately conform to traditional
gender roles and historical expectations.

Before the action begins in Wilson's play of the 1960s, *Two Trains Running*,
the one female character, Risa, has engaged in a radical and intensely personal
protest against the objectification of women. Frustrated by men who deny
her humanity by observing her body as a sex object, Risa takes a razor and
scars her legs, seven scars on one leg, eight on the other. Holloway, an older
black man and a daily visitor to the restaurant where Risa works, interprets
her self-mutilation for the other male characters:

> I know Risa. She one of them gals that matured quick and every man that
> seen her since she was twelve years old think she ought to go lay up with

them somewhere. She don't want that. She figure if she made her legs ugly that would force everybody to look at her and see what kind of personality she is. (50)

Risa later reiterates Holloway's contention: "That's why I did it. To make them ugly" (69).

Risa's ostensively irrational revolt against objectification lends itself to interpretations based on recent feminist theory and theatrical criticism. Feminist theatrical criticism has reacted against traditional gender categories and questioned the construction of women on stage. In *Feminism and Theatre* Sue-Ellen Case writes:

> Overall, feminist semiotics concentrates on the notion of "woman as sign." From this perspective, a live woman standing on the stage is not a biological or natural reality, but "a fictional construct, a distillate from diverse but congruent discourses in dominant western cultures." In other words, the conventions of the stage produce a meaning for the sign "woman," which is based upon their cultural associations with the female gender.[1]

Because traditional theater is constructed from and intended for the "male gaze," feminist theatrical criticism and practice attempts to "deconstruct" traditional "signs of woman" onstage. In *Two Trains Running*, Risa literally "deconstructs" herself as woman. She defies traditional expectations and exists outside cultural codes of femininity. Her employer, Memphis, with disdain proclaims:

> A man would be happy to have a woman like that except she done ruined herself. She ain't right with herself . . . how she gonna be right with you. Anybody take a razor and cut up herself ain't right. . . . Something ain't right with a woman don't want no man. That ain't natural. If she say she like women that be another thing. It ain't natural but that be something else. But somebody that's all confused about herself and don't want nobody I can't figure out where to put her. (50)

Although unintended, Memphis's words support the effectiveness of Risa's political strategy and feminist deconstruction. No longer is she viewed simply as a sexual object or a possession for "some man to lay up with." Her scarification and the corresponding reaction by men emphasize the interlocking systems of women's oppression and objectification noted by Patricia Hill Collins in her book *Black Feminist Thought*.[2]

Risa's scarification also calls attention to Western standards of beauty. Historically black women have combated Western concepts of beauty that valorize fair skin, blue eyes, and long blond hair while denigrating dark skin and kinky hair. As Collins maintains, "Current standards of beauty require either/or dichotomous thinking: in order for one individual to be judged beautiful, another individual—the Other—must be deemed ugly."[3] In African tradition standards of beauty are markedly different. In certain African tribes, such as the Tiv of northern Nigeria, scarification is a rite of religious and social significance. Scarification renders women of the Tiv tribe beautiful, thus inverting Risa's belief that by scarring her legs she makes herself ugly. Wilson has long argued in words and writings that black Americans need to recapture their "African-ness." By considering Risa's action in an African context, beauty is shown to be a social construct rather than a physical reality.

In the December 1991 production of *Two Trains Running* at the Kennedy Center in Washington, D.C., the staging by director Lloyd Richards and the movement and speech patterns created by actor Cynthia Martells further emphasized Risa's rebellion against objectification. Martells as the character Risa moves and speaks extremely slowly. As a result, her pattern of walking is symbolically liberated of cultural signs commonly attributed to gender or ethnicity. She subverts what Jill Dolan identifies as traditional representation where "the female body is imaged within representation only as the site of male desire."[4] Martells's first languid cross from behind the restaurant counter to a downstage right table disrupts traditional gender representations, while foregrounding in the spectator's mind the painful visual image of the scars on her legs.

Risa remains largely silent as the men converse about important issues. Her position within Memphis's restaurant supports Hortense J. Spillers's view that "in a very real sense black American women are invisible to various public discourse."[5] Adapting Collins's terminology, Risa is an "outsider-within" the male world of Memphis's restaurant. Risa's location "within" the restaurant's labor system but "outside" the male network of conversation and associations provides her with a unique perspective on the men as well as on her own subordination. While the men talk and debate around her, demand her services, and make overtures toward her, Martells as Risa in the Kennedy Center production continues to move at her own rhythm. Even as Memphis orders her about and demands that she hurry, Risa never stirs from her deliberate pace and thus responds with quiet defiance. Thus, Martells's exaggerated movement pattern renders her silence visible and emphasizes her removal as woman from the men's topic of discourse.

As the action of the play develops, Risa's nascent feminist consciousness and protest against objectification come into direct conflict with her burgeoning love relationship with the character Sterling. Reminiscent of a fairy-tale knight in shining armor, Sterling, recently paroled from prison, and with an unpolished charm and sincerity, enters the restaurant and rescues Risa from her sheltered, introverted existence. Despite his refreshing differences from the other men, Sterling desires Risa not for her independent feminist spirit but for her ability to fulfill traditional gender roles. "Woman, you everything a man need. Know how to cook . . . pay nice attention to yourself . . . except for those legs" (68). Sterling explains to Risa that her objectification by men is a reality of the world that she as a woman must accept:

> Risa . . . You in the world, baby. You a woman in the world. You here like everybody else. You got to make the best of it. Quite naturally when men see you with that big ass and them pretty legs they gonna try and talk you into a bed somewhere. That's common sense. They be less than a man if they didn't. (69)

Risa does not protest or question this pronouncement. Instead, true to conventional narrative structure, she ultimately succumbs to Sterling's advances. Thus, her revolt against male hegemony is unfulfilled and even contradicted by the dramatic action.

Clearly, Risa's relationship with Sterling generates changes in her behavior, attitude, and appearance. Even though she has adamantly expressed a dislike for crowds, Sterling is able to coax Risa into attending a Malcolm X rally with him. Despite her stated desire to avoid entanglements with men and her protestation that Sterling "just want what everybody else wants," she relents and becomes involved with Sterling. Their eventual union, a result of Sterling's persistent efforts to overcome Risa's apprehension, represents what Case terms "the reification of the male and female sexuality as a battle in which the female is defeated."[6] Still, at the moment when they first embrace, Wilson does present Risa as the aggressor. Risa wants Sterling, but only on her terms. Sterling asks her, "You wanna be kissing cousins," and kisses her lightly. She tells him, "I want to be your only cousin" and kisses him passionately. Yet this one act of self-assertion does not negate the male victory and the female defeat. In the scene directly following their embrace, Martells, in the Kennedy Center production, returns to the stage dressed for the first time in high heels, jewelry, makeup, and a dress. Her new appearance signifies her defeat. Her new acceptance of her "femininity" is visually revealed to the spectators. Rather than remain independent and alone, Risa chooses a traditional heterosexual union with Sterling and conforms to conventional expectations.

In contrast, Ma Rainey, the title character of *Ma Rainey's Black Bottom*, remains a fiercely independent woman throughout the action of the play. From her first entrance onto the stage, Ma is a woman in control. She commands her band members as well as her white record producer, Sturdyvant, and her manager, Irvin. Ma demonstrates a practical understanding of the material hierarchy and her place within it. Recognizing that the purpose of the recording session is to record *her* voice and *her* music, Ma does not allow herself to be objectified but uses her position as desired musical commodity to legitimate her authority. She reminds Irvin, "What band? The band work for me! I say what goes!" (60). As the play opens, all the men, the band members as well as Sturdyvant and Irvin, await the arrival of Ma so that the session can begin. The audience also awaits with anticipation Ma's arrival. With her chaotic entrance, well into the play's first act, Wilson focuses the spectators' attention on Ma and further establishes her significance.

The legendary Gertrude Pridgett "Ma" Rainey continually challenged the conventional limits and expectations of gender. Rather than being subjugated to a limited and powerless role as simply a singer with the band, she became the dominant force in her musical group, the bandleader. As bandleader she kept a tight control over her music. She alone decided how the music would be played and when she would record and perform. Musicians were kept happy because Ma understood that maintaining quality musicians depended on their receiving equitable compensation.[7] As the leader of her own band, Ma displaced the traditional positioning of women within the musical industry's hierarchy.

Through her music and its lyrical content, her public performances and stylistic flair, Ma Rainey developed an image that contradicted conventional representations of black female sexuality. Since the horrors and inequities endured by slave women on the plantation, the American patriarchal system has denied or misrepresented black women's sexuality. Historically, mainstream American culture limited black female sexuality to two stereotypical images—the wanton black whore and the asexual black mammy. In *Sex and Racism in America*, Calvin Hernton argues that in American public discourse black women disappear as legitimate subjects of female sexuality.[8] Still, Michelle Russell posits the blues and black female blues singers as important historical sources of black women's sexual empowerment. Russell writes that the blues "are the expression of a particular social process by which poor black women have commented on all the major theoretical, practical and political questions facing us and have created a mass audience who listens to what we say in that form."[9] Through the activity of singing the blues, Ma Rainey and other black women positively acknowledge their sexuality.

As the black female singer asserts control over the content and form of her song, she equally declares control over her own sexuality. "She is in the moment of performance the primary subject of her own being. Her sexuality is precisely the physical expression of the highest self-regard and, often, the sheer pleasure she takes in her own powers."[10] Russell writes that blues legend Bessie Smith, through her music and performances, "humanized" black female sexuality. Russell's words can also be applied to her rival and contemporary, Ma Rainey:

> With her black women in American culture could no longer be regarded as sexual object. She made us sexual subjects, the first step in taking control. She transformed our collective shame at being rape victims, treated like a dog, or worse, the meat dogs eat, by emphasizing the value of our allure. In so doing she humanized sexuality for black women.[11]

Ma Rainey's songs display an earthy and forthright, crude and sassy sensuality. Daphne Harrison in *Black Pearls* recounts the "same ambivalence about whether to go or stay, or to call him back or 'crown' him, to brag about other men or moan about the lost one, to defy sexual norms, appeared in her blues and were dealt with equally well."[12] In addition, Ma Rainey's flair for comedy showed in her music and performance style. In the play *Ma Rainey's Black Bottom* Ma Rainey and her band perform the title song. She sings,

> They say your black bottom is really good
> Come on and show me your black bottom
> I want to learn that dance. (70)

The comedy as well as the sexual connotations and innuendos are evident. Sandra G. Shannon maintains, furthermore, that the song expresses an equally important coded message: "To Ma Rainey's black audience, the image of a black bottom undoubtedly conveys sexual overtones and lively folk humor, yet the title also sends a stinging message of disrespect to their white oppressors."[13] Ma Rainey's blues music expressed and transcended the pain, oppression, and alienation experienced by Southern blacks during the period known as the Great Migration to the North.

By traditional standards of Western beauty, Ma Rainey would have been perceived as an ugly woman. Yet, as Shannon notes, "Those who truly connected with her ethos were not distracted by what critical Northern blacks and whites perceived as her physical ugliness."[14] Ma Rainey became known for her flamboyance. She adorned herself with lavish gowns and extravagant gold jewelry. Through her performance the image of the heavyset black woman as mammy figure was subverted and transformed into a symbol of sexuality and style. Traditional Western beauty standards were revealed to be a socially constructed means of oppressing black women.

Even in her personal sex life Ma Rainey refused to conform to traditional gender expectations. She was a bisexual with acknowledged lesbian relationships. According to Harrison, "Rainey's and Bessie Smith's episodes with women lovers are indicative of the independent stance they and other blues singers took on issues of personal choice."[15] Her lesbianism and the public knowledge of it further testified to Ma Rainey's personal revolt against male hegemony and her ability to survive outside male domination and social norms.

While Ma Rainey's own activities in life attempted to subvert the male-dominated, heterosexual status quo, the events of Wilson's play appear to uphold it. Decidedly more overt than the physical exchanges between Ma and Dussie Mae, her younger lesbian or bisexual companion, is the sexual embrace shared by Dussie Mae and the rebellious young trumpet player, Levee. Protected by the privacy of the downstairs band room, they exchange a passionate kiss. Their stolen embrace emphasizes Levee's fateful defiance of Ma Rainey's authority. Significantly, Dussie Mae jeopardizes her financially stable—Ma has supplied her with money and clothing—but nontraditional lesbian relationship with Ma Rainey for an extremely tenuous, but conventional heterosexual affair with Levee. Implicit is the message that relationships with men are more valuable than relationships with other women.

Although placing Ma's chaotic entrance late in the first act draws the audience's attention to her, it also provides Wilson with the time to establish interest and involvement in the lives of the band members who await Ma Rainey's arrival. As Shannon explains: "Ma Rainey's tardiness also serves as a means of Equalizing her role in the play with those of her band members: She becomes one who *interrupts* rather than instigates the ongoing action of the play."[16] The construction of the set further emphasizes the collective voice of the band, while silencing the presence and power of Ma Rainey. Ma

Rainey remains above, on the surface, in the recording studio. In the band room below, the domain of the men, the drama simmers. When Ma Rainey enters this environment, she *interrupts* the men. In the stories and conflicts of these men, she is powerless.

Interestingly, the only song other than "Ma Rainey's Black Bottom" that Ma Rainey sings in the play is "Hear Me Talking to You." The song is performed twice, in contrasting styles and with different ramifications. In the first act the song is rehearsed down in the band room by the male band alone. Cutler asks Slow Drag to sing for the tardy Ma Rainey. Slow Drag's cross-gender rendition of "Hear Me Talking to You"—a man singing as a woman singing to a man—suggests a critique of restrictive gender roles and potentially symbolizes the artificiality of gender. Slow Drag's version of the song, however, emphasizes principally the song's humor and cynically mocks the theme of female empowerment. When Slow Drag sings, "You want to be my man, You got to fetch it with you when you come," the audience laughs. Thus, Slow Drag's male voice undermines the song's messages of female control and self-definition. As the lights fade up in the recording studio late in the second act, Ma sings:

> Ah you hear me talking to you
> I don't bite my tongue
> You wants to be my man
> You got to fetch it with you when you come. (83)

Ma's reinterpretation of "Hear Me Talking to You" restores a spirit of black female assertiveness. Her rendition of the song, however, is abbreviated. She sings only this refrain. Furthermore, Wilson places Ma's version of the song after significant events of the play have shifted audience attention away from her and onto Levee.

Throughout the play, Ma's character remains largely unchanged, an iconic symbol framed in the spectator's mind by its historical significance. The mercurial and self-destructive Levee, on the other hand, explodes before the sensibilities of the audience with passion and fury. His frailties, his ambition, his disastrous battle for acceptance, all are exposed to the audience. Levee wants the power and success that Ma has acquired and more. He embodies the disillusionment and ultimate frustration that many blacks experience under white oppression. According to Wilson, "Levee is trying to wrestle with the process of life the same as all of us. His question is 'How can I live this life in a society that refuses to allow me to contribute to its welfare—how can I live this life and remain a whole person?'"[17] To Levee, Ma is only an obstacle, a symbol of the old "jug-band music" rather than the new rhythms of jazz.

In the final confrontation between Ma and Levee, she fires him for insubordination. Levee's dismissal by Ma Rainey is only a further step in his process of self-destruction. His fateful decline, complicated by his senseless murder of Toledo, provides the tragic conclusion to this drama. Significantly, the murder occurs after Ma has gathered her entourage and left the recording studio. Just as she does not determine the action at the outset of the play, she does not determine its conclusion.

Ma Rainey and Risa, in *Two Trains Running*, are women who exist outside of traditional norms. Both as a lesbian and as a bandleader, Ma Rainey defies patriarchal domination and wields power. Risa's extreme and self-destructive action also places her outside the patriarchy. While Risa eventually chooses to conform to the status quo through her relationship with Sterling and her newly discovered femininity, Ma Rainey remains independent.

For Ma Rainey, however, independence is not without cost. Despite her veneer of indomitability, Ma must struggle against the interlocking systems of racial and gender oppression. Her entrance into the play is delayed because of an altercation with the police and a white cab driver. As a black person in Chicago in 1927, she is unable to hail a cab. Singing the blues empowers her and provides her with the forum to subvert oppression. In a private moment, Ma explains to Cutler that she sings the blues because "that's life's way of talking. You don't sing to feel better. You sing 'cause that's a way of understanding life" (67). The inability to overcome social constraints frustrates both Ma Rainey and Levee, but the structure of the play silences Ma Rainey and removes her from the men's discourse. Wilson thus privileges the narrative and actions of the men. While the world of the band consumes and destroys Levee, Ma Rainey exits to an uncertain and racist world accompanied by the perfidious, materialistic Dussie Mae.

In *Joe Turner's Come and Gone*, the female characters attempt to function not outside but within the patriarchy and traditional gender roles. Molly Cunningham and Mattie Campbell are both defined by their relationships with men. David Barbour views these young black women as polar opposites: "Mattie Campbell, who is constantly being taken and abandoned by her lovers; and Molly Cunningham, Mattie's opposite number, who makes a career out of men."[18] These women, however, are not so much opposites as spiritual sisters, victimized by men in the past and looking for solutions in the present. Mattie enlists the help of Bynum, the binder of souls, to find her husband, Jack Carper, who left her. "Ain't said nothing. Just started walking. I could see where he disappeared. Didn't look back. Just kept walking" (224). Molly too has been left by a man. "Come home one day and he was packing his trunk. Told me the time comes for even the best of friends must part. Say he gonna send me a Special Delivery some old day" (225). Molly, unlike Mattie, determines not to wait for this man or any man, that "one's just as good as the other" and to trust nobody but "the good Lord above."

Both women, at different points, become involved with Jeremy, a confident and ingratiating young boarder at Seth and Bertha's Pittsburgh boardinghouse. For Mattie, Jeremy offers the possibility of stability, a replacement for her missing husband. For Molly, the attraction to Jeremy is not stability but adventure, as he offers her an opportunity to travel. While Jeremy moves Mattie into his room at the boardinghouse, he asks Molly to leave with him and "travel around and see some places." Just as Risa in *Two Trains Running* asserts certain limits for her relationship with Sterling, Molly sets down critical ground rules for her travels with Jeremy:

> *Molly:* Molly don't work. And Molly ain't up for sale.
> *Jeremy:* Sure, Baby. You ain't got to work with Jeremy.
> *Molly:* There's one more thing.
> *Jeremy:* What's that sugar?
> *Molly:* Molly ain't going South. (260)

Within the context of Jeremy's involvement with these two women, Wilson explores the principles of need, desire, and privilege in male and female relationships. Bynum lectures Jeremy, "A woman is everything a man *needs*. To a smart man she is water and berries" (245). After he first meets Molly, Jeremy turns to Bynum and responds, "Mr. Bynum, you know what? I think I know what you was talking about now" (247). Yet his male power and privilege affects Jeremy's perception of need. In a manner of courtship similar to that used by Sterling in *Two Trains Running*, Jeremy informs both Molly and Mattie that it is they who *need* a man. He tells Mattie: "A woman like you need a man. Maybe you let me be your man? . . . A woman can't be by her lonesome" (226). He informs Molly, who exudes independence: "A woman like you can make it anywhere you go. But you can make it better if you got a man to protect you" (262).

While Molly establishes the terms for her partnership with Jeremy, she still succumbs to his enticements. In so doing she conforms to his belief that a woman should not be alone. In fact, the actions of both Mattie and Molly reinforce the patriarchal principle that a woman needs a man. Once Mattie has lost Jeremy to Molly, she too is not content to face the world as a single black woman. As the play ends, she "rushes out after" Herald Loomis, the play's brooding central figure, who literally "looms" out over the boarding-house and its inhabitants.

Loomis, like Mattie and Molly, has been abandoned by love. As a man, however, his experience is quite different. Along with his daughter, Zonia, he travels to the boardinghouse in search of his wife, Martha. Martha left years earlier, after Joe Turner, the brother of the governor of Tennessee, who con-fined black men in slavelike servitude for seven years, kidnapped Herald Loomis and placed him in bondage. With monomaniacal determination, Loomis now undertakes the search for his wife. With the assistance of the mysterious Bynum, the binder of souls, Loomis comes to understand his search as a spiritual and practical quest to find his "song," a connection to a past lost while enslaved. His search concerns much more than abandoned love. He, unlike Mattie and Molly, journeys toward self-knowledge, spiritual and psychological liberation.

Hilary DeVries points out: "Loomis's search for his own past symbolizes the quest of an entire race."[19] Wilson believes that black Americans must re-discover "their song," their connection with their African heritage.[20] In the play's final scene, Loomis draws a knife and cuts his own chest. He shouts, "I don't need anyone to bleed for me. I can bleed for myself" (288). He bleeds for himself, but he also symbolically bleeds for black America in search of its collective song. Unshackled from the painful psychological burdens of servi-tude, Loomis rediscovers his lost identity and shines. His personal transcen-dence "heralds" to black Americans that they must regain their African past and reorient themselves in the future.

Even as the ending of *Joe Turner's Come and Gone* produces a radical new beginning for Herald Loomis, it fails to alter the traditional limitations on the women of the play. Loomis, despite the protestations of Zonia, hands over the child to her mother, Martha. "Whatever I know I tried to teach her. Now she need to learn from her mother whatever you got to teach her" (287). While Martha is now bound to her maternal duty, Loomis is bound only to his metaphysical search for self. Bynum explains to Loomis, "I bound that little girl to her mother. That's who I bound. You binding yourself. You bond to your song, all you got to do is stand up and sing it" (287). Loomis scars himself, exorcises his past, stands alone and liberated. The women, on the other hand, must endure a different reality. They are limited to and by their relationships with men. Mattie, hurt and abandoned by previous lovers, now runs off after Loomis. Martha, distraught at the loss of Loomis years ago, found refuge in Christian faith and the church of Reverend Tolliver. Love of God has replaced her connubial love. The message of African retention and spiritual transcendence offered by the pilgrimage and self-sacrifice of Herald Loomis does not empower these women.

The dialectic of feminist assertion and traditional conformity is again evident in *The Piano Lesson*. At the play's outset, Berniece, the one female character, stands in direct opposition to the male protagonist, her brother, Boy Willie. The intransigence of Boy Willie and Berniece over a piano, their shared inheritance, forms the play's central conflict. Boy Willie intends to sell the piano. Berniece, on the other hand, believes the piano must be kept in the family. She treasures the piano because of its sacred, sentimental, and spiritual value. This unique piano that their great-grandfather intricately carved with family portraits and that their father gave his life trying to reclaim is a powerful symbol of the family's heritage. According to Wilson, "The real issue is the piano, the legacy. How are you going to use it?"[21] Berniece and Boy Willie are separated not only by divergent perspectives on heritage but also by gender and acknowledgment of gender roles. While Boy Willie acknowledges the legacy of his father as a critical motivating force, Berniece pays homage to her mother. She presses Boy Willie to recognize their mother's role in the tragic history of the piano:

> Money can't buy what that piano cost. You can't sell your soul for money. . . . Mama Ola polished this piano with her tears for seventeen years. She rubbed on it till her hands bled. Then she rubbed the blood in . . . mixed up with the rest of the blood on it. You always talking about your daddy, but you ain't looked to see what his foolishness cost your mother. (50–52)

Berniece, as she reflects on her mother, represents and defends the world and worth of women. She recognizes the value of love, spirituality, suffering, and sacrifice and how they are devalued in the traditions and rituals of the patriarchy.

Like Molly and Mattie in *Joe Turner*, Berniece has been victimized by love. She lost her husband, Crawley, three years before the time when the play is set. He was gunned down by the sheriff, when he attempted to help Boy Willie steal lumber. Since Crawley's death, Berniece has purposefully resisted any involvement with other men. She holds Boy Willie responsible for

Crawley's death and refuses to recognize Crawley's own culpability. Boy Willie, her father, and Crawley all are representatives of a destructive world of men that she has observed as an "outsider-within" and rejects. She admonishes Boy Willie and her other male relatives: "I look at you and you all the same. You. Papa Charles. Wining Boy. Doaker, Crawley . . . you're all alike. And what it lead to? More killing and more thieving. I ain't never seen it come to nothing" (52). She blames this violent and irrational male order for her pain, suffering, and loss.

While the women in other Wilson plays acquiesce to the principle that "a woman needs a man to be complete," Berniece vocally rejects this dictum. Avery's tactics in his courtship of Berniece parallel those employed by Jeremy in *Joe Turner* and Sterling in *Two Trains Running*. Berniece's responses, however, are quite different from those of Molly or Mattie or Risa. When Avery chastises her for pushing him away and not accepting his love, she responds:

> You trying to tell me a woman can't be nothing without a man. But you alright, huh? You can just walk out of here without me—without a woman—and still be a man. That's alright. Ain't nobody gonna ask you, "Avery, who you got to love you?" That's alright for you. But everybody gonna be worried about Berniece. "How Berniece gonna take care of herself? How she gonna raise that child without a man? Wonder what she do with herself. How she gonna live like that?" Everybody got all kinds of questions for Berniece. Everybody telling me I can't be a woman unless I got a man. Well, you tell me, Avery—you know—how much woman am I? (67)

Berniece decries the double standard of social acceptability that is applied to single men and single women. She questions the traditional perception of women as defined solely by and in relation to men. She asserts her independence.

After warding off Avery, however, she succumbs to the charms of Boy Willie's friend Lymon. They share a passionate embrace. In fact, in an early draft of *The Piano Lesson*, Lymon and Berniece after the embrace went upstairs to bed together. The existing scene between Berniece and Lymon contrasts sharply with the earlier scene between Berniece and Avery. Berniece and Lymon share a spirit of attraction and desire unknown in her relationship with Avery. Yet, neither Berniece nor Lymon ever articulates the rationale for their unlikely embrace. Without articulation, their brief passion dissipates the impact of Berniece's earlier protest. Following directly after the encounter with Avery, this scene suggests that Berniece does in fact need a man, but that Avery is just not the right one.

Just as the embrace with Sterling changes Risa, Berniece is altered by her encounter with Lymon. Berniece rediscovers a sexual, sensual self that has been suppressed ever since Crawley died three years ago. Her rejuvenation through passion also provides the impetus for her spiritual reconciliation with Boy Willie at the culmination of the play. In the scene with Lymon, Berniece becomes the object of Lymon's desire. Lymon pursues her and, in the convention of traditional male-female sexual pursuits, vanquishes her. After their embrace, Berniece, uncertain of its meaning, retreats upstairs. Lymon remains below, smiling and relishing his victory. Wilson's stage directions reaffirm this victory: "Berniece exits upstairs. Lymon picks up his suit and strokes it lovingly with the full knowledge that it is indeed a magic suit" (80).

The idea of a woman "needing a man" is also implicit in the action of *Fences*. It underlines Rose Maxson's reasons for marrying her husband, Troy, and remaining married to him despite his infidelity. Rose Maxson in *Fences* reflects strong traditional values associated with black women and yet asserts a strong feminist voice. Unlike the other women discussed, she is both wife and mother. In these roles she sacrifices self, supports her family, and holds it together. Barbara Christian notes that in African American communities, "the idea that mothers should lead lives of sacrifice has become the norm."[22] Rose embodies this norm. Christian observes that the literature of black males has often perpetuated this image.[23] Yet with Rose, Wilson expands on the stereotype while exploring this question of need as well as consistent truths of black female experience as wife and mother.

Rose exudes both love and strength. Each Friday her husband, Troy, hands over his paycheck to Rose. He relinquishes this element of economic authority, and she controls the household budget. From a position of "outsider-within" she observes the weekly payday rituals of the men. When necessary and from a distance, she participates, playfully teasing Troy, always bolstering his authority and publicly demonstrating her support for her man. As mother she nurtures her son, Cory. Aggressively, she defends Cory against the stubborn will of his father.

Rose understands that she has consigned herself to the limits imposed upon her by marriage and social expectations. Unlike Risa or Berniece, Rose articulates her perspective and the motivation for her actions. When Troy rationalizes his infidelity to her, she reaffirms her commitment to the relationship and castigates him for not doing the same.

> But I held onto you, Troy. I took all my feelings, my wants and needs, my dreams and I buried them inside you. I planted a seed and watched and prayed over it. I planted myself inside you and waited to bloom. And it didn't take me no eighteen years to find out the soil was hard and rocky and it wasn't never gonna bloom. But I held onto you, Troy. I held tighter. You was my husband. I owed you everything I had. Every part of me I could find to give you. And upstairs in that room, with the darkness falling in on me, I gave everything I had to try and erase the doubt that you wasn't the finest man in the world. And wherever you was going I wanted to be there with you. 'Cause you was my husband, 'cause that's the only way I was gonna survive as your wife. (165)

Rose's verbal assault on Troy earns the audience's sympathy. Faced with the realities and imperfections of marriage, she determined to make their marriage work. Still, Rose clearly accepts her own material oppression. "I *owed* you everything I had," she says. Troy's adultery provides that catalyst that propels her to reassess her position, to gain a greater self-awareness and to change.

Quite powerfully, Rose, hurt and betrayed, asserts her independence. When Troy presents her with his illegitimate, motherless daughter, Rose informs him, "Okay Troy. You're right. I'll take care of your baby for 'cause, like you say, she's innocent and you can't visit the sins of the father upon the child. A motherless child has got a hard time. From right now . . . this child has a mother. But you a womanless man" (173). In the Broadway production, when Mary Alice as Rose accented this line by taking the baby and then slamming the back door in Troy's face, the audience, particularly black female spectators, erupted with cheers and applause. For at that moment Rose stands as a champion of black women, of any woman who has suffered under the constraints of a restrictive and inequitable marriage.

The avenues into which Rose channels her new freedom, nevertheless, affirm rather than assault traditional gender limitations and hegemonic legitimacy. She finds solace in the church and the mothering of her adopted daughter, Raynell. While Rose spiritually distances herself from Troy, she does not leave the marriage. The church becomes a surrogate. Collins argues that institutions such as the church can be "contradictory locations," where black women not only learn independence but also "learn to subordinate our interests as women to the allegedly greater good of the larger African American community."[24] Thus Rose, despite her spiritual independence, continues to conform to the traditional expectations and limitations placed on women. Black feminist scholar bell hooks criticizes the play and Rose for their conformity:

> *Fences* poignantly portrays complex and negative contradictions within black masculinity in a white supremacist context. However, patriarchy is not critiqued, and even though tragic expressions of conventional masculinity are evoked, sexist values are re-inscribed via the black woman's redemption message as the play ends.[25]

Rose's words at the end of the play, however, both critique and confirm the patriarchy. She tells Cory, who has returned for his father's funeral:

> That was my first mistake. Not to make him leave some room for me, for my part in the matter. But at that time I wanted that. I wanted a house that I could sing in. And that's what your daddy gave me. I didn't know to keep his strength I had to give up little pieces of mine. I did that. I took his life as mine and mixed up the pieces so that I couldn't hardly tell which was which anymore. It was my choice. It was my life and I didn't have to live it like that. But that's what life offered me in the way of being a woman, and I took it. (189–90)

As a black woman in 1957, Rose had extremely restricted options. Marriage required compromise and, quite often for women, a loss of self. The traditional nature of their marriage allowed Troy to dominate, while Rose suppressed her will and desires. Rose reflects on this reality, on a historic truth experienced by many black women. Thus her words call attention to the limitations of gender roles and critique the patriarchal system that created these limitations. Yet Rose also professes her own complicity. Rose's acceptance of the blame, her internalization of external conditions of oppression, prevent her from challenging the status quo. She chooses to accept her subservient position in her marriage; this she believes is what "life offers her as a woman."

The constraints placed on Wilson's female characters compel them to make choices. For Rose, Risa, Berniece, the cost of asserting an independent feminist voice is too high. Instead, they choose to conform. Despite her strength of character, insight, and awareness, Rose passively accepts "what life offers her as a woman." While Risa radically protests women's objectification by men through scarring her body, she later submits to a conventional relationship with Sterling. The alternative of independence offered by Ma Rainey cannot be perceived as viable, for her voice is largely silenced by the structure of Wilson's play. Clearly in *Ma Rainey* and his other works to date, Wilson privileges the discourse of men. Instead of relating to each other, women in Wilson's dramaturgy are represented by and limited to their interactions with men. Consequently, for these women, involvement with men becomes all the more valuable. As a result, the choices that these women make are conservative ones that reaffirm the traditional patriarchal order.

Dolan finds that the genre of realism is itself "a conservative force that reproduces and reinforces dominant culture relationships."[26] Wilson's dramaturgy, however, defies established limits of realism and moves toward a more ritualistic, mystical, and lyrical theater. His female characters, thus, defy and yet comply with the orthodoxy of realism. As Wilson probes the historical interaction of culture, race, and class, considerations of gender will continue to develop.

..................

## NOTES

1. Case, *Feminism and Theatre*, p. 118.
2. Collins, *Black Feminist Thought*, p. 69.
3. Ibid., p. 83.
4. Dolan, *Feminist Spectator*, p. 84.
5. Spillers, "Interstices," p. 74.
6. Case, *Feminism and Theatre*, p. 124.
7. Harrison, *Black Pearls*, p. 37.
8. Hernton, *Sex and Racism in America*, p. 166.
9. Russell, "Slave Codes," pp. 131–32.
10. Spillers, "Interstices," pp. 88–89.
11. Russell, "Slave Codes," p. 133.
12. Harrison, *Black Pearls*, p. 39.
13. Shannon, "The Long Wait," p. 140.
14. Ibid., p. 138.
15. Harrison, *Black Pearls*, p. 104.
16. Shannon, "The Long Wait," p. 139.
17. Powers, "Interview," p. 53.
18. Barbour, "Wilson's Here to Stay," p. 8.
19. DeVries, "Song," p. 25.
20. Ibid., p. 23.

21. Ibid., p. 25.

22. Christian, *Black Feminist Criticism*, p. 234.

23. Ibid., p. 236.

24. Collins, *Black Feminist Thought*, p. 86.

25. hooks, *Yearning*, p. 18.

26. Dolan, *Feminist Spectator*, p. 108.

..................

## WORKS CITED

Barbour, David. "August Wilson's Here to Stay." *Theatre Week*, April 18–25, 1988, pp. 7–10.

Case, Sue-Ellen. *Feminism and Theatre*. New York: Methuen, 1988.

Christian, Barbara. *Black Feminist Criticism*. New York: Pergamon Press, 1985.

Collins, Patricia Hill. *Black Feminist Thought*. Boston: Unwin Hyman, 1990.

Dolan, Jill. *The Feminist Spectator As Critic*. Ann Arbor: University of Michigan Press, 1990.

DeVries, Hilary. "A Song in Search of Itself." *American Theatre*, January 1987, pp. 22–25.

Harrison, Daphne. *Black Pearls*. New Brunswick: Rutgers University Press, 1990.

Hernton, Calvin. *Sex and Racism in America*. New York: Grove Press, 1965.

hooks, bell. *Yearning: Race, Gender, and Cultural Politics*. Boston: South End Press, 1990.

Powers, Kim. "An Interview with August Wilson." *Theater* 16, no. 1 (1986): 50–55.

Russell, Michelle. "Slave Codes and Liner Notes." In *All the Women Are White, All the Men Are Black: But Some of Us Are Brave*, edited by Gloria T. Hull, Patricia Bell Scott, Barbara Smith. Old Westbury, N.Y.: Feminist Press, 1981.

Shannon, Sandra G. "The Long Wait: August Wilson's *Ma Rainey's Black Bottom*." *Black American Literature Forum* 25, no. 1 (1991): 135–46.

Spillers, Hortense J. "Interstices: A Small Drama of Words." In *Pleasure and Danger: Exploring Female Sexuality*, edited by Carole S. Vance. Boston: Routledge and Kegan Paul, 1984.

Wilson, August. *The Piano Lesson*. New York: New American Library, Plume, 1990.

———. *Three Plays: "Ma Rainey's Black Bottom," "Fences," "Joe Turner's Come and Gone."* Pittsburgh: University of Pittsburgh Press, 1991.

———. "Two Trains Running." *Theater* 22, no. 1 (Winter 1990–91): 40–72.

MISSY DEHN KUBITSCHEK

# August Wilson's Gender Lesson

Like much African American literature of the last two decades, August Wilson's cycle of plays takes its readers/viewers on an extended historical examination of gendered interactions in the black community. Although his earliest play, *Ma Rainey's Black Bottom* (1984), does not focus on gender to the same extent as his later works, it sets the premises under which they develop their statements: the presence of a powerful African American spirituality and the difficulty of preserving it in an economic system controlled by white racists. *Fences* (1985) forcefully demonstrates the spiritual alienation of men and women from one another, and of men from their children. The play shows men and women speaking different languages, reflecting different understandings of the spiritual cosmos. *Joe Turner's Come and Gone* (1986) both describes an earlier shared understanding, if not a shared language, and explores its historical disruption. While the main characters of *Fences* and *Joe Turner* are male, the plays assert the presence of women's experiences and push toward their recognition. Taking a much stronger position, *The Piano Lesson* (1987) presents "missing" women's history and viewpoints as essential to overcoming alienation in a system where men and women initially speak not only different but opposing languages. The male and female characters of *Piano Lesson* redevelop an overlapping spiritual language and ritual that express, protect, and invigorate them as a community.

Although *Ma Rainey's Black Bottom* has the least explicit exploration of gender, it sets the premise of racist oppression within which gender roles operate. And when Ma voices her sense of the limitations of her powers outside of the blues, her imagery underscores her gender: "As soon as they get my voice down on them recording machines, then it's just like if I'd be some whore and they roll over and put their pants on. Ain't got no use for me then" (79). As Margaret Glover has noted, *Ma Rainey* represents the dilemmas of trying to exercise an African American spirituality within a racist European commercial setting. The recording moguls and Ma Rainey struggle for control, Ma fully aware that her signature on the release—the written word that controls the rights to her orality—marks the end of her power. Toledo's despairing statement "We done sold who we are in order to be someone else. We's imitation white men" (94), testifies to the vampirish effect of white economic control. Even conforming, becoming an imitation white man, does not guarantee access to the system, of course, since Sturdyvant can simply dismiss his promises to Levee. Levee clearly demonstrates the channeling of African American creativity into individualistic, patriarchal modes that will neither reward the individual creator nor mesh with Ma's and Cutler's more communal blues aesthetic. The manipulation that constitutes the interaction between Ma Rainey and the white businessmen—which Levee ineptly attempts to practice—cannot, apparently, be limited to black/white contexts. Levee and Dussie Mae also attempt to manipulate each other, Levee maneuvering for free sex, Dussie Mae for a higher price and status. Dussie Mae thus accepts the status that Ma resists so vigorously. The clashes between the white recording industry and frustrated black spiritualities reiterate the historical gender roles of slavery: Black women become sexual commodities, and black men die.

Centered on the economic disruption of black men's and women's relationships, *Fences* shows men and women speaking the different languages imposed/derived from their unconscious acceptance of an implicitly Eurocentric view of separate male and female spheres. The development of a situation in which men and women are speaking different languages that no longer refer to the same spiritual realities can be approached through a juxtaposition of two models of gender relations. Nineteenth-century European models divide sex roles into separate spheres in a hierarchical schema. A second set of models derives from the experiences of women in traditional nonindustrial societies or in minority communities in the United States.

Delineated by Paula Gunn Allen's *The Sacred Hoop* and Trinh Minh-ha's *Woman, Native, Other,* and implied by other works such as Gloria Anzaldua's *Borderlands/La Frontera* and bell hooks's *Feminist Theory: From Margin to Center,* this second paradigm represents men and women as possessing somewhat different spiritual gifts and hence different social responsibilities, but sharing some areas of influence. Men's and women's spheres of activity are fundamentally connected, mutually contributive parts of community. Anzaldua's project resembles in some ways Audre Lorde's *Zami* in attempting to create an empowering myth. To do so, she concentrates on pre-Aztec artifacts to postulate a nonviolent, egalitarian, matriarchal society displaced by the patriarchal and classist Aztecs.

More concerned with demonstrable historical reality, Gunn Allen delineates a traditional tribal system in which Indian men are primarily responsible for issues involving change while women are concerned with continuity; her discussion presents a worldview based on thoroughgoing interconnectedness—not only between the sexes but between human beings and the rest of the natural world, including the landscape—that precludes fixed hierarchy. Her analysis of contemporary Indian societies indicates Indian women's progressive loss of prestige as Western roles increasingly obscure traditional ones.[1] Trinh Minh-ha attacks the colonialist anthropological approach to gender in vernacular societies as mere prototype for European sex roles. She examines the relative power and importance of women as "ungendered" workers in industrial societies and gendered, noninterchangeable contributors to vernacular societies. Whether expressed in Anzaldua's, Gunn Allen's, and hooks's communally based conception of self or in Trinh Minh-ha's postmodernist vocabulary of the nonunitary self, these models of overlapping male and female influences present women as possessing real powers. Their power does not depend on patriarchal definition or permission, but (like men's power), remains subject to continual negotiation in response to social change.

In African American history, Eugene Genovese, Jacqueline Jones, and Paula Giddings have shown the paradigm of sex roles to have been contested territory. Separate spheres were for black Americans unachievable in the nineteenth century and available only to a small middle class in the twentieth. Historically, the separate-spheres ideology has combined with white male economic control to erode African American families and communities by preventing black men from achieving the only culturally endorsed definition of manhood and by subordinating the activities of black women, sometimes making them competitive in formerly common arenas of endeavor. *Fences* explores the damage that results when European constructions of sex roles separate, hierarchically order, and then alienate men and women; at the same time, the play suggests a palimpsest of a more empowering traditional model.

Troy Maxson's definition of his manhood centers on his ability to support his family economically, though he intermittently glimpses the inadequacy of this conception. He describes, for example, his own father's economically pressured definition of his children as workers, and only workers, with considerable pain. He also recognizes his father's lack of joy, his selfishness, his demeaning treatment of his children, his abuse of his wife. Simultaneously

Troy says, "He wasn't good for nobody" (51) but affirms that he strove to accomplish the one thing necessary, securing the necessities for his family.

Under this superimposed definition of manhood, another, broader, definition struggles to reemerge, the sense that economic relations ought not to be the whole of a father's relationship to his children. Troy cannot express such an idea directly. Though he suffered for lack of his father's love (and was further deprived when his mother left), he tries to force Cory to be satisfied with the same father/son relationship:

> "It's my job. It's my responsibility! You understand that? A man got to take care of his family. You live in my house . . . sleep you behind on my bedclothes . . . fill you belly up with my food . . . cause you my son. You my flesh and blood. Not 'cause I like you! Cause it's my duty to take care of you. I owe a responsibility to you." (38)

His intermittent recognition of his father's inadequacy does not lead to any other conception of fatherhood.

Trying not to fail Cory as he failed Lyons (imprisonment prevented him from supporting his first family), Troy virtually re-creates the destructive relationship between his father and himself. Not only does he insist on Cory's working for salary, he identifies the family's resources—the house and its furnishings, food—as his own property, his son as a dependent rather than a contributor. Troy expresses disgust at Lyons's easy acceptance of such a relationship; only a boy accepts such a position, and only because he has no choice.

Troy's bitterness at whites' power to exclude him from prestigious and well-paid labor (major league baseball) makes the likenesses between himself and Cory into threats. Unable to recognize changes in social conditions, he sees Cory's talents as a temptation to irresponsibility. He insists on conditions that make it impossible for Cory to satisfy his work requirement and also to attend necessary athletic practices. Although he claims to be protecting Cory from inevitable disappointment, he is deforming another generation with Procrustean gender definitions.

Following his only model, he plays his father's role with a slightly different script. Troy breaks from his father at fourteen, but the separation is temporary, geographic rather than temperamental or psychic; he understands his father later, when "I could feel him kicking in my blood and knew that the only thing that separated us was the matter of a few years" (53). Given the

economic conditions and his understanding of his role, Troy can only re-
create in another generation the economic exploitation and competition between father and son.

*Fences* demonstrates that, as the European/Victorian doctrine of separate
spheres combines with very limited economic opportunities, relationships
between black men and women deteriorate. The very list of characters for
*Fences* testifies to patriarchal hegemony, with its implications of subordination for women—all but one of the characters are identified solely by their
relationship to Troy, as "Troy's oldest son" or "Troy's wife"; significantly, Cory
is identified as "Troy and Rose's son," an assertion of women's ongoing presence and importance for heritage.

Men's and women's languages in *Fences* reflect the separation of their
spheres of activity. In their most intensely emotional scene (act 2, scene 1),
Troy and Rose attempt to communicate with metaphors that diverge sharply.
Troy repeatedly uses baseball metaphors that Rose implicitly rejects by returning always to the concrete level of action:

> *Rose:* You should have held me tight. You should have grabbed me and
> held on.
> *Troy:* I stood on first base for eighteen years and I thought . . . well,
> goddamn it . . . go on for it!
> *Rose:* We're not talking about baseball! We're talking about you going off
> to lay in bed with another woman. (69–70)

Troy's account doesn't lose track of the concrete level, but his metaphorical
expression is confined to—and confines—the experience to an arena that he
has only limited access to and that excludes Rose entirely. Troy chooses baseball, the game whose racial segregation has prevented his enjoying the economic or status benefits of his athletic prowess, as his vehicle. But baseball is,
of course, also sex-segregated. Troy hopes for "one of them boys to knock me
in" because metaphorically and literally, it has become impossible for any
woman to play on his team, to advance him in his competitive quest. Instead,
Rose disappears entirely from the metaphor, and Alberta is objectified, a base
to steal. Inevitably Rose refuses the metaphor that excludes her and includes
women only as objects.

Whereas Troy's metaphor comes from the social (and therefore hierarchical) world, Rose's metaphor in this scene derives from the natural world. Her
expression emphasizes her expectation that her experience will partake of the

cycle of living things, and her frustration that it does not come to fulfillment: "I took all my feelings, my wants and needs, my dreams and I buried them inside you. I planted a seed and watched and prayed over it. I planted myself inside you and waited to bloom. And it didn't take me no eighteen years to find out the soil was hard and rocky and it wasn't never gonna bloom" (71). In his role as divine fool, Gabriel underlines Rose's connections to nature by giving her flowers and commenting that she shares their essence. Rose's imagery, moreover, leaves open the possibility of shared ground as Troy's does not, for Troy at least appears in Rose's imagery, even though he is represented as an environment of dubious hospitality. Rose's natural imagery suggests continuity, as Troy's game imagery suggests a discrete series, and although women's experience provides the source of this natural imagery, the experience is itself not socially limited to one gender.

*Fences* does not, of course, present black men as failed human beings and women as the preservers of undamaged original spiritualities (a conception that would result from the separate-spheres doctrine's idealization of women's purity). The division into separate spheres affects Rose as well as Troy. Her impassioned denunciation of his affair and its results reveals the conflict between European and African ideals of kinship: "And you know I ain't never wanted no half nothing in my family. My whole family is half. Everybody got different fathers and mothers . . . my two sisters and my brother. Can't hardly tell who's who. Can't never sit down and talk about Papa and Mama. It's your papa and your mama and my papa and my mama" (68). On the one hand, Rose is angry about a kind of confused ancestral heritage, the lack of archetypal Mama and Papa, and their replacement by lowercase, less powerful specifics. On the other, her idea of a proper family reflects the European, nuclear ideal rather than the traditional African or African American conception of extended family.

The last scene shows the simultaneous influence of both paradigms. On the one hand, Raynell, like Rose, is associated with the natural world of the garden while Cory appears in military uniform, a clear suggestion of continued separation of sex roles. On the other hand, a shared spirituality persists. Troy's father's song, "Old Blue," for instance, survives because both Raynell and Cory have heard Troy's version. Singing it together, they ritually evoke the ancestors.

More important, both Rose and Gabriel reclaim spiritual powers by refusing European systems and returning to traditional understandings and roles. Rose, however equivocally, finally refuses the role offered to her by separate spheres—female victim of a superior male power—to embrace her own responsibility for constructing a shared space with Troy:

> When I first met your daddy I thought . . . Here is a man I can lay down with and make a baby. . . . I thought, Rose Lee, here is a man that you can open yourself up to and be filled to bursting. . . .
>
> When your daddy walked through the house he was so big he filled it up. That was my first mistake. Not to make him leave some room for me. For my part in the matter. But at that time I wanted that. I wanted a house that I could sing in. And that's what your daddy gave me. I didn't know to keep up his strength I had to give up little pieces of mine. I did that. . . . It was my choice. It was my life and I didn't have to live it like that. But that's what life offered me in the way of being a woman and I took it. (97–98, first ellipsis Wilson's)

Troy controlled what should have been their shared space because Rose did not claim and exercise her power. Rose does not blame Troy, however, indicating that a different outcome would have been possible if she had understood the implications of ceding power. At the same time, she implies that her choice was not entirely determined by personality: "That's what life offered me in the way of being a woman."

*Fences* shows mutual autonomy with shared responsibilities as a more fulfilling paradigm than that of separate spheres. Rose tells Cory directly that reclaiming her power and independence made her happier. Although she had initially rejected traditional ideas of kinship, referring to Raynell as "your baby," Rose went on to agree to Troy's request to care for her with "this child got a mother. But you a womanless man" (79). Thus, she no longer accepted Troy's presence throughout the shared house; instead, as the price of having shared responsibilities for Raynell, she insisted on redefining the whole relationship. The timing of Rose's communication of joint responsibility—Cory is engaged—makes an alternative available to her son that he did not witness in their home. Troy's mother had left by the time he rejected his father, and with no other model to emulate, Troy inevitably re-creates his father's role and vision. Rose's presence—more important, her communication—opens other possibilities for Cory.

In a more direct and absolute critique of Western models, Gabriel replaces a failed Christianity with an empowering African spirituality. Convinced that it's time for him to perform the role that Christianity assigns to the Archangel Gabriel, Gabriel decides to end the world by blowing his trumpet. When the damaged instrument makes no noise, "a weight of impossible description . . . fall[s] away" (101). His consequent "frightful realization" makes him begin to dance, then to howl. This "atavistic signature and ritual" (101) of dance and sound then opens the gate of heaven, and the last words of the play are Gabriel's triumphant "That's the way that go!"

If *Fences* shows Gabriel's victory and reports Rose's partial fulfillment, it also shows the absence of a socially recognized paradigm of African American spirituality and the resultant gender-related problems. Wilson's next play, *Joe Turner's Come and Gone*, explores the historical fragmentation of this spiritual understanding. As part of its exposition, it dramatizes in more detail the dynamics of overlapping spheres for men's and women's activities.

Set in 1911, *Joe Turner* shows men and women using different languages to describe the same spiritual reality. With somewhat different talents and therefore responsibilities, they have independent arenas and rituals but also share a sphere of influence. Their spirituality is grounded in the ancestors, the anchor of present life. Seth's rules for the boardinghouse, for instance, come from his father. Similarly, Reuben receives instructions from the haint Miss Mabel, Seth's mother. Only immature characters like Jeremy and Molly strive to leave the past behind. Molly is determined not to have children. Clearly, detachment from the past denies the future too, and Molly and Jeremy live in an isolated present. All the other characters understand themselves to participate in a spirituality whose expressions differ with gender but whose essence remains continuous.

*Joe Turner* sharply distinguishes between European and African American uses of their spiritualities. Always in service to commerce, European spiritualities are completely amoral. Thus the white Rutherford Selig describes the historical progression of his family's use of their "finding" talent: They have been slavers, then bounty hunters looking for fugitive slaves, and finally just people finders for postwar blacks. The family's skill in locating people is purely "business," the ends contractual and monetary.[2] Displaying African American spiritual gifts to a commercially oriented white audience is never productive and usually dangerous. As in *Ma Rainey*, African American spirituality finds expression through music, and whites control the monetary rewards for musical expression. More perceptive than Levee, Jeremy discovers early the uselessness of playing his guitar for a white audience: The event is constructed as a contest, so that black players compete, and the promised financial reward never materializes. Jeremy's mentor, the rootworker Bynum, directs him to a more spiritually nurturant, black-controlled context for his music.

*Joe Turner* addresses African Americans' attempt to recover wholeness in the face of European attempts to control and possess their spirituality. Although music and dance in general are presented as spiritual idiom, song in particular expresses both an individual's essence and a communal identity. One identifies his/her own song through spiritual vision, so that although Bynum's father had a healing song, Bynum has a binding song. When Herald Loomis wonders why Joe Turner imprisoned him, Bynum answers, "What he wanted was your song. He wanted that song to be his. He thought by catching you he could learn that song" (73). Europeans are attracted by African American spirituality, but they misunderstand it. Whereas Europeans define culture as possessions (which can be appropriated), African Americans understand it as participation in communal ritual or expression.

*Joe Turner* presents two African American spiritual workers, Bertha and Bynum, who labor to ensure healthy continuity in their community. In general, same-gender advice seems to be better understood than trans-gender talk; that is, Bertha works well with Mattie, and Bynum with Loomis, to develop or restore individuals to a state in which they can maintain stable sexual and emotional relationships. When Bynum tries to persuade Mattie not to pursue the husband who abandoned her, he discourses on the dangers in using spiritual forces to bind artificially rather than reinforcing what clings of its own nature. His language is metaphorical, visionary, abstract:

And if he ain't supposed to come back . . . then he'll be in your bed one morning and it'll come up on him that he's in the wrong place. Then he's lost outside of time from his place that he's supposed to be in. Then both of you be lost and trapped outside of life and ain't no way for you to get back in it. (22)

When Bertha consoles Mattie, on the other hand, she uses concrete speech:

Jeremy ain't had enough to him. You need a man who's got some understanding and who willing to work with that understanding to come to the best he can. You got your time coming. You just tries too hard. . . . You get all that trouble off your mind and just when it look like you ain't never gonna find what you want . . . you look up and it's standing right there. That's how I met my Seth. (75)

Further, Bertha offers Mattie her own experience as a hopeful model. Both men and women seem most effective in counseling others of their own sex, then, and their languages differ almost as much as those of Troy and Rose in *Fences*.

*Joe Turner* concentrates on male-to-male spiritual communication, as Loomis becomes One Who Goes Before and Shows the Way in his turn; Bertha's spirituality appears explicitly in the stage directions, as Gabriel's does in *Fences*. Significantly, however, male and female shamans in *Joe Turner* share rituals and ritual space; African American spirituality does not assume or enforce separate, unequal spheres. First, women are not shut out of economic power—Bertha's kitchen is a source of revenue (through its importance to the boardinghouse). Second, whereas in *Fences* the location of Rose's spiritual power is offstage, in her church, in *Joe Turner* the kitchen is a ritual ground in which both Bertha and Bynum function. Here Bertha exorcises melancholy and refreshes the community through contagious laughter (87); here Bynum's call and response guides not only Loomis's understanding of his vision but the community's juba. Both shamans heal, and they address individuals or community according to need. Third, Bynum provides the clearest example of the divergence of African American and European understandings of men's and women's powers; his role would be unthinkable for a European male because it requires giving of oneself to bind others—the specifically female role of the separate-spheres paradigm.

*Joe Turner* shows the potential for the superimposition of the separate-spheres paradigm shown in *Fences*. Though he certainly enjoys group religious rituals like the juba, Seth in particular shows an impatience with those whose spirituality has been damaged by Joe Turner. The free-born son of free parents, raised in the North, economically secure if not independent, he could easily allow his practicality to turn to cynical dismissal of spirituality, as in his reply to Loomis's question about why Joe Turner preys on blacks: "He just want you to do his work for him. That's all" (73). Further, Joe Turner has disrupted the lives and marriages of many individual black men and women so that they cannot be resumed. *Joe Turner* posits the necessity of continued communication between men and women so that their gendered articulations continue to be understood as expressive of the same spiritual essence.

For black adults to move beyond Joe Turner's influences and reclaim their true selves—for them to rear healthy children and thus preserve their culture, Wilson implies—men and women must exchange stories of their divergent experiences. When Herald Loomis and his wife, Martha Pentecost, tell each other their histories since Loomis's imprisonment, their languages differ in much the same way as Bynum's and Bertha's do. Loomis again speaks in abstractions: "I just been waiting to look on your face to say my goodbye. That goodbye got so big at times, seem like it was going to swallow me up. Like Jonah in the whale's belly I set up in that goodbye for three years" (90). Martha corrects his abstractions, for instance, that she "ain't waited," with concrete answers: "You talking about Henry Thompson's place like I'm still gonna be working the land by myself. How I'm gonna do that? You wasn't gone but two months and Henry Thompson kicked me off his land" (90). As they exchange understandings, they can come to a negotiated understanding of their pasts and the necessary present actions.

The most pressing issue is how to care for their daughter, Zonia. Loomis's angriest accusation is that Martha left his daughter motherless, that she cut Zonia off from the necessary female ancestor. Martha responds that when her church moved, "I didn't leave her motherless, Herald. . . . I left her with my mama so she be safe" (89); she recognizes the same need as Loomis does and assures him that she provided Zonia with a surrogate mother. Reassured, Loomis feels comfortable yielding their daughter to Martha's care so that she "won't be no one-sided person" (90). Sadly, Herald shifts from "my daughter" to "your daughter," the possibility of "our" daughter having been destroyed by the disruption Joe Turner brought to their lives. Nevertheless, all three individuals survive, and all three understand that the others, while forced to separate from them, did not abandon them. As long as communication continues, children can be reared and adults healed through individual shamans and communal rituals.

*The Piano Lesson* expands on this idea of men's and women's exchanging their stories, moving from the individual level of *Joe Turner* to a tribal and historical level. Specifically, it insists on restoring women's narratives to history in order to reestablish an African American paradigm of differing but cooperative interactive male and female spiritualities. *Piano Lesson* reiterates themes from Wilson's earlier plays, beginning with the danger of earning a living with one's gift in a white-controlled context.[3] The long-term effects of a hostile economic system on African American relationships have intensified from the portrayal in *Fences*, for here the languages of the main male and female characters are not only divergent but opposed.

Men's and women's understandings of each other's spiritual visions have deteriorated in *Piano Lesson* so that even kinship ties are threatened. Boy Willie and Berniece both think the other is simply using spiritual ideas to manipulate—an ominous extension of Seth's skepticism toward Bynum in *Joe Turner*. Boy Willie, for instance, initially believes that Berniece invents her glimpse of Sutter's ghost to accuse him of complicity in Sutter's death (13–15). Berniece, on the other hand, believes the Yellow Dog ghosts to be a convenient fiction invented to deny guilt for murders (34, 52), an extension of her belief that Boy Willie's irresponsibility ultimately caused her husband Crawley's death.

While denying these gendered accusations of bad faith, *Piano Lesson* asserts the validity of both male and female perspectives when they are not used to oppose one another. Boy Willie's description of the Yellow Dog ghosts articulates a reality present to the other male characters, all of whom believe in the ghosts. Further, elements of his narrative blend into the vision that leads Avery to become a Christian preacher, suggesting an enduring, valid male spiritual vision. Despite their gaps in understanding, men and women still inhabit the same spiritual world: a male character, Doaker, has seen Sutter's ghost even before Berniece, and by the end of the play, all the characters have witnessed his emanation. Sutter symbolizes a historic, persistent white economic control over black lives. Clearly the black community must exorcise him to reestablish kinship ties.

The dispute between Berniece and Boy Willie amounts to a battle over whose vision will define and control the family's actions. Most centrally, whether the piano is the ancestral and spiritual heritage or whether it is simply a rather heavy and financially valuable material object depends upon the controlling spiritual vision. Initially, because the visions are opposed, the negotiation or compromise possible to overlapping spheres remains impossible. *Piano Lesson* presents both of the separate, opposed visions as incomplete and unsustaining.

The woman's viewpoint honors the presence of spirituality in the material world but cannot participate in it; the man's point of view recognizes only avenging spirits, not protective ones, and his concentration on economics without reference to women's vision leaves him vulnerable to alienation (cf. Troy in *Fences*). Berniece finds the piano's history so painful that she can neither use it herself nor tell her daughter Maretha its (and their) story. The spiritual power of the ancestors literally embodied in the piano's carvings thus remains unused, and the past exists only as a burden to Berniece. For her, selling the piano would re-create slavery, selling the ancestors to whites again. Her unwillingness to use the piano, or even to inform Maretha of its significance, makes Boy Willie consider her definition of it merely sentimental.

Confident of his rights to exchange the piano-property for the land-property now belonging to Sutter's brother, Boy Willie appeals to gender solidarity to dismiss Berniece's objections. To his surprise and chagrin, Doaker does not support him. Doaker, of course, participated in taking the piano back from Sutter, and Doaker has seen Sutter's ghost, while Boy Willie is still unconvinced of its existence: Because Doaker is a generation older, neither his experience nor his vision diverges so completely from Berniece's as Boy Willie's does.

With compromise between the gendered visions impossible, only superior force can make one set of definitions dominate. When Boy Willie tries to remove the piano over Berniece's objections, she trains Crawley's gun on him. Intrafamilial violence seems the inevitable result of opposing visions. When their conflict intensifies, its relation to separate spheres becomes clear. Berniece tries to exclude her brother from the house; he replies that he's in his uncle Doaker's house, not hers. They are, of course, speaking of the same physical structure. When Boy Willie draws an invisible line with his foot to separate his (or Doaker's) part of the house from Berniece's, he symbolically creates the separate domains of a house divided. Historically, this division between men and women has been generations in the making—the slave master Sutter sells Mama Berniece and Boy Charles away from the original Boy Willie to buy the piano; Wining Boy leaves Cleotha, despite loving her; the second Boy Charles risks his life and loses, thus leaving Mama Ola, to reclaim the piano—but only in this generation does separation threaten to become fatal black-on-black violence.

The danger to the African American family is heightened after Sutter's ghost exposes the insufficiency of all three competing spiritual understandings, none of which can expel him. Boy Willie seeks simply to dispose of the piano-as-past. Under the symbolic weight of Sutter's ghost, however—which Boy Willie can't at this point see—the piano remains immovably heavy: Racist economics will not allow blacks to claim their material heritages, and African American men cannot move amid purely economic visions. The ghost of Sutter remains passive until Boy Willie mocks Avery's blessing, almost as though the parody empowers the malevolent spirit. Attacked by the ghost, Boy Willie has only physical strength to rely on, useless in dealing with incorporeal beings. His materialist vision cannot detach or defend him from vicious historical racist forces still active in the present.

Berniece's understanding also has clear limitations. First, she is unable to develop a sexually and emotionally fulfilling relationship. In addition, she is so tormented by the past that she can't pass on to Maretha the traditional knowledge necessary for defending self-respect. Berniece is afraid of losing her ability to function in the present, as she thinks Mama Ola did, by remaining too involved in the past: "Sometimes late at night I could hear my mama talking to them [the people represented in the carvings]. I said that wasn't gonna happen to me. I don't play that piano cause I don't want to wake them spirits. They never be walking around this house" (70). Berniece's vision cannot compel others, like Boy Willie, because it preserves apparently disempowering definitions.

Avery offers a third inadequate spiritual vision grounded in Western spirituality, particularly Christianity. Ironically, given the traditionally African American nature of his call to preaching, he urges Berniece to use religious faith for a particularly Euro-American task: "With the strength of God you can put the past behind you, Berniece" (71). To Berniece, putting the past behind her means selling the piano's sleeping presences, abandoning the ancestors. Further, Avery wants her to play "Ship of Zion," whose lyrics refer to Christ as captain of a heavily laden ship sailing to heaven. The spiritual is itself part of the past; in addition, ships are a multilayered signifier in African American experience, including the powerful images of slavers and of Garvey-ite repatriation.[4] Avery selects only one layer of these imbricated associations. His attempt to separate a convenient meaning from a more complex context anticipates Boy Willie's accusation, "You gonna go at the Bible halfway" (89). Avery ministers within a tradition that institutionalizes patriarchal power, which supposedly gives him, but not Berniece, power to bless. Not surprisingly, Avery finds himself helpless to exorcise Sutter, the powers of his spiritual vision defeated by the forces of racism.

To exorcise Sutter, the African American family must move beyond gendered visions that are separate and opposed, back to an ancestral spirituality. Throughout the play, the conditions that direct Berniece to invoke the ancestors successfully have developed despite the apparent conflict between the sexes. Most important, *The Piano Lesson* insists on restoring women's stories to historical accounts. The play not only includes black women's histories but also insists on the presence and influence of white women as well: Through Ophelia, *Piano Lesson* is the first of Wilson's works to indicate the presence of Josephine Turner. The white female plays a relatively passive part in this history. Unlike her husband, Sutter, Ophelia never appears except in the characters' stories. Further, her activity is limited to motivating force—Sutter sold slaves to buy her a piano for their wedding anniversary; when she pined for them, he ordered that their pictures be carved on the instrument—but she is at least present, named.

To reunite African American families divided by this European influence, the reiteration of black women's history is crucial. *Piano Lesson* here uses a pattern quite similar to that of Toni Morrison's *Song of Solomon*, where the story of the heroic flying African, Solomon, is complemented by the story of his homebound wife Ryna's grief. When Boy Willie tells the story of Boy Charles's heroic reclamation of the piano, Berniece answers him with Mama Ola's history: "You always talking about your daddy but you ain't never stopped to look at what his foolishness cost your mama. Seventeen years' worth of cold nights and an empty bed" (52). Neither story is by itself complete; to have any hope of re-creating a fuller understanding of men's and women's experiences, which participate in spiritualities and finally constitute them, individuals must have access to the totality of the information available. Thus, Boy Willie tells Maretha the story of the Yellow Dog ghosts (85) and directs that both she and Berniece must keep playing the piano.

Neither opposing view has prevailed. African American victory here does not occur in terms of Boy Willie's original terms (possession of Sutter's lands) nor does it occur in Berniece's original terms (museumlike preservation of potentially spiritual artifacts). When Berniece and Boy Willie combine forces to fight Sutter, Boy Willie accepts help from sources whose existence he has previously denied. For her part, Berniece not only remembers Mama Ola's use of the piano to communicate with forebears but uses it herself, participating in a traditional black female spirituality that honors male and female ancestors.

Despite a heartening victory, the future of the Charles family and the larger African American family is far from settled: the Loomis family cannot be what it was before Joe Turner's interference. But as the Loomises exchange stories and recognize that their child needs both male and female influences, so also this family returns to a working relationship, signified by Maretha's embrace of Boy Willie. In common with many contemporary African American works, August Wilson's plays explore gender in African American culture with increasing urgency. Morrison's *Tar Baby*, Naylor's *Mama Day*, and Marshall's *Praisesong for the Widow* coincide with Wilson's work in showing men and women who speak different languages to describe the same spiritual essence, and these writers obviously hope for future generations to overcome current estrangements caused or worsened by adherence to Euro-American models. If *Joe Turner* shows where African American culture has been, *The Piano Lesson* shows the way back, which is also the way forward.

## NOTES

1. In this light, bell hooks has critiqued white bourgeois feminism in two ways: first, for violating women's senses of themselves by insisting that only access to the male sphere is empowering; and second, for forcing women to internalize ideas of themselves as victims when in fact their community's paradigm can offer empowerment. Mechal Sobel's *Trabelin' On*, subtitled *The Slave Journey to an Afro-Baptist Faith*, details the modulations of African belief systems under European influence in another field. Specifically addressing the spiritual powers of women in the African sacred cosmos, it shows their persistence in African American religion.

2. Within the play's framework, not only the uses but the very existence of European spirituality are questionable. Bertha, for example, scoffs at Selig's—and by implication all Europeans'—claim to any spiritual gifts. She explains Selig's success as the natural result of finding what he has earlier put in place himself.

3. Glover, "Two Notes on August Wilson," p. 69.

4. Railroads too are powerfully multivalent in this play, signifying the underground railroad of escape, mobility in Wining Boy's blues, employment in Doaker's song, a fiery trap in the Yellow Dog ghost narrative, and the way home for Boy Willie. A train is heard during the exorcism scene as well, suggesting its economic connection to Sutter.

## WORKS CITED

Allen, Paula Gunn. *The Sacred Hoop: Recovering the Feminine in American Indian Traditions*. Boston: Beacon, 1986.

Anzaldua, Gloria. *Borderlands/La Frontera*. San Francisco: Spinsters/Aunt Lute, 1987.

Collins, Patricia Hill. *Black Feminist Thought*. Boston: Unwin Hyman, 1990.

Gates, Henry Louis, Jr., ed. *Reading Black, Reading Feminist*. New York: Penguin/Meridian, 1990.

Genovese, Eugene. *Roll, Jordan, Roll*. 1972. Reprint. New York: Random/Vintage, 1976.

Glover, Margaret. "Two Notes on August Wilson: The Songs of a Marked Man." *Theater* 19, no. 3 (1988): 69–73.

hooks, bell. *Feminist Theory: From Margin to Center*. Boston: South End Press, 1984.

Jones, Jacqueline. *Labor of Love, Labor of Sorrow*. 1985. Reprint. New York: Vintage, 1986.

Sobel, Mechal. *Trabelin' On: The Slave Journey to an Afro-Baptist Faith.* 1979. Reprint. Princeton: Princeton University Press, 1988.

Trinh, Minh-ha. *Woman, Native, Other.* Bloomington: Indiana University Press, 1989.

Wilson, August. *Fences.* New York: New American Library/Signet, 1986.

———. *Joe Turner's Come and Gone.* New York: New American Library, Plume, 1988.

———. *Ma Rainey's Black Bottom.* New York: New American Library, Plume, 1985.

———. *The Piano Lesson.* New York: New American Library, Plume, 1990.

# I Want a Black Director

Eddie Murphy said that to me. We were sitting in his house in New Jersey discussing the possibility of Paramount Pictures' purchasing the rights to my play *Fences*. The subject was film directors. I said I wanted a black director for the film, and he said, "I don't want to hire nobody just 'cause they black." My response was immediate. "Neither do I," I said. What Mr. Murphy meant I am not sure. I meant that I wanted to hire somebody talented, who understood the play and saw the possibilities of the film, who would approach my work with the same amount of passion and measure of respect with which I approach it, and finally, who shared the same cultural responsibilities of the characters. That was more than three years ago. I have not talked to Mr. Murphy about the subject since. Paramount Pictures did purchase the rights to make the film in 1987. What I thought of as a straightforward, logical request has been greeted by blank, vacant stares and the pious shaking of heads as if in response to my unfortunate naiveté. I usually have had to repeat my request, "I want a black director," as though it were a complex statement rendered in a foreign tongue. I have often heard the same verbatim response, "We don't want to hire anyone just because they are black." It has taken me three years to learn to read the implication in that statement. What is being implied is that the only qualification any black has is the color of his skin. For some occupations this seems to work just fine. I doubt if anyone has ever heard the owner or the coach of an NBA team say they didn't want to hire anybody just because he was black.

In the film industry the prevailing attitude is that a black director couldn't do the job and that to insist upon one is to make the film "unmakeable," partly because no one is going to turn a budget of $15 million over to a black director. That this is routinely done for novice white directors is beside the point. The ideas of ability and qualification are certainly not new to blacks. The skills of black lawyers, doctors, dentists, accountants, and mechanics are often greeted with skepticism, even from other blacks. "Man, you sure you know what you doing?"

At the time of my last meeting with Paramount Pictures in January 1990, a well-known, highly respected white director wanted very much to direct the film. Since I don't go to the movies I don't know his work, but he is universally praised for his sensitive and intelligent direction. I accept that he is a very fine film director. But he is not black. He is not a product of black American culture—a culture that was honed out of the black experience and fired in the kiln of slavery and survival—and he does not share the sensibilities of black Americans. I have been asked if I am not, by rejecting him on the basis of his race, doing the same thing Paramount Pictures is doing by not hiring a black director? That is a fair, if shortsighted, question which deserves a response.

First, I am not carrying a banner for black directors. I think they should carry their own. I am not trying to get work for black directors. I am trying to get the film of my play made in the best possible way. As Americans of various races we share a broad cultural ground, a commonality of society that links its various and diverse elements into a cohesive whole that can be defined as "American." We share certain mythologies. A history. We share political and economic systems and a rapidly developing, if suspect, ethos. Within these commonalities are specifics. Specific ideas and attitudes that are not shared on the common cultural ground. These remain the property and possession of the people who develop them, and on that "field of manners and rituals of intercourse" (to use James Baldwin's eloquent phrase), lives are played out. At the point where they intercept and link to the broad commonality of American culture, they influence how that culture is shared and to what purpose.

.................

White American society is made up of various European *ethnic* groups which share a common history and sensibility. Black Americans are a *racial* group which do not share the same sensibilities. The specifics of our cultural history are very much different. We are an African people who have been here since the early seventeenth century. We have a different way of responding to the world. We have different ideas about religion, different manners of social intercourse. We have different ideas about style, about language. We have different aesthetics. Someone who does not share the specifics of a culture remains an outsider, no matter how astute a student they are or how well meaning their intentions. I declined a white director not on the basis of race but on the basis of culture. White directors are not qualified for the job.

The job requires someone who shares the specifics of the culture of black Americans.

The suggestion from a high-ranking Paramount executive that they simply hire a "human being" made me realize that something else is going on here. What is going on here is something very old. It has to do with how Africans were first viewed in this country, the residuals of which still affect and infest our society. The early plantation owners, unfamiliar and uninterested in African culture, viewed their slaves as slow, dull-witted, childlike, and otherwise incapable of grasping complex ideas. This was, if incorrect, at least an honest view. African culture, its style and content, was so incongruent with European sensibilities and beliefs that Africans *seemed* primitive and slow and dull-witted. Elsewhere there were whites who bore a different witness and testimony. On Nantucket Island, for example, sailors who had sailed around the world on whaling expeditions and had been exposed to various cultures saw Africans as black-skinned humans of a different culture capable of all the diversity of human conduct and endeavor.

The shortsightedness of the plantation owners must be thought of as willful. While viewing African slaves with curiosity, they did not allow that curiosity to lead to an examination of the people or their culture. To do so would have been to extend a hand of welcome into the human community. This would have led to a cultural exchange of ideas, postures, worldviews, language concepts, eating habits, attitudes, style, concepts of beauty and justice, responses to pleasure and pain, and a myriad of other cultural identities. It was easier, and a point of justification for their ideas of Christianity, to ignore Africans by consigning them to the status of subhumans, whom they in their benevolence had rescued from the dark ages that reigned in the jungles of Africa.

Their assigning of Africans, and others of different cultures, to a subhuman status had been sanctioned by the founding fathers, who were writing about equality and self-evident truths while systematically eliminating the native population and lending support and credence, through their documents and laws, to the enslavement of blacks in the South.

I suspect that to pursue a crosscultural exchange would have done a violent damage to the plantation owners' idea of the correctness of their being and their manner. They insisted that their ideas about the world and how to live in it were the only correct and valid ideas about human life. Their manners and their being reigned supreme. This led to the idea of white supremacy.

Such an idea cannot exist without something to measure it against. If whites were intelligent, then blacks must be ugly. If they are imaginative, then blacks must be dull. These notions, while not embraced by all whites in the society, led to the creation of a linguistic environment in which they could grow and prosper. They became part of the society's consciousness and part of its truth. *Webster's Third New International Dictionary* gives the following character definitions listed under "black" and "white":

> **White:** free from blemish, moral stain, or impurity: outstandingly righteous; innocent; not marked by malignant influence; notably pleasing or auspicious; fortunate; notably ardent; decent; in a fair upright manner; a sterling man; etc.
>
> **Black:** outrageously wicked; a villain; dishonorable; expressing or indicating disgrace, discredit, or guilt; connected with the devil; expressing menace; sullen; hostile; unqualified; committing violation of public regulations, illicit, illegal; affected by some undesirable condition; etc.

No wonder I had been greeted with incredulous looks when I suggested a black director for *Fences*. I sat in the offices of Paramount Pictures suggesting that someone who was affected by an undesirable condition, who was a violator of public regulations, who was sullen, unqualified, and marked by a malignant influence, direct the film. While they were offering a sterling man, who was free from blemish, notably pleasing, fair and upright, decent, and outstandingly righteous—with a reputation to boot!

Despite such a linguistic environment, the culture of black Americans has emerged and defined itself in strong and effective vehicles that have become the flagbearers for self-determination and self-identity. In the face of such, those who are opposed to the ideas of a "foreign" culture's permeating the ideal of an American culture founded on the icons of Europe seek to dilute and control it by setting themselves up as the assayers of its value and the custodians of its offspring. Therein lies the crux of the matter as it relates to Paramount Pictures and the film *Fences*—whether we as blacks are going to have control over our own culture and its products.

Some Americans, both black and white, do not see any value to black American lives that do not contribute to the leisure or profit of white America. Some Americans, both black and white, would deny that a black American culture even exists. Some Americans, both black and white, would say that by insisting on a black director for *Fences* I am doing irreparable harm to the efforts of black directors who have spent the last fifteen years trying to get Hollywood to ignore the fact that they are black. The origins of such ideas are so very old and shallow that I am amazed to see them so vividly displayed in 1990.

What to do? Let's make a rule. Blacks don't direct Italian films. Italians don't direct Jewish films. Jews don't direct black American films. That might account for about 3 percent of the films that are made in this country. The other 97 percent—the action-adventure, horror, comedy, romance, suspense, western, or any combination thereof, that the Hollywood and independent mills grind out—let it be every man for himself.

As I write this I am still waiting for Paramount to hire a director for the film *Fences*. I want somebody talented, who understands the play and sees the possibilities of the film, who would approach my work with the same amount of passion and measure of respect with which I approach it, and who shares the same cultural sensibilities of the characters. The last time I looked, all those directors were black. I want to hire them just because of that.

...............

**NOTE**

This essay appeared originally as an opinion column in *Spin* magazine. It was excerpted and reprinted in the *New York Times* Arts and Leisure section, under the title "I Want a Black Director." It is reprinted here in its entirety.

MICHAEL AWKWARD

# "The Crookeds with the Straights": *Fences*, Race, and the Politics of Adaptation

...........................................................

*A co-incidence of contingencies among individual subjects who interact*
*as members of some community will operate for them as noncontingency*
*and be interpreted by them accordingly.*
—*Barbara Herrnstein Smith,* Contingencies of Value

*We must remember that ideology also functions overtly, censoring and*
*editing in the name of moral, economic, and political righteousness.*
—*Donald F. Larsson, "Novel into Film: Some Preliminary*
  *Considerations"*

*How can a whole people share a single subjectivity?*
—*Vincent Crapanzano, "Hermes' Dilemma: The Masking of*
  *Subversion in Ethnographic Description"*

.................

**I**

In his suggestion in "I Want a Black Director" that racial positionality
largely determines the nature of a white director's interpretive and, ultimately,
filmic response to black authored texts, playwright August Wilson calls attention to the potential impact of ideological and cultural difference on filmic

adaptations of literary sources. Wilson's insistence to executives of Paramount Pictures, the studio which in 1987 purchased the film rights to the Pulitzer Prize–winning *Fences*, that a black person be found to direct the film version of this play startled many observers inside and outside of the Hollywood community because it represents "the kind of thorny racial issue that Hollywood, with its long-standing concern for the bottom line, is typically reluctant to address."[1] Among the forces of resistance with which the playwright must contend are the views of film and literature scholars which, almost without exception, are unsympathetic to claims that movie adaptations need necessarily position themselves as pictorial or even thematic realizations of their originary sources. Although film criticism over the last decade especially has become generally much more attentive to the impact of ideology on narrative, theories of adaptation have not moved radically away from the positions first espoused in 1957 by George Bluestone, who, in a seminal study of adaptation, *Novels into Film*, argues that the filmist need be only minimally concerned with reproducing significant aspects of the prompting textual event. For Bluestone, those who expect more from films possess naive views of the relationship between films and their literary sources, because the filmed adaptation "becomes a different thing in the same sense that a historical painting becomes a different thing from the historical event it illustrates. . . . In the last analysis, each is autonomous, and each is characterized by unique and specific properties."[2]

What happens, therefore, when the filmist undertakes the adaptation of a novel, given the inevitable mutation, is that he does not convert the novel at all. What he adapts is a kind of paraphrase of the novel—the novel viewed as raw material.

Following Bluestone's example, contemporary studies of film adaptation have focused generally on the formal and aesthetic similarities and differences between these diverse modes of storytelling, assuming that calls for investigation of the motivations for specific alterations reflect, in the words of Neil Sinyard, either "ignorance" about film's responsibilities to originary texts or "a tone of academic superiority and condescension towards the newer art form."[3] Thus, despite narrative criticism's recent focus on the ways in which ideologies are reproduced and reinforced in filmic and other representations, theories of adaptation continue to insist that to examine in a potentially critical way the trajectory of film's appropriation of the "raw material" even of works which may be said to represent challenges to hegemonic points of view is to participate in a retrograde and hopelessly naive interpretive endeavor. As a consequence, discussions like Wilson's (or, for that matter, the hotly contested debates about Steven Spielberg's adaptation of Alice Walker's black feminist novel, *The Color Purple*[4]) enter the national consciousness without the sound theoretical interventionist possibilities that leftist academics are prepared to contribute to, say, debates about Clarence Thomas's fitness for Supreme Court ascendance; such debates centered on complex—but, for many of us, quite familiar—issues such as sexual politics, racial identity, the consequences of ideological predisposition, and, perhaps most perplexing for the diverse groups for whom Thomas's nomination hearings were watershed events, autobiographical narrative's limitations as an indisputable truth-telling device.

In part, the silence about difference and filmic adaptation—a process which Bluestone and virtually every scholar who has written on the subject equates with critical interpretation—might reflect our general unease with the full exegetical implications of foregrounding critical positionality. Contemporary theory's oft-articulated loss of faith in objectivity has turned the unavoidability of misreading into a commonplace, the inevitable consequence of language's, ideology's, and the human psyche's defining properties and limitations. That skepticism, however, has invaded our rhetoric about interpretation much more deeply than it has our analytical practices, which continue generally to be governed by a desire to uncover, if not the single true reading, then at the very least a truer reading than those of our ideological adversaries. To accept and operate wholeheartedly in terms of a sense of subjectivity's dominion over the critical project (without, for example, a Bloomian reliance on an intimate knowledge of a particularly narrow hegemonic literary tradition or, for that matter, the protection of a strategically articulated sense of affinity with some empowering ideology) is not necessarily to open the doors to a type of radical relativism, but it does force us to question the accuracy and veracity—in fact, the very possibility—of our own interpretive conclusions. If originary texts are, indeed, no more than interpretation's "raw material," which, within certain limits, the filmist generally can employ as he or she sees fit, then despite our best efforts, we may be no more effectively engaged with the texts which we critique than our ideological adversaries are.[5] And while the following discussion will not pretend to resolve this interpretive dilemma, it does strive to examine the motivations for Wilson's demands within the context of systems of meaning-making that see manifestations of ideology and definitions of race as powerful, though contestable, constructs.

## II

In "I Want a Black Director," Wilson says of "a well-known, highly respected white director [identified by James Greenberg as Barry Levinson, who] wanted very much to direct the film" version of *Fences*:

> I accept that he is a very fine film director. But he is not black. He is not a product of black American culture—a culture that was honed out of the black experience and fired in the kiln of slavery and survival—and he does not share the sensibilities of black Americans.

Wilson's perspectives do not represent in the strictest sense of the term—or perhaps in any sense—what Donald Larsson calls, in his reading of critical theory's utility in analyses of the politics of adaptation, a "new ideology."[6] Indeed, they demonstrate the continuing impact of a belief that the cultural manifestations of "race" or its performative dimensions remain ideally the province—the possession, if you will—of the group who has produced them. Notwithstanding the technical and discursive distinctions between music and film production, Wilson's argument is of a kind with a view that whites cannot offer emotively authentic renderings of the blues and, to cite a more contemporary manifestation of this perception at work, the belief expressed on T-shirts worn by some black youth which proclaim the exclusive and exclusionary nature of knowledge with the words "It's a black thing. You just wouldn't understand." Wilson articulates his views on the matter in the following way: "As Americans of various races we share a broad cultural ground, a commonality of society that links its diverse elements into a cohesive whole that can be defined as 'American.' We share certain mythologies. A history. We share political and economic systems and a rapidly developing, if suspect, ethos. Within these commonalities are specifics. Specific ideas and attitudes that are not shared on the common cultural ground. These remain the property and possession of the people who develop them, and on that 'field of manners and rituals of intercourse' (to use James Baldwin's eloquent phrase), lives are played out."

Challenges to the notion that race determines a predispositional fixity are currently widespread enough that we possess a shared term by which to call and thereby contain that notion: racial essentialism. In an attempt to protect himself from charges that his views are indeed essentialist, Wilson insists that he is referring not to biological but to cultural "qualifications"; he states that he "declined a white director not on the basis of race but on the basis of culture. . . . The job requires someone who shares the specifics of the culture of black Americans." According to Wilson, "no matter how astute a student or how well meaning their intentions," non-blacks will always remain "outsider[s]" with limited access to the specific meanings of that culture's "ethos."

Wilson's articulation of his sense of directorial qualifications might be said both to confirm and to challenge what has become for many an indisputable truism: that race is a trope, a necessary fiction used by both hegemonic and anti-hegemonic forces in our complex battles for power. We might be able to observe further some of the dimensions of Wilson's comment in relationship to this truism if we consider it in the context of the useful insights offered by Michael Omi and Howard Winant. Omi and Winant employ the term "racial formation" in an effort to displace views that race is either "something fixed, concrete and objective" or "mere illusion, which an ideal social order would eliminate." According to these scholars, race is

> an unstable and "decentered" complex of social meanings constantly being transformed by political struggle. . . . The crucial task . . . is to suggest how the widely disparate circumstances of individual and group racial identities, and of the racial institutions and social practices with which these identities are intertwined, are formed and transformed over time. This takes place . . . through political contestation over racial meanings.[7]

Rather than being either condemned to fixity or assigned a significant status merely because of an imperfect practice of democracy, race for Omi and Winant is best understood as a meaningful entity whose precise definitions are continually under dispute even in the very institutions and social practices whose self-appointed task is to represent and clarify its precise meanings. This definition of race, while supporting Wilson's analysis in that it emphasizes the centrality of learned modes of interacting with and interpreting the world, insists that we examine Wilson's and all statements which seek to describe and ascribe definitive racial characteristics as explicitly or implicitly formative constructs. In other words, constructions of race such as Omi and Winant's hold that definitions espoused by sources both within and outside a given group participate in forming and transforming race's meaning(s) and must, therefore, be scrutinized carefully.

In that respect, Omi and Winant's formulations correspond with the explicitly postmodernist interrogations of the meanings of culture offered by James Clifford in his introduction to the collection *Writing Culture*, where he outlines his reasons for believing that we need to be more judicious in defining that term. Insisting that we be attentive to the operation of ideology in constructions of cultural meaning that present "partial truths" about a people as indisputable defining characteristics, Clifford argues that culture is not "a unified corpus of symbols and meanings that can be definitively interpreted. Culture is contested, temporal, and emergent. Representation and explanation—both by insiders and outsiders—is implicated in this emergence."[8]

Clifford is concerned primarily with articulating his sense of the potentialities and the limitations of the Western ethnographical enterprise in postmodernist interpretive contexts. But given the fact that Clifford also implicates cultural "insiders" as ideologically motivated contributors to a belief in perspectival unanimity and fixity, he urges us to test these views in the context of intracultural acts of meaning-making such as that which Wilson provides in "I Want a Black Director." For while Clifford calls for a more judicious investigation of the "other's" cultural difference(s) by those white Euro-American scholars who profit from ethnography's disciplinary authority, he insists also that his readers recognize the persuasiveness of postmodernist perspectives in the examination of our own cultural milieu, for even at home, as it were, "there is no whole picture that can be 'filled in,' since the perception and filling of a gap lead to the awareness of other gaps."[9]

With notions of race and culture in mind provided by Omi and Winant and Clifford, I will interrogate below what appear to me to be both the persuasive elements and the conceptual "gaps" in Wilson's efforts to undermine pejorative hegemonic notions of black people by proposing a definition of Afro-American culture as an essentially unitary, fixed, and historically static entity.

..................

## III

Wilson asserts that even at the level of language production and usage in American culture, ideology is in evidence, as is best exemplified by the fact that whiteness is defined as "free from blemish, moral stain or impurity," and blackness is seen as "outrageously wicked; . . . expressing menace; sullen, hostile; unqualified." But if the chromatic terms which we employ as shorthand to connote race are, indeed, obviously contaminated with the taint of (caucacentric) cultural bias, with the stain of ideology, so too is the discourse Wilson produces to describe and protect blackness. For while aspects of black American identity are indeed containable under Wilson's designation of the race as "an African people," despite our spatiotemporal distance from that continent, the group as a whole reflects the widest possible range of conscious and unconscious connection to Africa as originary source. Certainly it is not the case that all of the sometimes competing institutions and institutionally empowered individuals that speak for or in the name of black Americans are in agreement about the constitutive qualities of black "religion," "manners of social intercourse," "style," "language," and/or "esthetics"—or, more to the point, about the significance of these modes of action and being for Africa's late-twentieth-century descendants on American shores—despite the fact that Wilson acts as though, with some notable exceptions, these modes of difference are generally agreed upon by "[w]e . . . African people." While it is apparent that he is writing, as we will see even more clearly below, primarily with the forces of white hegemony in mind whose historical control over the dissemination of black cultural production has served to reinforce pejorative interpretations of black character, he also takes to task those Afro-Americans who as a rule question "[t]he skills of black lawyers, doctors, dentists, accountants and mechanics," thereby evincing their internalization of white hegemony's negative representation of blackness.

Ultimately, Wilson is concerned not simply with the persistence and conceptual brilliance of these cultural forms but with claiming ownership over them, with promoting his belief, in other words, that "these remain the property and possession of the people who develop them." Regardless of whether we feel that certain manners of religious practice or modes of expression are more authentic or intrinsically more black than others, we must acknowledge that his notion that Afro-Americans "own" cultural forms belies both anthropology's sense of the manner in which culture is practiced in the world and, more important, the ways in which cultures interact in ethnically and racially diverse nations such as America. Despite my profound differences with aspects of Werner Sollors's project, clearly he is correct in asserting that ethnically and racially circumscribed cultures borrow from one another continuously in a multicultural America.[10] Because our advanced capitalist society makes forms of culture available to all with the resources to purchase or otherwise interact with them, black culture's contemporary dissemination cannot be said to occur only in relatively homogeneous spheres like black neighborhoods, urban and/or rural or, for that matter, in Pentecostal, Baptist, or African Methodist churches. Aspects of these modes of cultural production are, in fact, bought and sold in a manner not wholly distinguishable from soap, mouthwash, and designer basketball sneakers.[11] Indisputably, some part of a contemporary Afro-American's education in blackness, as it were, is influenced by these modes of cultural dissemination in a manner similar to an interested suburban white youth's interaction with such material, regardless of whether that Afro-American inhabits a predominantly black or racially heterogeneous environment. In part because aspects of black culture have for decades been the topic of sophisticated academic and mass cultural inquiry—often in the work of white scholars—it seems to me impossible to argue convincingly that whites cannot learn enough to internalize or reproduce features of the complex "ethos" of which Wilson speaks. Additionally, we must acknowledge here the difficulty for Afro-Americans who move outside of an exclusively black nexus to be imbibed with or necessarily employ significant features of that ethos in interracial situations such as their neighborhoods and work places, including the academy. And if the non-black "remains an outsider" to black culture, so too, in a sense, does the Afro-American him or herself, if we accept the notion espoused by Clifford and others that culture is being continuously (re)produced and, therefore, constantly altered.

Spokespersons for specific forms of black ideology throughout the twentieth century have invested significant amounts of intellectual energy in formulating and reproducing perceptions of black culture as a fixed entity with identifiable connections to a monolithic African sensibility. Whatever resistance is encouraged by formulations such as Clifford's to notions of a transhistorical, transnational blackness, the question of "property and possession"—what Wilson speaks of later in the essay as "control"—represents simultaneously much firmer and much more shaky ground for his insistence on finding a black director for his award-winning drama. Wilson speaks of his efforts as a logical response to the racialist climate in which Afro-American art is created: "Despite such a linguistic environment, the culture of black Americans has emerged and defined itself in strong and effective vehicles that have become the flag bearers for self-determination and self-identity. In the face of such, those who are opposed to the ideas of a 'foreign' culture's permeating the ideal of an American culture founded on the icons of Europe seek to dilute and control it by setting themselves up as the assayers of its value and the custodians of its offspring. Therein lies the crux of the matter as it relates to Paramount Pictures and the film *Fences*— whether we as blacks are going to have control over our own culture and its products."

Wilson seeks, then, to contribute to the efforts of Afro-Americans to demonstrate an intellectual, technical, and entrepreneurial acumen by providing avenues whereby the "strong and effective vehicles" which members of the race have created to probe the consequences of black presence in the West can be disseminated without the diluting, distorting intervention of caucacentric protectionism. As ideological strategy, as a gesture whose intent is to intervene on centuries of white control over the representation—and the meanings—of blackness, Wilson's formulations are clearly defensible, for no one should deny him the right to use the cultural material which he has produced to serve the doubtlessly admirable political ends to which he is committed.

As self-conscious ideologue, then, it behooves Wilson to employ his significant power in an attempt to actualize his goals: namely, the dissemination of relatively undiluted narratives which highlight in aesthetically satisfying ways the presence of "black self-determination and self-identity." But his argument is weakened, in my view, by his efforts to polarize white and black means of access to Euro-American and "'foreign'" (in this case, black) cultural production. The problem is not that his exploration of traditional caucacentric perspectives on black art is unpersuasive but rather that he suggests, despite the technological advances that have made possible a wider dissemination of black cultural material, that an Afro-American ethos remains inherently less available to a white interpreter than, say, the aesthetics of Euro-American drama are to a black American such as himself. Wilson admits that much Afro-American art results from a process whereby black artists appropriate and transform Euro-American discursive forms by infusing them with what he calls "the ideas of a 'foreign' culture."[12] Hence, he would acknowledge the veracity of Henry Louis Gates's claim, for example, that in employing the Western dramatic form as a vessel for the expression of a black blues sensibility, he (and other black writers) "creates texts that are double-voiced in the sense that their literary antecedents are both white and black, but also modes of figuration lifted from the black vernacular tradition."[13] More to the point, Wilson insists that an identifiably Afro-American art derives from the abilities of its creators to master the formal "icons of Europe"—including, no doubt, Western dramatic principles—to the extent that such "vernacular" resonances and complex manifestations of black "self-determination" can be recorded despite the English language's status as a tool of caucentricism. The artistic ancestry of *Fences* is at least as much Euro-American as African, for the play's blues sensibilities (themselves an American invention) are figured in a text which displays its creator's obvious mastery of conventional Euro-American theatrical structure, pace, and methodology. Furthermore, its narrative events, particularly its exploration of family dynamics, appear—at least to me—intended self-consciously to recall, in particular, Arthur Miller's classic mid-twentieth century American drama, *Death of a Salesman*.[14]

Wilson's ruminations thus leave unanswered a crucial question: Why, if black Americans are able to gain a formal mastery over "the icons of Europe," are white Americans incapable of similar mastery of black "style," "language," and "esthetics"? While his suggestion that "[a]s Americans of various races, we share a broad cultural ground" would seem to indicate a belief that Euro-American literary genres represent dimensions of that common ground, their communal nature is merely a function of their wide institutional endorsement and dissemination in and by America's schools, book publishers, theater groups, and other avenues of cultural distribution. What makes this "broad cultural ground" possible, certainly, is not that American ideals and social practices are somehow more inherently accessible to a larger number of the nation's citizens than, say, call and response verbal forms or the adoption of a blues ethos as a means of responding to what is, for the vast majority of us, the inevitable pain of living in the world, but because centuries of American propagandists and other perpetuators of the self-evident truths of our nation's constitutive texts have worked tirelessly to convince the population to see its values as natural or, at the very least, superior to all other forms of human interaction and governance. Like American citizenry—like, for that matter, the production of dramatic texts deemed Broadway-worthy—participation in an ethos of blackness is a form of learned behavior which, with an even more effective propaganda machine behind it, might become for millions of the nation's non-black citizens part of that "broad cultural ground" which many share (if it has not already, to some extent, attained that status).

Just as, in recent years, the blues as recorded and concert event has been supported almost exclusively by white middle-class audiences, in its Broadway run *Fences*—a play whose central character, Troy Maxson, and general thematics (most succinctly articulated in Maxson's oft-repeated "take the crookeds with the straights") seem clearly infused with a blues sensibility— "appealed largely to the white theatergoers"[15] with the financial resources and inclination to witness its performance on the Great White Way. Furthermore, given the fact that much of what "Americans of various races" have in common—"certain mythologies," "history," "shared political and economic systems"—was created and/or typically presided over by whites, including the dramatic tradition in which Wilson participates so effectively, the playwright's identification of certain "broad . . . elements" as common American ground and, therefore, accessible to all with the willingness to develop the talent to use it, seems to me indisputably strategic, particularly if we consider this view in light of his unwillingness to acknowledge that, potentially, black cultural products are equally susceptible to white mastery. These are dangerous arguments, if only because they seem to echo those of unself-reflective white racists who, informed by a sense of perpetual Afro-American cultural outsiderness quite similar to Wilson's views on white interaction with black cultural forms, seek to justify their perceptions of exclusive caucasian rights to citizenship and, indeed, location on American shores.

..................

## IV

I want to turn now to Wilson's *Fences* itself, a text which we might consider one of the "strong and effective vehicles that have become the flag-bearers for [Afro-American] self-determination and self-identity." The play, which explores, among other matters, male intergenerational conflict and the motivations for and repercussions of the protagonist's extramarital affair, is peopled with characters who attempt to erect domestic and social boundaries—literal and figurative fences, if you will—as a means of marking both domestic space itself and its inhabitants as "property and possession" in order to shield them from the corruptive and/or murderous forces of the outside world while at the same time protecting the marking subject from the threat of abandonment. Ultimately, I want to investigate the play's examination of the possibilities of erecting protective fences around black familial space in terms of the quite different trajectory of Wilson's efforts to find a black film director in order to protect his creation from potentially contaminating caucacentric forces. While the playwright orchestrates the search primarily for what are ideologically justifiable reasons, its perspectives appear on the surface at least to be at odds with *Fences'* inquiry into the advisability of protectionist imperatives.

An interrogation of boundaries commences in the play's first act, which offers a series of pointed delineations of the social and personal restrictions placed on racial and gendered interaction which the play's protagonist, Troy Maxson, seeks to negotiate. *Fences* begins with Troy and Jim Bono entering the former's partially fenced yard on "Friday night, payday, and the one night of the week the two men engage in a ritual of talk and drink" (1). This ritualistic space is filled immediately with discussion of contrasting means of responding to racially motivated socioeconomic inequality. In the first instance, Troy describes one such type of negotiation whose rejection serves as a means by which to introduce both Troy's subversive act and Wilson's own afrocentric thematics.

> *Troy:* I ain't lying. The nigger had a watermelon this big. Talking about . . . "What watermelon, Mr. Rand?" I liked to fell out! "What watermelon, Mr. Rand?" . . . And it sitting there big as life.
>
> *Bono:* What did Mr. Rand say?
>
> *Troy:* Ain't said nothing. Figure if the nigger too dumb to know he carrying a watermelon, he wasn't gonna get much sense out of him. Trying to hide that great big old watermelon under his coat. Afraid to let the white man see him carry it home. (1–2)

In its reference to watermelons, apparent black simpletons, and white male authority figures involved in a comic interchange about petty larceny, Troy's language recalls—and rejects vehemently as a mode of interracial interchange—a tradition of minstrelsy which, according to Houston Baker, is characterized by "nonsense, misappropriation, or mis-hearing."[16] At one time a popular theatrical behavior which operated as a dramatic formalizing of hegemonically enforced manners of black behavior, minstrelsy was a "device," according to Baker designed to remind white consciousness that black men and women are mis-speakers bereft of humanity—carefree devils strumming and humming all day—unless, in a gaslight misidentification, they are violent devils fit for lynching, a final exorcism that will leave whites alone.[17]

Wilson sets the stage, as it were, for a different style of black dramatic representation by offering, in the play's first words, discursive structures which both recall and forcefully repudiate this comically inflected modality whose social practice had previously constituted a means by which to contain both white and black violent impulses. In other words, the play's opening scene attempts to bracket or set containing boundaries around traditional notions of black theatrical representation, thereby insisting that what follows will not conform to the nonsense syllables and actions characteristic of black participation in the theater of America historically. After relegating this manner of negotiating social difference to the realm of the antiquated—Bono says pointedly, "I'm like you . . . I ain't got no time for them kind of people" (2)—the men then begin to discuss Troy's enactment of other, newer strategies of black behavior whose purpose is to effect social change.

*Troy:* I ain't worried about them firing me. They gonna fire me cause I asked a question? That's all I did. I went to Mr. Rand and asked him, "Why? Why you got the white mens driving and the colored lifting?" Told him, "What's the matter, don't I count? You think only white fellows got sense enough to drive a truck. That ain't no paper job! Hell, anybody can drive a truck. How come you got all whites driving and the colored lifting? He told me "take it to the union." Well, hell, that's what I done! Now they wanna come up with this pack of lies. (2–3)

If minstrel performances such as those of the watermelon-stealing "nigger" (and scores of other Afro-Americans in their interactions with representatives of a white hegemonic structure) might be effectively characterized in terms of the serious play with pejorative racist stereotypes and other extant cultural forms which Baker calls "the mastery of form," then Troy's insurgent act, which insists on white confirmation of its responsibilities to ensuring constitutionally guaranteed Afro-American rights, might be viewed as an instance of a black "deformation of mastery." For Baker, "deformation is a go(uer)rilla action in the face of acknowledged adversaries."[18] While watermelon theft seeks as its end the temporary satisfaction of black desire, deformation—a formal challenge to the racially hierarchical status quo—attempts to delegitimize permanently the hegemonic structures which have sought historically to contain and control that desire.

Troy and Bono move directly from the subject of negotiating interracial relations to an investigation of (hetero)sexual politics and dynamics. Specifically, they begin discussing "that Alberta gal" and the relative success of the efforts of males in their community—themselves included—in attracting her attention. Again they speak in terms of respecting (or rejecting) boundaries:

*Bono:* . . . I see where you be eyeing her.
*Troy:* I eye all the women. I don't miss nothing. Don't never let nobody tell you Troy Maxson don't eye the women.
*Bono:* You been doing more than eyeing her. You done bought her a drink or two.
*Troy:* Hell yeah, I bought her a drink! What that mean? I bought you one, too. What that mean cause I buy her a drink? I'm just being polite. (3)

What concerns Bono is that his friend, who Wilson's stage directions indicate is admirable to Bono because of his "honesty, capacity for hard work, and his strength" (1), is not cognizant of the potentially disruptive nature of his interest in Alberta to others' and Troy's own sense of his character and integrity. Indeed, as Bono later suggests, the threat of disruption, of dissolution of a lifestyle that she has come to see as normative, motivates Rose's desire to have a fence built around the Maxson home. As he tells Troy, "some people build fences to keep people out . . . and other people build fences to keep people in. Rose wants to hold on to you all. She loves you" (61). Specifically, Bono is worried that Troy's attention to Alberta, which he is aware includes not only the polite purchase of "a drink or two" but also frequent visits to her apartment, suggests that his best friend may overstep the boundaries of acceptable marital behavior, that his actions may compromise his sense of self and his relationship with Rose, whom both men describe as "a good woman" (62). Troy's extramarital desires trouble Bono not merely because of his concern for Troy's well-being but also because of his status as role model for Bono himself. As he tells Troy later in the play when he more directly confronts him with his suspicions:

> When you picked Rose, I was happy for you. That was the first time I knew you had any sense. I said . . . My man Troy knows what he's doing . . . I'm gonna follow this nigger . . . he might take me somewhere. I been following you too. I done learned a whole heap of things about life watching you. I done learned how to tell where the shit lies. How to tell it from the alfalfa. You done learned me a lot of things. You showed me how to not make the same mistakes . . . to take life as it comes along and keep putting one foot in front of the other. (62)

When Troy commences a more public relationship with Alberta, the affair eventuates in the dissolution of the rituals of friendship with Bono in part because the grounds upon which the intensity of the latter's admiration of the protagonist is based—evidence of Troy's clear-sightedness, his ability to understand and not be tempted to overstep the boundaries with which his life presents him—have been undercut.

One of *Fences'* most resonant examinations of boundaries appears in Troy's discussion with Lyons about the material and psychological benefits of gainful employment.

> *Troy:* I done learned my mistake and learned to do what's right by it. You still trying to get something for nothing. Life don't owe you nothing. You owe it to yourself. . . .

*Lyons:* You got your way of dealing with the world . . . I got mine. The only thing that matters to me is the music.

*Troy:* Yeah, I can see that! It don't matter how you gonna eat . . . where your next dollar is coming from. You telling the truth there.

*Lyons:* I know I got to eat. But I got to live too. I need something that gonna help me to get out of bed in the morning. Make me feel like I belong in the world. I don't bother nobody. I just stay with my music cause that's the only way I can find to live in the world. Otherwise there's no telling what I might do. (18)

Here we are presented with a contrast between what the play presents as two poles of available male behavior: Troy's hypermasculine sense of self-sacrifice and economic responsibility and Lyons's self-indulgent search for personal fulfillment. What is particularly striking about this scene is its principals' energetic articulation of positions which, at this moment in the history of their weekly ritual of filial money borrowing and paternal castigation, they preach much more energetically than practice. For Lyons is only minimally dedicated to his art (the stage directions which proceed his appearance describe him as "more caught up in the rituals and 'idea' of being a musician than in the actual practice of the music" [13]), and Troy has slipped from the lofty position from which he has somewhat self-righteously critiqued others. (Moreover, as we will see, Lyons's discourse of self-fulfillment and irresponsibility is later echoed in his father's description to Rose of the motivations for his infidelity.)

While in his talks with Lyons and, later, Cory about financial responsibility he demonstrates—though not without some authorial irony—some of the more admirable aspects of his character, in his discussion with his younger son about paternal displays of affection (both his own demonstrations and those of his father) Troy most poignantly displays both his most positive and most negative dimensions. After Troy asserts that his son's continued participation in football depends on a near-impossible commitment to both housework and store employment, Cory asks whether his father's generally harsh treatment of him is motivated by a lack of paternal affection. Troy responds:

Liked you? Who the hell say I got to like you? What law is there say I got to like you? Wanna stand up in my face and ask a dam fool-ass question like that. Talking about liking somebody. . . . I go out of here every morning . . . bust my butt . . . putting up with them crackers everyday . . . cause I like you? You about the biggest fool I ever saw. . . . It's my job. It's my responsibility! You understand that? A man got to take care of his family. You live in my house . . . sleep you behind on my bedclothes . . . fill you belly up with my food . . . cause you my son. You my flesh and blood. Not 'cause I like you! Cause it's my duty to take care of you. I owe a responsibility to you! . . . Mr. Rand don't give me my money come payday cause he likes me. He gives me cause he owe me. . . . Don't you try and go through life worrying about if somebody like you or not. You best be making sure they doing right by you. You understand what I'm saying, boy? (37–38)

In Troy's estimation, Cory's question demonstrates that he is unaware of the boundaries of interpersonal responsibility, of the central role an economics of duty plays in profitable human interactions. While this perspective may encourage appropriate responses to a society characterized by deceit and institutionalized inequality, clearly it lacks the ability to foster an appreciation of the potential tenderness of intimate human relations. Put another way, Troy's economics of duty—learned from an abusive father so embittered by his parental "responsibility" to "eleven children" that "all his women run off and left him" (51)—leaves him poorly equipped to deal with the emotional demands of intimate personal relations. "[D]oing right," in such relations, is not merely providing clean sheets and nourishing foods, but also demonstrating an intense concern about the psychic welfare of those for whom one has assumed responsibility. Troy's discussion of familial duty, then, reflects inherent flaws in his worldview caused, it would appear, by his failure to attend to important aspects of intimacy.

I am suggesting, then, that at the point at which we meet him, Troy's code of living is defective because it leaves no space for a pursuit of self-fulfillment. While this self-protective mechanism of boundary maintenance serves effectively to check the impulse toward familial abandonment which Troy terms the "walking blues" (51), a condition manifested in the form of "a fellow moving around from place to place . . . woman to woman . . . searching out the New Land" (50), it is limited as a means of responding to the full range of human emotional possibilities.

Apparently, as his discussions with both Bono and Rose about his affair attest, he recognizes that the absence of joy in his own life renders him unable to reconcile his words and actions to the philosophical views by which he had been governed. When Troy states, for example, "I can't shake her loose,"

Bono insists that he remain true to his oft-stated perspectives on individual culpability and responsibility:

> *Bono:* You's in control . . . that's what you tell me all the time. You
>   responsible for what you do.
> *Troy:* I ain't ducking the responsibility of it. As long as it sets right in my
>   heart . . . then I'm okay. Cause that's all I listen to. It'll tell me right
>   from wrong every time. And I ain't talking about doing Rose no bad
>   turn. I love Rose. She done carried me a long ways and I love and
>   respect her for that. (63)

His intentions not to do Rose a "bad turn" and his faith in his "heart" notwithstanding, his manner of constructing his motives for infidelity makes it clear that the pursuit of self-fulfillment has served effectively to block his limited capacity to attend to his wife's feelings:

> It's just . . . She gives me a different idea . . . a different understanding
> about myself. I can step out of this house and get away from the pressures
> and problems . . . be a different man. I ain't got to wonder how I'm gonna
> pay the bills or get the roof fixed. I can just be a part of myself that I ain't
> never been . . . I can sit up in her house and laugh . . . I can laugh out loud
> . . . and it feels good. It reaches all the way down to the bottom of my
> shoes.
> (Pause)
> Rose, I can't give that up. (68–69)

After an interchange most notable, in my view, for its evidence of the participants' communicative gaps or discursive boundaries (he employs baseball metaphors, a mode of discourse which Rose considers inappropriate, telling him, "We're not talking about baseball! We're talking about you going off to lay in bed with another woman . . . and then bring it home to me"), Troy seeks to win his wife's sympathy by turning his attention to the difficulty he has encountered in being confronted with evidence of his inadequacy.

> *Troy:* Rose, you're not listening to me. I'm trying the best I can to explain
>   it to you. It's not easy for me to admit that I been standing in the same
>   place for eighteen years.
> *Rose:* I been standing with you! I been right here with you, Troy. I got a
>   life too. I gave eighteen years of my life to stand in the same spot with
>   you. Don't you think I ever wanted other things? What about my life?

> What about me. Don't you think it ever crossed my mind to want to
> know other men. That I wanted to lay up somewhere and forget about
> my responsibilities? That I wanted someone to make me laugh so I
> could feel good? You not the only one who's got wants and needs. But
> I held on to you, Troy. I took all my feelings, my wants and needs, my
> dreams and I buried them inside you. I planted a seed and watched
> and prayed over it. I planted myself inside you and waited to bloom.
> And it didn't take me no eighteen years to find out the soil was hard
> and rocky and it wasn't never gonna bloom. (70–71)

Rose shifts the discursive ground from a masculinist metaphorics of individually determined psychic and socioeconomic advancement to a nature-
centered figuration of the growth of the un(der)developed. In figuring the
interior spaces of the self-protective male as potential uterine site of her own
development, Rose defies—and, in fact, denies—the limitations of both the
biological and Troy's economics of duty. Just as Troy believes that imparting
to Cory his philosophy of financial self-support will allow him to discharge
his parental responsibilities in a sufficient manner, so, too, does he feel that
by sleeping every night with and turning over his weekly pay to Rose he
is meeting his marital duties. The costs of accommodating herself to this
worldview by containing and thereby ignoring her own desires are extremely
high for Rose, as she tells Cory upon his return to the house from which he
had been banished for his father's funeral:

> I married your daddy and settled down to cooking his supper and keeping
> clean sheets on the bed. When your daddy walked through the house he
> was so big he filled it up. That was my first mistake. Not to make him
> leave some room for me. For my part in the matter. But at that time I
> wanted that. I wanted a house that I could sing in. And that's what your
> daddy gave me. I didn't know to keep up his strength I had to give up
> little pieces of mine. I did that. . . . It was my choice. It was my life and I
> didn't have to live it like that. But that's what life offered me in the way of
> being a woman and I took it. I grabbed hold of it with both hands. (98)

Rose describes here the consequences of her efforts to achieve her desire
for material space, which include, most importantly, her failure to pursue
her own desires in order to direct her attentions to satisfying the wishes of
her forceful husband. Given the gender politics of the period and the direct

correlation between Rose's self-sacrifice and Troy's fairly stable and positive self-image—as she says, "to keep up his strength I had to give up little pieces of mine"—her immolation apparently was necessary in order to stave off the onset of a masculinist "walking blues." To put the matter somewhat differently, the cost of the maintenance of material space for even a restricted articulation of female song is the loss of verbal strength and the possibility of self-actualization within a domicile dominated by Troy's pragmatic economics of duty. The fences that Troy and Rose place around their marriage, their feelings, and their unarticulated desires for a more fulfilling existence are effective while these characters exclude intense self-investigation from their rituals of living. The price both pay for self-protection—for the protective barriers of "fences"—includes stagnation and the repression of cognition of intense dissatisfaction.

But how do we accommodate Wilson's figurations of the motivations for and consequences of the construction of self-protective fences—not the least of which is psychic inertia—with his protectionist insistence on finding a black director for the film version of his play, an insistence which seems to reflect a cynicism about the trajectory of racial progress over the last half-century on the level of *Fences'* protagonist, Troy? The play itself is infused with a poetics of progress and boundary breaking. For example, all of Troy's articulations of his sense of the fixity of race relations—his insistence that his inability to become a major league baseball player after his incarceration and a young Roberto Clemente's initial failure to become an everyday player for the Pittsburgh Pirates are solely a function of racism; his view of the inevitable fruitlessness of his son's attending college on an athletic scholarship—are effectively challenged either within the context of the play or by our historical knowledge of changes that have taken place in American race relations since the 1950s. Moreover, Wilson's self-composed epigraph to the play urges an understanding of the possibility of improving upon, of transcending, the negative aspects of a cultural legacy. Wilson writes:

> When the sins of our fathers visit us
> We do not have to play host.
> We can banish them with forgiveness
> As God, in His Largeness and Laws.

Indeed, it is the importance of "banish[ing]" "the sins of our fathers" "with forgiveness," while at the same time recognizing the significance of spiritually beneficial paternal gifts, that motivates Rose's concluding words to Cory, whose bitterness is so intense that he threatens not to attend Troy's funeral. She says to his son:

> I took on to Raynell [Troy's and Alberta's daughter] like she was all them babies I had wanted and never had. . . . Like I'd been blessed to relive a part of my life. And if the Lord see fit to keep up my strength . . . I'm gonna do her just like your daddy did you . . . I'm gonna give her the best of what's in me. (98)

Rose encourages Cory to move beyond the self-protective bitterness that he has employed to shield himself from his painful memory of his father's treatment of him and to strive to comprehend the nature of the psychic inheritance bequeathed him by Troy. Noting her own ability to come to terms with her husband's transgressive behavior, her capacity to—in the words of Troy's favorite saying—"take the crookeds with the straights," Rose urges Cory not to seek to erase the aspects of his character and imaginative repertoire which reflect his father, but instead to combine these characteristics with other conceptually persuasive modes of being in order to develop his own ethics of living. Rather than attempt to deny Troy's influence upon the formation of his identity, Rose challenges him to honor and improve upon that which was good about her husband.

In addition to its call for psychic generational advancement, Wilson's play reflects an awareness that socioeconomic progress has been a dimension of Afro-American life over the last three decades. When, for example, Troy complains to Mr. Rand and, subsequently, to the union about a systemic hierarchization of labor in the garbage collection company for which he works, he is promoted to the status of driver, thereby achieving a measure of racial justice of the sort he believes was denied him during a prestigious baseball career confined by major league strictures to the Negro Leagues. But Wilson is also cognizant of the cost of those changes, including the onset of socioeconomic stratification of members of the Afro-American community, as is evidenced by the fact that Troy considers retiring soon after he is promoted because occupying the heretofore exclusively white space as driver is akin to "working by yourself" (83). More important, Wilson seems to recognize that comprehensive transformations in American race relations are necessary before the fact of greater access for a select few to the promises explicit in the recorded ideals of the nation's founding fathers—its constitutional "gifts," as it were—will ameliorate the effects of the sins of these fathers and their off-spring committed on the bodies and minds of black countrymen and women in the white citizens' imperfect and often racist pursuit of strategically limited aspects of these ideals. Whatever we make of Troy's affair with Alberta, clearly his psychic inertia before he starts to date her is in large part a function of a personal history in which he had to confront as a skilled sports laborer the racist boundaries to constitutionally guaranteed opportunity.

Until more-comprehensive changes are made to the basic structure of American society where the questions of racial and cultural differences are concerned—changes that will affect the grammar of motives upon which significant aspects of our shared culture is constructed—seemingly important transformations such as Troy's improved employment status, August Wilson's own success as a dramatist, and Hollywood's recent interest in sophisticated representations of Afro-American life such as *Fences* will constitute merely local, individual victories. Wilson seems cognizant of one of American hegemony's strategies of operation vis-à-vis the oppressed wherein it presents impressive gifts to individual members of disenfranchised groups as a substitute for a wider redistribution of its socioeconomic and cultural assets, and he is apparently less concerned with personal profit from the returns for a film version of his play than in employing the cultural capital he has earned in order to assist efforts to ensure the continued alteration of racist American discourse that always already questions Afro-American qualifications.

Despite his insistence at some points in "I Want a Black Director" to the contrary, whether or not whites can understand and disseminate the culturally specific aspects of *Fences* is not the most central issue in Wilson's formulation of his position. Of preeminent importance to the playwright, I believe, is whether, given the persistence of caucacentric discourse and actions in our nation, Afro-Americans can afford to allow patterns of expressive cultural distribution to continue wherein blacks remain pawns to the whims and racialist will of white entrepreneurial forces interested primarily in economic bottom lines rather than in working to destroy the still-evident barriers to social, economic, and cultural power for a large portion of the black population. If Wilson's play and his polemic do indeed complement each other in their examinations of the dangers of boundaries, that complementarity is reflected in his skepticism about the benefits of minimal alteration in the nation's practice of racial politics. The sins of the nation's white founding fathers and its sons and daughters—including the fences they constructed by way of its governing laws, bylaws, and historical practices whose intent seems to be to encourage Afro-American inequality virtually in perpetuity—can be banished only through herculean energy and ideologically informed activity because, however pronounced our desire to forgive and move on, they visit us continuously.

..................

## NOTES

This essay was written during my 1992 stay at Princeton University as President's Postdoctoral Fellow in Afro-American Studies. I wish to thank Princeton and my home institution, the University of Michigan, for their support, and Alan Nadel, who offered quite helpful editorial suggestions.

1. Greenberg, "Did Hollywood Sit on 'Fences,'" p. 13.

2. Bluestone, *Novels into Film*, p. 1.

3. Sinyard, *Filming Literature*, 117. A look at two analyses of filmic adaptations might suffice to demonstrate this tendency within scholarship to minimize the importance of issues such as those which Wilson considers central. Hulseberg argues that "our own biases and predilections, and experience and value of all sorts hover about our dealings with an individual work" (p. 57), and that "many comparisons of novels and films are sensed as moral ones, the idea being that the filmmaker has an obligation to 'restate,' in his fashion, the essence of the novel, and that anything less constitutes a kind of vulgar cultural cannibalism, an abuse of the high art of fiction" (p. 58). Hulseberg locates cultural cooptation not in the exchange between directors and counterhegemonic texts—where Wilson places it—but in American society's simplistic distinctions between high and low art, between the written literary text as bourgeois form of consumption and its formally and diegetically unfaithful filmic rendering. Conversely, Larsson focuses at points on contemporary critical notions of ideology, even going so far as to reference an Althusserian notion of ideology as "the way in which people live the relationship between themselves and the conditions of their existence" (p. 79). However, rather than seeing the enactment of ideology potentially as a result of an attempt to neutralize the impact of counterhegemonic ideological energies, Larsson foregrounds historical difference—what he refers to as "a change in lived relationships"—as the primary motivation for tangible differences between originary text and filmic adaptation. In addition to considerations of the ways in which historical differences transform the texts we receive from earlier periods, I believe that we need also a theory of adaptation which encourages our serious consideration of the textual transformations that take place within historical periods if we want more fully to investigate ideology's continuous

impact on narrative and form. For other discussions of filmic adaptations, see Cohen, "Eisenstein's Subversive Adaptation"; Sinyard, *Filming Literature*; and Giddings, Selby, and Wensley, *Screening the Novel.*

4. For discussions of Steven Spielberg's adaptation of Alice Walker's novel, see Bobo, "Sifting through the Controversy"; Early, "*The Color Purple* as Everybody's Protest Art"; and Wallace, "Blues for Mr. Speilberg."

5. According to Cohen, "adaptation is a truly artistic feat when the new version carries with it a hidden criticism of its model, or at least implicit (through a process we should call 'deconstruction') certain key contradictions implanted or glossed over in the original" ("Eisenstein's Subversive Adaptation," p. 245). Cohen's contention, I believe, is merely a poststructuralist-inflected articulation of Bluestone's perspectives, and is echoed in Neil Sinyard's assertion that the best adaptations of books for film can often be approached as an activity of literary "criticism . . . [as] a critical essay which stresses what it sees as the main theme. Like a critical essay, the film adaptation selects some episodes, excludes others, offers preferred alternatives. . . . [Film adaptors] are also not afraid . . . to take liberties with character and structure when they feel they have more convincing readings to offer than the original, to emphasise some features and disregard others. In other words, they go for intensity of illumination more than a shapeless inclusiveness" (p. 117). While we need not accept black filmmaker Warrington Hudlin's view that a white film director inevitably seeks to bracket the ideological thrust or black focus of Afro-American texts because of his inability otherwise "to find an emotional center that he can identify with" (Greenberg, p. 18), clearly views such as Sinyard's and Cohen's might cause concern for any artist who wishes to see his or her ideas reflected on the screen, particularly authors like Wilson who have what they feel are historically justifiable suspicions about white filmmakers' appropriations of black texts.

6. Larsson, "Novel into Film," p. 80.

7. Omi and Winant, *Racial Formation,* pp. 68–69.

8. Clifford, "Introduction: Partial Truths," p. 19.

9. Ibid., p. 18.

10. For my discussion of Sollors's response in "A Critique of Pure Pluralism" to contemporary Afro-Americanist and other forms of ethnic and/or gendered interrogation of the significance of critical positionality, see "Negotiations of Power." Sollors's extended discussion of these matters occurs in *Beyond Ethnicity.*

11. As is perhaps most perversely—and tragically—manifested in the murder of black urban youth by other blacks in order to steal the $100-plus court shoes, it is clear that certain trends in Afro-American communities can be regarded as direct responses to the commodification of aspects of black cultural style.

12. I have identified this adaptive process elsewhere as denigration. See Awkward, *Inspiriting Influences*, particularly pp. 8–14.

13. Gates, xxiii.

14. Indeed, whatever the differences between Wilson's and Miller's family dramas (and they are significant), a recitation of some of the most central of *Fences'* concerns—intergenerational male conflict; the motivations for and far-reaching impact of marital infidelity; the consequences for the patriarchical figure of not achieving the American dream; a wife's victimization in and complicity with her husband's self-delusional efforts to maintain a positive sense of self despite evidence of his failures; paternal socialization of male offspring through sports; the thematic centrality of death; and, finally, a concluding requiem in which mother, close male friend, and sons assess the meanings of the patriarch's life just before attending his funeral—suggests that Wilson's play would not have been possible in its present form without the precursoral presence of Miller's canonical white American middle-class family drama.

15. Greenberg, "Did Hollywood Sit on 'Fences,'" p. 18.

16. Baker, *Modernism and the Harlem Renaissance*, p. 18.

17. Ibid., p. 21.

18. Ibid., p. 50.

. . . . . . . . . . . . . . . . .

## WORKS CITED

Awkward, Michael. *Inspiriting Influences: Tradition, Revision, and Afro-American Women's Novels*. New York: Columbia University Press, 1989.

———. "Negotiations of Power: White Critics, Black Texts and the Self-Referential Impulse." *American Literary History* 2 (1990): 581–605.

Baker, Houston A., Jr. *Modernism and the Harlem Renaissance*. Chicago: University of Chicago Press, 1987.

Bluestone, George. *Novels into Film*. Berkeley: University of California Press, 1985.

Bobo, Jacqueline. "Sifting through the Controversy: Reading *The Color Purple*," *Callaloo* 13 (1990): 332–42.

Clifford, James. "Introduction: Partial Truths." In *Writing Culture: The Poetics and Politics of Ethnography*, edited by James Clifford and George E. Marcus, pp. 1–26. Berkeley: University of California Press, 1986.

Cohen, Keith. "Eisenstein's Subversive Adaptation." In *The Classic American Novel and the Movies*, edited by Gerald Peary and Roger Shatzkin, pp. 239–56. New York: Ungar, 1977.

———. *Film and Fiction: The Dynamics of Exchange.* New Haven and London: Yale University Press, 1979.

Crapanzano, Vincent. "Hermes' Dilemma: The Masking of Subversion in Ethnographic Description." In *Writing Culture: The Poetics and Politics of Ethnography*, edited by James Clifford and George E. Marcus, pp. 51–76. Berkeley: University of California Press, 1986.

Early, Gerald. *Tuxedo Junction: Essays in American Culture.* New York: Ecco, 1989.

Giddings, Robert, Keith Selby, and Chris Wensley. *Screening the Novel: The Theory and Practice of Literary Dramatization.* London: Macmillan, 1990.

Greenberg, James. "Did Hollywood Sit on 'Fences' over Hiring a Black Director?" *New York Times*, 27 January 1991, Arts and Leisure, sec. 2, pp. 13, 18.

Hulseberg, Richard. "Novels and Films: A Limited Inquiry." *Literature and Film Quarterly* 6 (1978): 57–65.

Larsson, Donald. "Novel into Film: Some Preliminary Reconsiderations." In *Transformations in Literature and Film*, edited by Leon Golden, pp. 69–83. Tallahassee: University Presses of Florida, 1982.

Omi, Michael, and Howard Winant. *Racial Formation in the United States: From the 1960s to the 1980s.* London: Routledge and Kegan Paul, 1986.

Sinyard, Neil. *Filming Literature: The Art of Screen Adaptation.* New York: St. Martin's, 1986.

Smith, Barbara Herrnstein. *Contingencies of Value: Alternative Perspectives for Critical Theory.* Cambridge: Harvard University Press, 1988.

Sollors, Werner. *Beyond Ethnicity: Consent and Descent in American Culture.* New York: Oxford University Press, 1986.

———. "A Critique of Pure Pluralism." In *Reconstructing American Literary History*, edited by Sacvan Bercovitch, pp. 250-79. Cambridge: Harvard University Press, 1986.

Wallace, Michelle. *Invisibility Blues: From Pop to Theory.* London and New York: Verso, 1990.

Wilson, August. *Fences.* New York: New American Library, Plume, 1986.

———. "I Want a Black Director." *New York Times*, 26 September 1990, sec. 1, p. 15.

SANDRA G. SHANNON

# Annotated Bibliography of Works by and about August Wilson

· · · · · · · · · · · · · · · · · · · · · · · · · · · · · · · · · · · · · · · · · · · · · · · · · · · · ·

Critical assessment of August Wilson's plays has increased in scope and in momentum over the last decade. Although he wrote his first play in 1973 (*Recycle*), serious attention to his work did not come until the early 1980s with the Broadway success of *Ma Rainey's Black Bottom* (1981). Now Wilson is one of the most-written-about dramatists in America, capturing the respect and admiration of some of New York's toughest critics and inspiring a wellspring of scholarly activity about the plays that make up his proposed ten-play chronicle of the black experience. Published commentary on his work has likewise evolved from an abundance of theater reviews of works staged along a familiar path from the Yale Repertory Theater to Broadway.

Every effort was made to include as many references to Wilson's work as possible in the annotated bibliography that follows. However, because of an already voluminous and steadily increasing supply of published material on him and his work (some of which has yet to be cataloged and therefore remains irretrievable), several references may not be included here. Extensive though it may be, this annotated bibliography is not all-inclusive; it is instead intended as a starting place for anyone doing preliminary research on August Wilson.

The bibliography is the result of a two-year research mission funded by a faculty research grant from Howard University that allowed me to make several productive trips to the Yale School of Drama Library to examine what is the largest and most organized collection of published information on Wilson to date. Housed here is a repository of news clippings and cataloged information on the various performances staged specifically at the Yale Repertory Theater as well as at various other locales throughout the United States.

In some instances parts of certain citations may not include page numbers or dates, largely because of the abbreviated format used by the New England Newsclip Service, an official news-collecting firm to which the Yale School of Drama Library subscribes.

In addition to the New England Newsclip Service, St. Louis University librarian Chester S. Bunnell graciously donated his working bibliography on August Wilson to the project. Howard University graduate student Charles Tita also assisted me by conducting a thorough search for pertinent materials at the Library of Congress and at major university libraries in the Washington, D.C., area. Homero Lurns, my English department colleague, was very helpful as a human resource in providing me not only with recent clippings of news on Wilson but also—since he is a black music buff—much insight into his use of the blues. Other sources below were located by consulting the *New York Times Theater Reviews* and relying upon my own detectivelike fervor to collect and read every published item pertinent to August Wilson.

## BY WILSON

PLAYS

*Black Bart and the Sacred Hills.* Unpublished script, written in 1977. Produced in St. Paul, Minnesota, in 1981.
   Sprawling musical satire featuring twenty-seven characters based upon a series of poems about a legendary rustler named Black Bart. Considered to be Wilson's debut as a serious dramatist.
*The Coldest Day of the Year.* Unpublished script, written in 1977. Produced in 1989.
   One-act experiment with ritual and absurdist drama. Encounter between a man and a woman at a bus stop during the bleakest part of winter.
*Eskimo Song Duel: The Case of the Borrowed Wife.* Unpublished script, written in 1979. One of several short scripts written while employed at the Science Museum of Minnesota.
   Eight-page war of words between a skilled Eskimo huntsman and a clumsy, undeserving rival husband. Wife goes to the superior huntsman, who wins verbal contest.
*An Evening with Margaret Mead.* Unpublished script, date unavailable. One of several short scripts written while employed at the Science Museum of Minnesota. One-woman play composed of comments by Mead as she considers an invitation to deliver a lecture at the Pacific Arts Council.
*Fences.* Written in 1983. Produced in New Haven in 1985; in New York in 1987.

Published in New York by New American Library in 1986; earned Wilson his first Pulitzer Prize in drama in 1987.

Plight of an urban black family on the eve of the Civil Rights Movement. The protagonist is Troy Maxson, Pittsburgh garbageman, one-time prisoner, and would-be major leaguer turned tyrant.

*Fullerton Street.* Unpublished script, written in 1980. No productions mounted.

Originally intended to be Wilson's play of the 1940s, *Fullerton Street* examines blacks as urban Northerners.

*The Homecoming.* Unpublished script, written in 1976. Produced in 1989.

Seventeen-page fictitious rendering of itinerant blues singer-guitarist Blind Lemon Jefferson, who died of exposure in Chicago in 1930.

*How Coyote Got His Special Power and Used It to Help the People.* Unpublished script; date unknown. One of several scripts written while employed at the Science Museum of Minnesota.

Nine-page beast fable recalling how several wild animals acquired their names and their instinctive callings.

"The Janitor." Published in *Short Pieces from the New Dramatists,* edited by Stan Chervin, pp. 81–82. New York: Broadway Play Publishing, 1985.

Four-minute play about a black cleaning man who becomes a celebrity-for-an-instant when he exchanges broom handle for microphone set up in preparation for a National Youth Conference.

*Jitney!* Written in 1979. Produced in 1982. Accepted by the Minneapolis Playwrights' Center for performance in 1980. Also performed in 1985 at the Martin Luther King Center in Saint Paul, Minnesota.

Set in 1971, the play is about black men who work as jitney drivers in Pittsburgh.

*Joe Turner's Come and Gone.* Written in 1984. Produced at Yale Repertory Theater in New Haven in 1986 and at Washington, D.C. Arena Stage in 1988. Work-in-progress published in *Theater* 19 (1988): 70–71; published in 1988 in New York by New American Library.

Examines costs of cultural fragmentation that followed Emancipation and mass Northern exodus. A 1911 Pittsburgh boardinghouse is beacon to weary travelers seeking family members and sense of direction in the world.

*Ma Rainey's Black Bottom.* Written in 1982. Opened in New Haven on 6 April 1984, and in New York at Broadway's Cort Theater in 1984. Published in 1985 in New York by New American Library.

Plight of black blues musicians in 1920s Chicago. First play to bring Wilson critical acclaim and first of cycle of plays performed on Broadway.

*The Mill Hand's Lunch Bucket.* Produced in New York in 1983.

Original title given to *Joe Turner's Come and Gone.*

*The Piano Lesson.* Written in 1986. Initially presented as a staged reading at the

Eugene O'Neill Theater Center's 1987 National Playwrights' Conference. Opened on Broadway on 16 April 1990, at the Walter Kerr Theater. Published in New York by Plume in 1990. Earned Wilson a second Pulitzer Prize in drama in 1990. A century-old piano holds a black family hostage until they are convinced to confront their past. Set in 1936, the play relegates the hardships of the Depression to the background and focuses upon what the characters do with their cultural legacy.

*Recycle.* Unpublished script. Written in 1973. Produced at a community theater in Pittsburgh. Further information unavailable.

*Rite of Passage.* According to Wilson, his "first play." Further information unavailable.

"Testimonies: Four Monologues." *Anteus* 66 (Spring 1991): 474–79.

Reprint of selected monologues that appeared in *Two Trains Running.* Includes moving dialogue by Holloway and Memphis.

"Two Trains Running." Written in 1989. Produced at Yale Repertory Theater in 1990. Work-in-progress published in *Theater* 22, no. 1 (1991): 40–72.

Set in a soon-to-be-demolished restaurant in Pittsburgh's Hill District in 1968, a sounding board for several disenchanted black men living in the midst of the decade's political and social turmoil.

## SELECTED POETRY

"Bessie." *Black Lines* 1 (Summer 1971): 68.

"For Malcolm X and Others." *Negro Digest* 18 (September 1969): 58.

"Morning Song." *Black Lines* 1 (Summer 1971): 68.

"Muhammad Ali." *Black World* 21 (September 1972): 60–61.

"Theme One: The Variations." In *The Poetry of Black America: Anthology of the Twentieth Century,* edited by Arnold Adoff. New York: Harper and Row, 1973.

## COLLECTIONS

*Contemporary American Plays: An Anthology.* Abridged ed. New York: Literary Volunteers of New York City, 1990.

Wilson, August. "Fences." In *The Best Plays of 1986–1987.* New York: Dodd, Mead, 1988.

———. *Fences and Ma Rainey's Black Bottom.* Harmondsworth, Eng.: Penguin, 1988.

———. "Ma Rainey's Black Bottom." [Excerpt] in *Best Plays of 1984–1985,* edited by Otis L. Guernsey and Jeffrey Sweet. New York: Dodd, 1986.

———. *Three Plays.* Pittsburgh: University of Pittsburgh Press, 1991.

CRITICAL INTRODUCTIONS WRITTEN BY WILSON

Foreword to *Romare Bearden: His Life and Art*, by Myron Schwartzman. New York: Harry N. Abrams, 1990.

Penny, Rob. *Black Tones of Truth*. Pittsburgh: Oduduwa Productions, 1970.

PERIODICAL PUBLICATIONS

"Characters behind History Teach Wilson about Plays." *New York Times*, 12 April 1992, sec. H, p. 5.

Wilson explains his early fascination with the forces of history that ultimately led to writing plays that "dealt with black life and manners for each decade of the 20th century." He also discovered a correlation between history and culture. The histories of his characters "would not only represent the culture but illuminate the historical context both of the period in which the play is set and the continuum of black life in America that stretches back to the early 17th century."

"I Want a Black Director." *Spin*, October 1990 and *New York Times*, 26 September 1990. (See also "So You Want a Black Director for Your Movie?" *New York Times* [letters] (12 October 1990).

Wilson expresses his frustration over Paramount Pictures' reluctance to hire a black director for a proposed film version of *Fences*. He lambasts Eddie Murphy, who he thinks can influence Paramount in this direction, for his comment "I don't want to hire nobody just 'cause they're black." Although he has sold rights to the play for a reported $500,000, he still insists that the play demands the sensitivities of a black director to do it justice.

———. "Hero Worship on Sunday Afternoon." *26 Super Bowl Game Program*. Los Angeles: NFL Properties, 1992.

Memoir discussing experience of seeing first football game.

"How to Write a Play like August Wilson." *New York Times*, 10 March 1991, sec. H, pp. 5–17.

Adapted from a talk by August Wilson at the Poetry Center of the Ninety-second Street Y in Manhattan in early 1991. Wilson describes process for developing characters: "The first thing to do," says the playwright, "is create characters who know everything. Then, if there are problems, ask them."

———. Memory of actor Robert Judd. In *Broadway Day and Night*, pp. 114–16. New York: Simon and Schuster, 1992.

———. "The Legacy of Malcolm X." *Life*, December 1992, pp. 84–94.

Personal reflections on Malcolm X: Malcolm's message and meaning for African American culture, then and now. Also discusses Malcolm's involvement in and separation from the Nation of Islam.

INTERVIEWS

Byrne, David. "August Wilson's 'The Piano Lesson.'" *Theater* 19 (1988): 2.

Evans, Barbara. *Pittsburgh Magazine* 20 (September 1989): 12.

Gussow, Mel. "Fine-Tuning 'The Piano Lesson.'" *New York Times Magazine*, 10 September 1989, p. 518.

Henderson, Heather. "Building Fences: An Interview with Mary Alice and James Earl Jones." *Theater* 16 (Summer/Fall 1985): 67–70.

Hunter-Gault, C. "On Broadway: Everybody's America." *Vogue*, August 1988, pp. 200–201.

Mitgang, Herbert. "Wilson, From Poetry to Broadway Success." *New York Times*, 22 October 1984.

Moyers, Bill. "August Wilson's America." *American Theater*, June 1989, p. 10.

———. "August Wilson." In *A World of Ideas: Conversations with Thoughtful Men and Women about American Life Today and the Ideas Shaping Our Future*, edited by Bill Moyers, pp. 167–80. New York: Doubleday, 1989. (Content same as above reference by Moyers.)

O'Neill, Michael C. "Interview." In *American Playwrights Since 1945*, edited by Philip Kolin. New York: Greenwood, 1989.

O'Steen, Kathleen. "Writer's Block? What's That, Asks 'Fences' Author August Wilson." *Variety* 327 (10 June 1987): 83.

Palmer, Don. "Interview with August Wilson: He Gives a Voice to the Nameless Masses." *New York Newsday*, 20 April 1987, p. 47.

Powers, Kim. "An Interview with August Wilson." *Theater* 16, no. 1 (Fall/Winter 1984): 50–55.

Savran, David. *In Their Own Words: Contemporary American Playwrights*. New York: Theater Communications Group, 1988.

Schafer, Yvonne. "An Interview with August Wilson." *Journal of Dramatic Theory and Criticism* 4 (1989): 161–73.

Sheppard, Vera. "August Wilson: An Interview." *National Forum: Phi Kappa Pi Journal* 70 (Summer 1990): 7–11.

Watlington, Dennis. "Hurdling Fences." *Vanity Fair*, April 1989, pp. 102–13.

## ABOUT WILSON

BIOGRAPHICAL PIECES

*American Drama Criticism: Supplement II.* Compiled by Floyd Eugene Eddlemen, pp. 206–7. 2d ed. Hamden, Conn.: 1989.

"August Wilson." *Current Biography* 48 (August 1987): 53–56.

Berry, Jane. "Inspired in a Deli." *Tucson (Arizona) Citizen*, 30 December 1987.

Brown, Chip. "The Light in August." *Esquire*, April 1989, pp. 116–25.

Charles, Nick. "August Wilson: Stages of Black America." *Emerge*, April 1990, pp. 62–65.

*Chicago Tribune.* 16 September 1984, p. 13; 9 February 1986, p. 7; 10 April 1987.

*Christian Science Monitor.* 16 October 1984, p. 29; 27 March 1987.

Christianson, Richard. "Wilson, August." In *Contemporary Playwrights*, edited by D. L. Kirkpatrick, 571–72. Chicago and London: St. James, 1988.

*Contemporary Authors.* Vols. 115 and 122 (1985).

*Contemporary Black Playwrights and Their Plays.* Edited by Bernard L. Peterson, Jr., pp. 505–6. New York: Greenwood, 1988.

*Contemporary Dramatists.* 1988.

*Contemporary Literary Criticism.* Vol. 39 (1985).

*Current Biography* 48 (August 1987): 53.

*Current Biography Yearbook, 1987.* Edited by Charles Moritz, pp. 607–10. New York: Wilson, 1987.

DeVries, Hilary. "A Song in Search of Itself." *American Theater* 3 (January 1987): 22–25.

Dworkin, Norine. "August Wilson Chronicles Blacks Decade by Decade." *Asbury Press-Sun*, 15 April 1990, pp. F1, F6. *Essence*, August 1987, p. 51.

"Exorcising the Demons of Memory." *Time*, 11 April 1988, p. 77.

Freedman, S. G. "A Voice from the Streets." *New York Times Magazine*, 15 May 1987, pp. 36–50.

Grewing, Colleen. "August Wilson." *Where/Washington*, November 1991, pp. 17–19.

Hawley, David. "The Making of a Playwright." *Minnesota Pioneer Press Dispatch*, 26 March 1987, pp. C1–C3.

Henry, William. "Exorcising the Demons of Memory: August Wilson Exults in the Blues and Etches Slavery's Legacy." *Time* (11 April 1988).

Johnson, Malcolm. "Wilson: Acclaim Doesn't Alter His Mission." *Hartford Courant*, 28 April 1985, pp. F5–F7.

Kowinski, William. "The Play Looks Good on Paper—But Will It Fly?" *Smithsonian*, March 1992, pp. 78–87.

Livingston, Sandra. "August Wilson: Regards from Broadway." *MPLS/St. Paul* 13 (September 1985): 184.

Mirsky, Jennifer. "The Natural Voice." *Yale Daily News*, December 1987, pp. 8–9.

*New York Newsday*, 20 April 1987, p. 47.

*New York Times*, 22 October 1984, p. 12.

*New York Times Magazine*, 15 March 1987, p. 36.

*Newsday*, 7 October 1984, p. 7.

O'Neill, Michael C. "August Wilson." In *American Playwrights Since 1945*, edited by Philip Kolin, pp. 518–27. New York: Greenwood, 1989.

Pointsett, Alex. "August Wilson: Hottest New Playwright." *Ebony* 43 (November 1987): 68.

Reed, Ishmael. "In Search of August Wilson." Connoisseur 217 (March 1987): 92–97.

Rosenburg, David. "From Poet to Playwright." *Fairpress,* 29 March 1990, p. D3.

Rothstein, Mervyn. "Round Five for the Theatrical Heavyweight." *New York Times,* 15 April 1990, pp. 1–8.

Rush, Theresa Gunnels, Carol Fairbanks Myers, and Ester Spring Arata. *Black American Writers Past and Present,* 2: 779. Metuchen, N.J.: Scarecrow, 1975.

Shannon, Sandra. "August Wilson." *Encyclopedia of World Biography: 20th Century Supplement,* edited by David Eggenberger, 17: 563–65.

Staples, Brent. "Spotlight: August Wilson." *Essence* 18 (August 1987): 50–51.

Stayton, Richard. "August Wilson Lets His Characters Go." *Los Angeles Herald Examiner,* 31 May 1987, pp. C2–C4.

Vaughan, Peter. "The History of August Wilson: His Plays Are Drawn from a Deeper Well than His Own Experience." *Minneapolis Star Tribune,* 22 April 1990, pp. F1–F9.

———. "Wilson's Prize Stories Come from His Past." *Minneapolis Star Tribune,* 18 April 1987, p. C8.

Winn, Steven. "Playwright August Wilson Forges an African Identity for the American Stage." *San Francisco Examiner,* 8 February 1987, pp. C5–C7.

WILSON-RICHARDS COLLABORATION

Backalenick, Irene. "Fine-Tuning the Piano Lesson: An Interview with Lloyd Richards." *Theater Week,* 16–22 April 1990, pp. 16–19.

———. "A Lesson from Lloyd Richards: Subtle Imposition over Auteurist Vision." *Theater Week,* 16 April 1990, pp. 17–19.

Cole, Gloria. "Theater-Maker at Yale: Lloyd Richards Is Stepping Down But Leaving a Rich Legacy Behind." *Fairpress,* 21 June 1990, p. 20.

DeVries, Hilary. "Drama Lesson." *Boston Globe Magazine,* 24 June 1990, p. 20.

Erstein, Hap. "Richards, Wilson Team Up on Prize Dramas." *Washington Times,* 8 November 1991, pp. E1, E5.

Freedman, Samuel. "Leaving His Imprint on Broadway." *New York Times,* 22 November 1987.

Friedman, Rosalind. "A Pairing of Great Talents at the Yale Rep." *Commentary, WMNR Fine Arts 88.1 FM,* 23 November 1987.

Gussow, Mel. "Fine-Tuning 'The Piano Lesson.'" *New York Times Magazine,* 10 September 1989, p. 18.

Killen, Tom. "Black Theater Triumphant: A Dynamic Duo from the Yale Repertory." *The World and I* (December 1987): 236–39.

Matousek, Mark. "Sure Bets." *Harpers Bazaar*, April 1990.

Migler, R. "An Elegant Duet." *Gentleman's Quarterly* 60 (April 1990): 114.

Rosenfeld, Megan. "Yale Dynamo of Drama." *Washington Post*, 11 November 1990, pp. G1–G10.

Shannon, Sandra. "From Lorraine Hansberry to August Wilson: An Interview with Lloyd Richards." *Callaloo* 14 (Winter 1991): 124–35.

White, F. "Drama Dean Lloyd Richards: Center Stage on Broadway and at Yale." *Ebony* 40 (January 1985): 86–90.
   Traces Richards's career up to opening of *Ma Rainey*.

## ABOUT PLAYS

CRITICISM

Barbour, David. "August Wilson's Here to Stay." *Theater Week*, 18–25 April 1988, pp. 8–14.
   Dispels three misconceptions about Wilson: that plays require actual historical research, that he deliberately follows the tradition of great American playwrights, and that he approaches each play with a prearranged plan. Excellent analysis of *Joe Turner*.

Ching, Mei-Ling. "Wrestling against History." *Theater* 19 (Summer/Fall 1988): 70–71.
   Analysis of *Piano Lesson* identifies blending of Christianity and African cosmology as the source of its spiritual landscape. Same holds true for other plays.

Glover, Margaret. "Two Notes on August Wilson: The Songs of a Marked Man." *Theater* 19 (Summer/Fall 1988): 69–70.
   Uncovers a recurring paradox in Wilson's plays: "Music gave the black man a place in the white man's world, but at the cost of losing his right to that music and the part of himself he put in it." Demonstrates tendency in several characters directly or indirectly affected by music.

Harrison, Paul C. "August Wilson's Blues Poetics." In *August Wilson: Three Plays*. Pittsburgh: University of Pittsburgh Press, 1991.
   Situates Wilson's work squarely within the African American blues tradition. Discusses his efforts to sustain the "African continuum."

Rosenburg, David. "From Poet to Playwright: August Wilson's Cycle of Plays Chronicle and Explore the Black Experience." *Fairpress*, 29 March 1990, p. D3.
   Defends Wilson's use of history as a catalyst for "our own memories set against a collective background."

Rothstein, Mervyn. "Round Five for the Theatrical Heavyweight." *New York Times*, 15 April 1990, 1–8.

*Piano Lesson*'s Broadway opening occasions biographical piece and informative treatment of Wilson's artistic agenda.

Shannon, Sandra. "Conversing with the Past: August Wilson's *Joe Turner's Come and Gone* and *The Piano Lesson.*" *CEA-Magazine: The Journal of the College English Association.* Middle English Group 4 (Fall 1991): 33–41.

Argues that "[by] inviting contemporary African-American audiences to experience the emotional and psychological milieu of their ancestors, [Wilson] encourages renewed interaction, communion, and, ultimately, conversations with their past." Discusses *Joe Turner's Come and Gone* and *The Piano Lesson* to support her premise.

———. "The Fences That They Build: August Wilson's Portrayal of African-American Women." *Obsidian II: Black Literature in Review* 6 (Summer 1991): 1–17.

Argues against the label "victim" and asserts that Wilson's African American women exhibit power through their choices.

———. "The Good Christian's Come and Gone: The Shifting Role of Religion in August Wilson's Plays." *MELUS: The Journal of the Society for the Study of Multi-Ethnic Literature of the United States* 16 (Fall 1989–90): 127–42.

Demonstrates how Wilson's belief that "God does not hear the prayers of black people" influences consistent portrayals of black men as blasphemers and nonbelievers.

———. "The Long Wait: August Wilson's *Ma Rainey's Black Bottom.*" *Black American Literature Forum* 25 (Spring 1991): 151–62.

Establishes a correlation between the sluggish pace of play and its thematic message, underscoring a pattern of economic and political stagnation among blacks in America. Offers structural explanation for decision to deemphasize Ma Rainey and focus upon her band members instead.

Smith, Philip E. "Ma Rainey's Black Bottom: Playing the Blues as Equipment for Living." *Within the Dramatic Spectrum: The University of Florida Department of Classics Comparative Drama Conference Papers* 6 (1986): 177–86.

Argues that *Ma Rainey's Black Bottom* is an enactment of the blues temperament as a form of survival for blacks. "Wilson's characters present American blacks' strategies for survival and their dissemination of attitudes toward exploitation by means of playing the blues, singing the blues, telling the blues, and living the blues."

Wilde, Lisa. "Reclaiming the Past: Narrative and Memory in August Wilson's 'Two Trains Running.'" *Theater* 22 (Fall/Winter 1990–91): 73–74.

Observes that Wilson dredges up characters and their circumstances from "his own memory" and thus saves their "stories from obscurity."

REVIEWS OF INDIVIDUAL PLAYS

### *Ma Rainey's Black Bottom*

Aronson, Jeffrey. "Ma Rainey Stunning in Emotional Drama." *Fairpress*, 25 April 1984.

Aubrey, Dan. "'Ma Rainey'—A Hit in the Making." *Evening Times*, 28 September 1984.

"August Wilson Has Hit in London." *New York Times*, 27 November 1989.
    Play's success at London's Royal National Theater. Now Wilson is confident "that his message and characters transcend borders."

Banciforte, Richard. "'Ma Rainey's Black Bottom.'" *Good Times*, 23 October– 5 November 1984.
    Straightforward but not overly laudatory appraisal of *Ma Rainey's Black Bottom*'s Broadway run.

Barnes, Clive. "'Ma Rainey'—The Black Experience." *New York Post*, 12 October 1984.
    "An essentially political play" with excessive explanations and abrupt, rather predictable ending.

Baxter, Robert. "A 500-Event Season at Annenberg Center." *Courier-Post*, 23 September 1984, pp. 1, 5.
    Play praised as kind the Annenberg Center looks for—about "important social issues."

———. "'Ma Rainey' Explores Blacks' Tortured Search for Identity." *Courier-Post*, 24 September 1984, p. 6C.
    Review of Philadelphia opening. Notes abundance of anger and sees "long first act" as "padded." Praises Charles Dutton for portrayal of Levee.

Beaufort, John. *Christian Science Monitor*, 16 October 1984, p. 31.
    Glowing appraisal of Broadway opening, commending Theresa Merritt's portrayal of legendary blues singer.

Berman, Paul. "Review of *Ma Rainey's Black Bottom*." *Nation* 239 (8 December 1984): 626–28.
    Sensitive analysis of play as another in a long line of "black music stories, a dialectical exercise between bias and bigotry."

Blank, Ed. "Cast Is Solid in Broadway's 'Ma Rainey's.'" *Pittsburgh Press*, 27 November 1984.
    Notes undeniable naturalism, flawed structure, and overreliance upon "anecdotes and reminiscences."

Blumenthal, Eileen. "True Blues." *Village Voice*, 23 October 1984.
    "Clever" structure but simplistic formula: "childhood trauma-plus-new-betrayal-equals-psychotic explosion."

Brown, Carol. "Big Hit: Play Spawned at O'Neill Center Gets Rave Reviews on Broadway." *New London Day*, 8 November 1984, pp. 1, 16.
Play's progress from the O'Neill to Broadway, with brief conversation between Brown and Wilson.

Brown, Rob. "'Ma Rainey' Is Sad, Angry, Powerful." *Briston/Valley Press*, 13 April 1984.
Too much time developing a communal bond among musicians and not enough streamlining the content; Ma Rainey is vaguely drawn, despite Theresa Merritt's hard work; play exudes sadness and anger about hopeless circumstances for African Americans of the 1920s.

Bushnell, Scott. "Playwright Wilson's Work on Blues Makes Debut." *The Hour*, Norwalk, 11 April 1984, p. 17.
Chronicles three-month behind-the-scenes work by Richards and Wilson, leading to inclusion in 1984 Yale Rep's spring program. Wilson's background also covered.

Butterfield, John. "Angry and Eloquent: *Ma Rainey's Black Bottom*." *Rutgers Daily Targum*, 25 October 1984, p. 5.

Campbell, James. "American Soul." *Times Literary Supplement*, 3–9 November 1989.
Indicts Wilson for stereotyping the police and record producers; band members lack decent lines and play hides behind the gimmick of having a band onstage.

Campbell, Mary. "Merritt Sings 'Those Nasty Blues' in 'Ma Rainey's Black Bottom.'" *Greenfield Recorder*, 3 October 1984.
Merritt reminisces about parallels between her own life and Ma Rainey's; chronicles her struggle to raise a family and pursue a singing and acting career.

———. "Theresa Merritt Takes 'Ma' from Yale to Broadway." *New London Day*, 30 September 1984.
Merritt expresses concern over "nasty suggestive lyrics" she would have to sing as Ma Rainey; focuses upon Merritt's background and decision to play the lead.

Caruso, Michael. "'Ma Rainey': A Strong If Flawed New Play." *Main Line Times* (Philadelphia), 27 September 1984, p. 17.
Wilson fails "to establish a single mode of communication. . . . Too frequently he relies upon humor."

Christiansen, Richard. "Broadway Awaits 'Ma Rainey.'" *Sunday Post*, 23 September 1984, pp. D1, D7.
Draws parallels between *Ma Rainey's Black Bottom* and *A Raisin in the Sun* (1959). Describes Wilson's measures to improve upon dialogue.

———. "New Playwright Ignites with 'Ma Rainey's Black Bottom.'" *Chicago Tribune*, 15 October 1984, p. 1–2.
Cousin to such dramas as *A Raisin in the Sun, Dutchman, Blues for Mr. Charlie*,

and *A Soldier's Play*; "striking beauty of both its literary and theatrical poetry" best distinguishes it from the pack.

Cole, Gloria. "Rep's 'Ma Rainey': 'Stunning, Haunting Theater.'" *Fairfield Citizen News*, 19 April 1984.
Yearns for more of Ma Rainey's music and less rhetoric.

Collins, William. "'Ma Rainey' Owes a Debt to an Influential Reviewer." *Philadelphia Inquirer*, 15 October 1984.
Suggests Frank Rich's rave reviews of the Yale Rep's rendition of *Ma Rainey's Black Bottom* controlled Broadway reception; emphasizes politics of reception.

Day, Richard. "A New Playwright Makes Auspicious Debut at Yale." *Bridgeport Post*.
"Textbook example of the playwright's art"; lessons include the causal equations of black-on-black violence and reasons the illiterate fear and/or hate the better educated among their race.

Dickey, Michelle. "*Ma Rainey's Black Bottom* at the Yale Rep: Even the Musical Novice Will Like This One." *Old Lyme Gazette*, 12 April 1984, p. 9.

Drake, Sylvie. "'Rainey': A Verbal Jam Session." *Los Angeles Times*, 24 November 1984, pp. 1, 3.
"Freshest old-fashioned play to hit Broadway since *Ceremonies in Dark Old Men*."

Feldberg, Robert. "'Ma Rainey' Makes Memorable Drama." *Record*, 12 October 1984, p. 7.
"Rebuttal to those who say that contemporary American playwrights are obsessed with narrow, personal concerns"; points out Wilson's focus upon what whites have done to blacks and upon "what oppression causes blacks to do to blacks."

Fisher, John. "'Ma Rainey's' Statement Needs Some Refinement." *Buck County Courier Times*, 26 September 1984.
Commends Wilson's ability to let audiences in on the lives of Ma's band members yet criticizes imbalance in beefy portrayals of Toledo and Levee and limited development of Ma Rainey.

Freedman, Samuel. "The Debt That Black Writers Owe to Jazz and the Blues." *International Herald Tribune*, 22 October 1984, p. 16. Same material as in "What Black Writers Owe to Music."

———. "A Playwright Talks about the Blues." *New York Times*, 13 April 1984, p. C3.
Describes Wilson's work in terms of Ralph Ellison, Langston Hughes, Richard Wright, Amiri Baraka, and Louis Armstrong. "Wilson has made the blues a metaphor, or, more precisely, several metaphors for black life."

———. "What Black Writers Owe to Music." *New York Times*, 14 October 1984, 1–17.

Explores affiliation with the blues tradition: "Black music tends to be both spiritual and political."

Gale, William K. "'Ma Rainey' Actors Say Play's Racism Is Real." *Providence Rhode Island Journal*, 17 January 1988, pp. B8–B9.

Actors who play Cutler, Toledo, Slow Drag, and Levee recall incidents in their own lives that parallel struggles of Wilson's characters.

———. "'Ma Rainey': A Beautiful Telling of the Truth. *Providence Sunday Journal*, 27 January 1985.

Ponders how "truthful" play makes it to Broadway in 1984.

Gerard, Jeremy. "Broadway Sings the Blues." *Dallas Morning News*, 15 October 1984, pp. F1, F2.

Interesting labeling of the play structure as blues: "a schematic pattern wherein the arguments are set like a theme and variations."

Gill, Brendan. "Hard Times." *New Yorker*, 22 October 1984, p. 152.

Play's awkwardness similar to that of Williams's *The Glass Menagerie*; suggests its transcendent brilliance.

Gittelsohn, John. "Play Swings to Jazz Strains." *Burlington Free Press*, 24 April 1984, p. D1.

Goff, Paul. "'Ma Rainey' States the Obvious about Blacks' Blues." *North Penn Reporter*, 26 September 1984.

Singles out blues as play's pivotal theme; criticizes Wilson's preference for telling rather than showing.

Gordon, Ronni. "'Ma Rainey' Hits Rock Bottom at Yale Rep." *Morning Union*, 10 April 1984, p. 21.

Groome, Clark. "A New Play That Knows How to Sing the Blues." *Chesnutt Hill Local* (Philadelphia), 27 September 1984, p. 39.

Gross, Charles. "Blacks on the Great White Way." *Press Journal/Valley Star*, 29 November 1984, p. 8.

Gunner, Marjorie. "On and Off Broadway." *New York Voice*, 20 October 1984.

Ending not artificial; final scene "throws a searing flashback light on the whole Black experience in America, like a look back in a dark tunnel."

Harris, Mark. "Wilson's 'Ma Rainey': Blues and Bluster." *After Hours*, 13 April 1984, p. 2.

Views play through a prism of Jewish experience during the holocaust, concluding that it tells an oft-repeated story of oppression without a new angle.

———. "A Writer's First Work Gets a Rep Production." *After Hours*, 13 April 1984.

Reflects a recent conversation with Wilson, revealing his focus upon "social dislocation" and his belief that "it's important for young blacks in America to see that their lives are just as serious and as important as yours are."

Haun, Harry. "Staging Black Lives: On and Off-Broadway, Playwright Struggle to Bring Form to Experience." *Daily News*, 2 December 1984.
Play did not scare away Broadway white audiences as had been predicted by critics after Yale Repertory Theater run.

Heinz, Mona. "Ma Rainey and the Journey of the Blues." *Center Stage: A Theater's Journal* 3 (Fall 1990): 2–3.
Collection of memorabilia surrounding Ma Rainey and her contributions to blues, including excerpt from Sandra Lieb's *Mother of the Blues*, excerpt of "One-Way Ticket" by Langston Hughes, excerpt from LeRoi Jones's *Blues People*, and extensive chronology of Gertrude Pridgett "Ma" Rainey.

Henry, William. "They Defied the Doom Sayers: Three Unlikely Survivors on Broadway Reap Tony Nomination." *Time*, 20 May 1985, p. 87.
Ponders play's potential for success.

Hess, Evelyn A. "Zellerbach Hosts Local Premiere of 'Ma Rainey's Black Bottom.'" Periodical title and page unavailable on newsclip.
Yearns for more actual blues numbers; emphasizes play's mixture of humor and actual performance to temper emphasis upon racial issues in the 1920s recording industry.

Hill, Holly. "Brilliant Drama, Bitter Irony." *London Times*, 6 November 1984.
Adopts Euripides's *The Trojan Women* as frame of reference for play and briefly alludes to *A Raisin in the Sun*.

Hogrefe, Jeffrey. "On Broadway." *Washington Post*, 23 October 1984, p. C7.
Favorable review.

Hummler, Richard. Review of "Ma Rainey's Black Bottom." *Variety*, 17 October 1984, p. 156.
Sensitive assessment noting "over-reliance on reminiscences of past events that the audience cannot experience and contrivances that challenge credibility for plot expedience."

Isaacs, Robert. "You Don't Get 'Ma Rainey,' But Play Has Good Moments." *Waterbury Republican*, 13 April 1984.
Disappointed that play is not about Ma Rainey.

Johnson, Malcolm. "Ma Rainey's Burning, Visceral Attack on American Racism." *Hartford Courant*, 7 April 1984, p. 1.
Sensitive and informative review of premiere at Yale Repertory Theater.

———. "'Ma Rainey' Cuts to Bitter Heart of Chicago Blues." *Hartford Courant*, 8 April 1984, p. B15. Reprinted in Saturday *Courant*.
Brief sensitive review of Yale Repertory opening; play is "burning visceral attack on American racism" as it "cuts to the heart and soul of the blues, and [lays] bare the humiliations of blacks at the hands of white America."

———. "Yale Rep's 'Ma Rainey' Withstands Broadway Test." *Hartford Courant*, 21 October 1984.

Notes very few changes in cast as play opened on Broadway; observes transitions are still difficult because of upscaled emotions and more "fun and games" in the Broadway production.

Kaplan, D. A. "Blues Age Featured in Yale Rep Drama." *Evening Sentinel*, 13 April 1984.

Katz, Judi. "Review of *Ma Rainey's Black Bottom*: Yale Repertory Theater." *WYBC Current Attractions*, 14 April 1984.
Radio review highlights Wilson's use of "humor, music and heavy drama to make his points."

Kauffmann, Stanley. "Bottoms Up." *Saturday Review* 11 (January/February 1985): 83, 90.
Central flaw is that play "is split figuratively, just as the set is split literally, between the musicians and the star."

Kaufman, David. "Been Down So Long It Looks Like Down to Us." *Aquarian Weekly*, 31 October 1984, p. 11.
Kaufman praises play at the expense of Michael Bennett's *Dream Girls*.

Keezing, Henry. "'Ma Rainey' Stunning Drama." *Herald*, 13 April 1984.
Sensitive to Wilson's depiction of whites as "heavies" in the Yale Rep opening; provides background for the play's title and Ma's theme song.

Kemper, Steve. "Shuck and Jive." *New Haven Advocate*, 18 April 1984, p. 29.
Characters, like Chekhov's, do not change but "fill out" as their characters slowly transform into allegorical representatives of their culture.

Killens, Tom. "Playwright Busy Even without Play." *New Haven Register*.

Kissell, Howard. Review of "Ma Rainey's Black Bottom." *Women's Wear Daily*, 12 October 1984, p. 200.
Notes sharp and poignant dialogue and avoidance of jargon.

Kroll, Jack. "So Black and Blue." CIV *Newsweek*, 22 October 1984, p. 106.
Excellent account of the profound emotions of black musicians and relevance of the blues to their torment.

Kuchwara, Michael. "'Ma Rainey' Goes from Yale to Broadway." *New London Day*, 3 October 1984.

Lang, Joel. "Lloyd Richards: The Quiet Man of the Theater." *Hartford Courant*, 7 October 1984, pp. 12–19.

Leiter, Robert. Review of *Ma Rainey's Black Bottom*. *Hudson Review* 38 (Summer 1985): 299–300.
Finds Ma Rainey's talk superfluous and plot manufactured: "Wilson should have trusted his metaphoric imagination more and used the blues to comment on the action."

Le Sourd, Jacques. "Blues Takes Backseat in 'Ma Rainey's Black Bottom.'" *Gannett Westchester Newspapers*, 12 October 1984, pp. C1, C4.
Points out Wilson's method of "fictionalizing a genuine historical character" in

order to comment upon the black experience in America, and notes wellspring of black theater to come from Yale since Richards became Dean.

Lesser, Ruth. "Yale Rep's 'Ma Rainey': Effective, But Needs Focus." *Journal Courier*, 11 April 1984, pp. 30, 31.

Levine, Roslyn. "'Black Bottom' Gives Peek at Blues Culture." *Daily Pennsylvanian*.

"Ma Rainey's Black Bottom." *Variety*, 18 April 1984, p. 224.

Review of Yale Rep opening notes the overwriting in excessively long rehearsal scene, points to "verbal riffs and flourishes" of band members, and regrets failure to emphasize Ma Rainey's character more.

"Ma Rainey's Black Bottom by August Wilson at Yale Rep." *Weston Forum*, 24 April 1984.

Explains play's deceptive displacement of Ma Rainey through a band member's comments: "She didn't have to sing any words. She would just moan, and the audience would moan with her."

"'Ma Rainey's Black Bottom' Is a Winner on Broadway." *Jet*, 12 November 1984, pp. 62, 64.

"A heavy hard-hitting drama mixed lightly with a few blues tunes."

McNally, Owen. "Wilson's 'Ma Rainey' to Open on Broadway." *Hartford Courant*, 16 September 1984.

Mitgang, Herbert. "Wilson, From Poetry to Broadway Success." *New York Times*, 22 October 1984.

An insider's view at what it feels like for Wilson as a relatively unknown playwright coming to Broadway. Mitgang interviews Wilson and Richards in the seventy-two-year-old Cort Theater on Broadway. Wilson gives a detailed account of the conceptualization of Ma Rainey from his head to the page.

Morigi, Gilda. "Broadway Jottings." *American Jewish Life*, 26 October 1984, p. 13.

Praises play and seems baffled that blacks were offended by the repetition of "nigger" and by the play's journey through history back to a scene laden with racist images of their past. "Personally I saw two enormously talented casts of performers and musicians as evoking a bygone era and whatever went with it."

Mullinax, Gary. "'Ma Rainey' Gives Intense Look at Conflicts of Black Americans." *Wilmington* (Del.) *Morning News*, 25 September 1984.

Nelsen, Don. "Splendid Shake-Up." *Playbill*, December 1984, pp. 6–12.

Notes play's ability to shake up audiences rather than entertain them; provides background on play's conception and Wilson's early experiences with the O'Neill Center.

Nelson, Nels. "'Ma Rainey' at the Zellerbach." *Philadelphia Daily News*, 24 September 1984, p. 41.

Minimizes "messy, noisy, excessively verbal, a bit quirky and sometimes unintelligible" plot by calling Wilson a "dramatist of substance"; assesses play's racial turbulence.

Nemirow, Mark. "'Rainey' Generates Explosive Drama." *Chronicle*, 18 October 1984.
Play causes the actors and the audience to become one despite heavy humor of the first act.

Nemy, Enid. "Dutton Identifies with His Role in 'Ma Rainey.'" *New York Times*, 15 October 1984, p. C13.
Biographical piece on Dutton finds striking parallels between Levee and circumstances of his own life.

———. "'Ma Rainey,' A Hit at Yale, Coming to Town in October." *New York Times*, 29 June 1984.
Discusses acquisition of professional personnel for Broadway premiere.

———. "A 'Ma Rainey' Quartet Plays Its Own Special Music." *New York Times*, 28 October 1984, pp. 1, 6.
Commends band in light of its eclectic nature and short real-life rehearsal period.

———. "1985 Target Date for a Play about the O'Neills." *New York Times*, 31 August 1984.
Announces producers.

Newquist, Jay. "When Ma Sang the Blues She Brought Joy to the World." *New Haven Register*, 1 April 1984, pp. D1, D3.
Discusses the real Ma Rainey and sketches biography of Theresa Merritt, who played Ma.

Nourse, Joan T. "'Ma Rainey's' Blues Not Just Music." *Catholic Transcript*, 16 November 1984, p. 12.
Conveys far-reaching implications of the blues in the play.

Paglia, Bob. "'Ma Rainey's Black Bottom' at Yale Repertory Theater." WELI Radio 960 New Haven.
Sees major thematic question in the play as: Should the people be given what they want? Sees Levee and Ma Rainey's clash over her preference for older jug-band music as pivotal.

Palmer, Don. "The Tale of Ma Rainey's Blues." *City Sun*, 17–23 October 1984, pp. 13, 16.
Discusses Wilson's interest in blues, playwright's past, and artistic agenda.

Palmer, Robert. "The Real Ma Rainey Had a Certain Way with the Blues." *New York Times*, 28 October 1984, p. 6.
Excellent discussion of Ma Rainey's relationship with Bessie Smith and others, including Louis Armstrong, Fletcher Henderson, and Coleman Hawkins.

Porterfield, Sally. "'Ma Rainey's Black Bottom' at Yale Rep." *Tarmington Valley Herald* (Simsbury, Connecticut), 12 April 1984.

Insightful, albeit brief, commentary notes the way the play shifts from humor to violence in a matter of moments, and demonstrates "bitter fruits of oppression."

Pronechen, Joseph. "Yale's *Ma Rainey* Hits Bottom." *Trumbull Times*, 12 April 1984.

Regrets play's failure to become a musical.

Pryce, Vinette. "'Ma Rainey's Black Bottom': A Smash Well Worth the Price." *Daily Challenge*, 11 October 1984, pp. 6, 8.

Quinn, Michael. "'Ma Rainey's' New York Triumph." *New Haven Advocate*, 7 November 1984, p. 25.

Comprehensive review including assessment of effect on black viewers as told from the observations of Dutton.

Raidy, William. "'Ma Rainey's Black Bottom': A Dramatically Riveting Play." *Star Ledger*, 12 October 1984.

Traces the history of black employment in America back to the seventeenth century to discuss problems of black commercial enterprises that the play exemplifies; motivated to "sell herself cheap," Ma essentially imitates whites.

———. "Merritt Swings Smoothly from Classic to Bluesy 'Ma Rainey.'" *Sunday Star Ledger*, 11 November 1984.

Summarizes Merritt's life as a wife, mother, and artist.

"Rep Premieres *Ma Rainey's Black Bottom*." *Yale Weekly Bulletin and Calendar*, 9–23 April 1984, pp. 1–2.

Rich, Frank. "Ma Rainey" WQXR, 11 April 1984.

A brief newsclip for radio broadcast sees play as both a "scaborous comedy" and "most devastating American play" since *Raisin in the Sun*.

———. "Ma Rainey's Black Bottom." *New York Times*, 11 April 1984, p. C19.

Discusses *Ma Rainey's Black Bottom* in terms of O'Neill's *The Iceman Cometh* and Miller's *Death of a Salesman*, noting *Ma Rainey's Black Bottom* is "about the black American's search for identity—and it is also about the process by which any American sells his soul for what Arthur Miller calls the salesman's dream." Perceptively analyzes "Ma" Rainey's role as regal, monstrous, and lunatic.

———. "Wilson's 'Ma Rainey's' Open." *New York Times*, October 1984, pp. C1, C3.

Poignantly points out that play is "a seering inside account of what white racism does to its victims." Among the best all-round critiques of the play.

Richards, David. "Look! Ma!: 'Rainey' Brings Life to Tired Broadway." *Washington Post*, 18 November 1984, pp. H1, H4.

Expresses concern about the play's ambivalent focus.

Russell, Joan. "Ma Rainey Premieres at Yale." *Stratford Bard*, 18 April 1984, p. 12.

Cautions potential viewers about profanity yet believes this type of language "added to the high quality of the production."

Ryan, Richard. "'Ma Rainey' Pays Its Dues." *Staten Island Register*, 25 October 1984, p. 16.

Suggests that the blues determine the overall "down" mood of the play.

Schreck, Frank. "'Ma Rainey's Black Bottom.'" *Columbia Daily*, 25 October 1984.

Brief, intelligent, favorable review.

Siegel, Joel. WABC-TV 7, 11 October 1984, in *New York Theater Critics Review* 45 (1984): 200.

Notes Wilson's clever manipulation of place, time, and relationships.

Sikorski, Fran. "Ma Rainey's Beat Good." *Bethel* (Conn.) *Home News*, 18 April 1984.

Explains play's 1927 setting and Gertrude "Ma" Rainey's place in it; also focuses upon ways that technical aspects of the play's production were ironed out.

Simon, John. "'Black Bottom,' Black Sheep." *New York Post*, 22 October 1984, p. 95.

Generally negative review that describes Wilson as a "new black playwright . . . whose promise and provocation bode well, even if what he delivers is only intermittently drama."

Slade, George. "'Ma Rainey's Black Bottom.'" *Stages*, December 1984, p. 35.

Points out both structural and cosmetic changes made for Broadway debut.

Syna, Sy. "'Ma Rainey' Unsettling, Angry Allegorical Play." *New York Tribune*, 12 October 1984.

Sees play as too talkative and static.

Tapley, Mel. "'Ma Rainey's' Reveals Age-Old Struggle of Black Musicians." *Amsterdam News*, 20 October 1984, p. 23.

Explains how Wilson resurrects the tabooed word "nigger" and uses it as an invitation to see and think as these black musicians did in the 1920s. Although wincing at rapid-fire use of the word, Tapley discusses how Wilson uses it to "expose the real pain in the blues through the orchestrated remarks and eruptions."

Taylor, Markland. "Ma Rainey's Black Bottom." *Variety*, 18 April 1984.

Suggests that, as a minor figure, Ma Rainey could be eliminated from the play.

———. "'Ma Rainey': Uneven But Disarming." *New Haven Register*, 8 April 1984.

Praises play but calls for "a ruthlessly wielded blue pencil" to edit the "verbal riffs and flourishes"; blames overwriting for the lopsided scene depicting band members' conversations before Ma Rainey arrives; speculates that Wilson's excessive dialogue was used to soften the blow of racial indictments against white racism.

Thomas, Beth. "Yale Stage Has Hit in 'Ma Rainey.'" *New London Day*, 8 April 1984.

Traces development of play from first stage reading at the O'Neill Center; commends play for its "aura of a classic."

Thomas, Don. "A Powerful 'Ma Rainey' Merritt Seems Handpicked for the Role."
    *Big Red News*, 27 October 1984, p. 18.
    Praises play for not being a musical with blacks resigned to singing and dancing.
Tighe, Mary Ann. "A Rough, Raw, Jazz-filled Drama Makes It to Broadway on
    Ecstatic Word-of-Mouth." *Vogue*, October 1984, p. 95.
    Notes gamble Broadway backers face staging a black drama but thinks play will
    overcome this discouraging trend because of its word-of-mouth potential.
"Two World Premieres in New Haven." New from WMNR Fine Arts 88.1 FM
    *Theater Circuit/Broadcast*, 10–17 April 1984, pp. 1–4.
    Though largely impressed, the reviewer objects to Ma Rainey's depictions as
    unnecessarily mean and stereotyping of Jews as cheats.
Viagas, Robert. "'Black Bottom' and the Blues." *Fairpress*, 18 April 1984, p. C5.
    Considers Wilson's play "a particularly black story" and commends him for
    being "cynical without being depressing and [provoking] outrage without
    turning off the audience."
Wallach, Alan. "Ma Rainey: A Rich Experience." *Newsday*, 12 October 1984.
    Praises Wilson for being both entertaining and informing.
Watt, Douglass. "'Ma Rainey's': Mostly, It Swings." *Daily News*, New York, 12
    October 1984. Reprinted in *New York Theater Critics' Reviews* 45 (17 September
    1984):197.
    Believes play is "padded . . . though vivid, slice-of-life" that "marks time."
Weiss, Hedy. "'Rainey' Pours Out Black Men's Tale." *Chicago Sun Times*, 15
    January 1988.
    Underscores emphasis on musicians "as both valiant survivors and sacrificial
    victims."
White, Ellen. "Black Pride Won and Lost in Turbulent 'Ma Rainey.'" *New Haven
    Register*, 4 November 1984.
    Sees focus to be on "the use and abuse of power that talent brings, the backlash
    of oppression and self expression in the world of musical blues," with Ma Rainey
    as both tyrant and victim.
Williams, Ed. "Ma Rainey's Black Bottom: A Moving Portrayal of Times Gone
    By." *Scoop USA* (Philadelphia), 28 September 1984, p. 9.
    Praises Philadelphia production, noting, "It validates our black roots in America
    and demands we squeeze the very marrow out of them."
Wilson, Edwin. "On Broadway: Ma Rainey and Kipling." *Wall Street Journal*, 16
    October 1984, p. 26.
    Effectively uses the common sheet music phrase "vamp until ready" to
    characterize play's "abundance of atmosphere and banter and strong racial
    statement" but lack of substance and plot.
Winer, Linda. "'Ma Rainey' Gifted Storyteller's Debut." *USA Today*, 12 October
    1984, p. 4D.

Concludes that the unique work is "a drama with music" that lacks a strong overall plot.

Winship, Frederick. "'Ma Rainey's Black Bottom' Opens on Broadway." *Daily Challenge*, 15 October 1984, p. 6.

Apologetically labels the play "more a polemic than a drama."

Wood, Frank. "'Ma Rainey' Powerful Play about the Blues." *Daily Record* (New Jersey), 12 October 1984, p. 24.

Notes Broadway audiences were surprised to find, in place of "an evening of nostalgia and jazz," a riveting commentary on racism in the 1920s recording industry.

### *Joe Turner's Come and Gone*

Aucoin, Don. "Playwright Adds to His Cycle of Black History in America." *Boston Sunday Globe*, 11 May 1986, pp. 83, 86.

Yale Rep opening occasions another of a series of biographical looks at August Wilson.

Barbour, David. "August Wilson's Here to Stay: The Innovative Playwright Has a Genius for the Unexpected." *Theater Week*, 18–25 April 1988, pp. 8–14.

Clarifies misconceptions about August Wilson regarding historical research, influence on American playwrights, grand design of his work, impact of Lloyd Richards, and pressure that his success places upon him.

Barnes, Clive. "O'Neill in Blackface." *New York Post*, 28 March 1988.

Notes elements of O'Neill and Ibsen but stresses, "The idiom is the black theater, as is the language and the form."

Beaufort, John. "New Chapter in Wilson Saga of Black Life." *Christian Science Monitor*, 30 March 1988.

Thinks play has "moved beyond the conventional 'race play'. . . crimes of Joe Turner presented as part of the pattern of subjugation that black Americans have historically endured."

Bernstein, Richard. "August Wilson's Voice from the Past." *New York Times*, 27 March 1988, pp. 1, 34.

Discusses Wilson's dependence upon images and voices from his past; play inspired by Bearden collage.

Brown, Joe. "Staging the Black Experience: Playwright August Wilson and the Persistence of Vision." *Washington Post*, 4 October 1987, p. F1.

Reviews Wilson's early life in Pittsburgh and struggle for recognition as playwright; explains attraction to "old guys."

Carr, John C. "Pulitzer Prize Winner Brings His Stories to Arena." *Sunday Capital*, 4 October 1987, p. E9.

Favorable review of opening at Washington, D.C.'s Arena Stage with related interview.

Cohen, Ron. "'Joe Turner.'" *Women's Wear Daily*, 30 March 1988.
    Very favorable review.

Cole, Gloria. "Mysticism of Africa at Yale Rep." *Westport News*, 9 May 1986. Same review appears in *Fairfield Citizen News*, 14 May 1986, with the title "Yale Rep's 'Joe Turner'—Provocative Yet Elusive."
    Raises a unique criticism of *Joe Turner*'s enigmatic nature. Lack of objectivity prevents Wilson and Richards from editing the play or making it clearer.

Day, Richard. "A Coupla Black Folks Sitting Around Talking." *New England Newsclip*, 8 May 1986.
    Calls for improvements needed after Yale Rep premiere; identifies "verbosity, fragmentation and lack of logical progression to a meaningful solution."

Disch, Thomas. Review of *Joe Turner's Come and Gone*. *Nation*, 12 December 1987, 725–27.
    Considers boardinghouse setting "an ideal milieu for a well-made play" and "a microcosm of post-lapsarian, dog-eat-dog life."

"Dramaturgy in America: August Wilson's 'Joe Turner's Come and Gone.'" *Theater Magazine* 17 (1986): 3.

Erstein, Hap. "'Joe Turner' Is a Piece in the Puzzle of Identity." *Washington Times*, 9 October 1987, pp. E1, E10.
    Finds parallels "too close" to *Ma Rainey* but recognizes "a more matured writer, confident enough to experiment with less realistic events and more complex themes."

Fetherston, Drew. "Pinning 'Joe Turner's' Hopes on the Tony's." *New York Newsday*, 31 May 1988, pp. 7, 11.
    Notes that good reviews did not produce good run in New York.

"Flesh-and-Blood Icons." *America* 158 (16 April 1988): 410, 414.
    Sees characters as "flesh-and-blood icons of vanished generations and of racial memory" and entire play as "lyrical tragedy, a volcanic hymn to the human spirit."

Funsten, Ted. "Wilson's 'Joe Turner' at the Yale Rep." *Middletown Press*, 9 May 1986, pp. 7, 9.
    Conditionally admires play despite playwright's overburdening characters to convey an epiclike story line.

Gerard, Jeremy. "Broadway Is Offering Black Theater-Goers More Reason to Go." *New York Times*, 29 March 1988, p. C13.
    Black dramas, especially plays with serious themes, bring blacks into the theater.

Greenleaf, Jim. "'Joe Turner': Strong Story of Migrants." *Bristol Press*, 9 May 1986.

Hulbert, Dan. "'Joe Turner' Explores the Freedom that Binds." *Atlanta Journal and Constitution*, 1 November 1987.

Discusses Wilson's chances of completing his proposed cycle of plays, expressing reservation about Wilson's attempt to "connect 'Joe Turner' to the themes of his other plays: the need for blacks to reunite their families ('Fences') and to find their heritage."

Israel, Bob. "Joe Turner's Come and Gone: The Song of a People." *Rhode Island Herald*, 21–26 May 1986, p. 12.
Favorable review of Yale Rep opening.
Johnson, Malcolm. "Yale Rep's 'Joe Turner' Develops Slowly." *Hartford Courant*, 3 May 1986.
Points out some parallels with *Ma Rainey*—in particular, scenes in which characters rail against the white man's religion and take part in rituals of violent bloodletting; provides sensitive analysis of *Joe Turner*'s purposefully slow-building plot.
Killen, Tom. "Black Theater Triumphant: A Dynamic Duo from the Yale Repertory." *The World and I*, December 1987.
Focuses upon the Wilson-Richards collaboration that brought *Joe Turner's Come and Gone* to San Diego's Old Globe Theater.
Kirton, Wesley. "August Wilson Prepares for Arena Opening of *Joe Turner's Come and Gone*." *Metro Chronicle*, 1 October 1987.
Kissel, Howard. "The Reunion Rag." *Daily News*, 28 March 1988.
Points out noticeable absence of jazz reference despite the popularity of ragtime during the period.
Kleiman, Dena. "'Joe Turner,' The Spirit of Synergy." *New York Times*, 19 May 1986.
Richards tries to convince Wilson that audience needs to witness Loomis's quest for identity. Discusses dynamics of Wilson-Richards relationship.
Kroll, Jack. "August Wilson's Come to Stay." *Newsweek*, 11 April 1988, p. 324.
Thinks play is Wilson's "best play to date and a profoundly American one"; provides background on the playwright and explores briefly Wilson's creative process in writing play.
Lesser, Ruth. "With More Work 'Joe Turner' Could Succeed." *Journal-Courier*, 5 May 1986, p. 14.
Analyzes the play's cast and notes its need for "further development and fusion before the play can peak."
Marshall, Michael. "Spiritual Odyssey: August Wilson's *Joe Turner's Come and Gone*." *The World and I*, December 1987, pp. 240–41.
Sensitive analysis of the sufferings of *Joe Turner*'s characters.
Novick, Julius. "Wilson's 'Joe Turner': Good Intentions Unfulfilled." *New York Observer*, 18 April 1988.
Questions point of Loomis's self-scarification.
Oliver, Edith. "Boarding-House Blues." *New Yorker*, 11 April 1988, p. 107.

Rich, Frank. "Cutting to the Heart of the Way We Live." *New York Times*, 25 December 1988, p. H5.

Tribute in year-end wrap-up of 1988's theater season that places play in the company of others about the homeless.

———. "Panoramic History of Blacks in America in Wilson's 'Joe Turner.'" *New York Times*, 28 March 1988.

Observes that play is most significant in "what the characters do not say" and sees . . . thrust to be in [deciphering] the history that is dramatized in images and actions beyond the reach of logical narrative."

———. "Theater: 'Joe Turner' at Yale Rep." *New York Times*, 6 May 1986.

Regards the play as "its author's finest achievement yet."

Richards, David. "The Tortured Spirit of 'Joe Turner.'" *Washington Post*, 9 October 1987, pp. B1, B12.

Feels that Wilson stretches the naturalistic setting to suit his flight into the mystical.

Rousuck, J. Wynn. "August Wilson Has Come to Stay." *Sun*, 4 October 1987, pp. 1N, 11N.

Gives sweeping synopsis of Wilson's rise to fame.

———. "Wilson Probes Love and Loss." *Baltimore Sun*.

Review of Arena Stage opening observes that "characters come close to being stripped of their humanity by the obligation to serve the message of the play."

Schaefer, Stephen. "Wilson's Works Sweep USA Theaters." *USA Today*, 2 October 1987.

Underscores Wilson's sweeping national popularity by noting simultaneous productions of several of his works at regional theaters.

Scherer, M. A. "'Turner' Never Comes at All." *Evening Capital*, 13 October 1987.

Negative review of Arena Stage opening.

Sikorski, Fran. "Wilson's Joe Turner Premieres." *Lewisboro Ledger*, 21 May 1986, p. 78.

Smith, Michael. "Cliche Transformed by Poetry of Vision in Yale Rep's Play." *Day*, 19 May 1986, pp. F1, F5.

Considers play "full of love." Notes that play's characters "have an extraordinary sympathy for each other, an awareness of each other's desperations, a supportive communion beneath their differences, and have magical, mythic needs to appease."

Stearns, David. "'Turner' Comes to a Near Halt." *USA Today*, 29 March 1988.

Negative review of Arena Stage opening describes play as "people sitting in a room yelling at each other."

Tallmer, Jerry. "The Writer's 'Lunch Bucket.'" *New York Post*, 23 March 1988, p. 31.

Discusses Wilson's relation to Bearden.

Taylor, Markland. "Joe Turner's Come and Gone." *Variety*, 14 May 1986, p. 94.

Rehashes earlier review.

————. "Premiere Seems a Bit Premature." *New Haven Register*, 4 May 1986, pp. A36, A39.
Harshly criticizes premiere at Yale Rep.

Viagas, Robert. "Dramatic John Henrys Pound Hard to Get Their Due." *New Haven Register* (1 April 1990): B5.
Considers characters equivalent of John Henrys; playwright "raises these homeboy characters to American archetypes."

————. "A Shining Man: August Wilson Creates a New American Legend with Yale Rep's 'Joe Turner's Come and Gone.'" *Fairpress*, 14 May 1986.
Emphasizes the importance of the conjurer Bynum Walker to the play's theme of lost identity.

Watts, Douglass. "Second Thoughts on First Nights." *Daily News*, 8 April 1988.
Credits "Wilson's epic vision, power and poetic sense" with lifting play "to strange and compelling heights."

Wilson, Edwin. "A Major American Playwright." *Wall Street Journal*, 14 October 1987.
Sees the play as further confirmation that Wilson has achieved status as "a major American playwright."

————. "Theater: Will It Play on Broadway?" *Wall Street Journal*, 18 April 1988.
Considers effect of theater size on a play's success and concludes that *Joe Turner* will work in large or small theater.

Winer, Linda. "Joe Turner Enriches Wilson's Cycle." *New York Newsday*, 28 March 1988.
Wilson's play seen as companion piece to Toni Morrison's *Beloved*.

"Yale Rep Presents August Wilson Play." *Compass*, 7 May 1986.
Considers characters to be "refugees within the land," hopelessly displaced from their homes in Africa and America.


*Fences*

Adcock, Joe. "Rep's Richly Realized 'Fences' Stands as a Tribute to Humanity." *Seattle Post Intelligencer*, 21 March 1986, p. 5.
Notes play shifts from "good old-fashioned naturalism" to a "myth of life in black America."

Albrecht, Ernest. "'Fences' Breathes New Life, Humanity into Theater." *Home News*, 27 March 1987, p. 19.
Discusses depth of emotions in Wilson's characters.

Barnes, Clive. "Fiery Fences." *New York Post*, 27 March 1987.
Play demonstrates "what it's like to be a black man of pride and ambition from the South, trying to live and work in the industrial North in the years just before and just after World War II."

Beaufort, John. "'Fences' Probes Life of Blacks in 50's." *Christian Science Monitor,* 27 March 1987.

Commends play's "exceptional depth, eloquence, and power."

Christiansen, Richard. "Artist of the Year: August Wilson's Plays Reveal What It Means to Be Black in This Century." *Chicago Tribune,* 27 December 1987, 13: F8–F10.

Discusses Wilson's continuing refusal to compromise his art by writing Gabriel out of play to suit producer; includes good bio sketch of Wilson.

Collins, William. "Powerful 'Fences' Opens on Broadway." *Philadelphia Inquirer,* 27 March 1987, pp. 1C, 3C.

Discusses excitement in anticipation of Broadway opening.

Curry, Jack. "'Fences' Mends Its Family Conflicts Well." *USA Today,* 27 March 1987.

Measures play against "a black *Death of a Salesman.*"

Dufresne, David. "In Hollywood Dreams Don't Always Pan Out." *Day,* 1 April 1990, pp. F1, F4.

Discusses Wilson's fight with Paramount Pictures to have a black director for film version of play.

Feldberg, Robert. "A Study of Racism's Withering Power." *Record,* 27 March 1987, p. 8.

Considers play "not as gripping or balanced" as *Ma Rainey.*

Fiengold, Michael. "The Fall of Troy." *Village Voice,* 7 April 1987.

Concentrates on the power of Wilson's words.

Freedman, Samuel. "Wilson's New 'Fences' Nurtures a Partnership." *New York Times,* 5 May 1985.

Explains how the Richards-Wilson collaboration works.

Frymer, Murry. "Flawed 'Fences' Rides the Broad Shoulders of James Earl Jones." *San Jose Mercury,* 13 February 1987, pp. 1D, 15D.

Doubts that *Fences* can survive despite James Earl Jones's fine performance.

Gerard, Jeremy. "Waterford to Broadway: Well-Travelled 'Fences.'" *New York Times,* 9 April 1987.

Points out how this play, unlike most, was nurtured every step of the way from New Haven to Broadway.

Greenberg, James. "Did Hollywood Sit on 'Fences'?" *New York Times,* 27 January 1991, pp. 16, 18.

Discusses four-year delay since Paramount purchased rights to *Fences.* Wilson's insistence on having a black director and Paramount's stalemate.

Henderson, Heather. "Building Fences: An Interview with Mary Alice and James Earl Jones." *Theater* 16 (Summer/Fall 1985): 67–70.

Henry, William A. "Righteous in His Own Backyard." *Time,* 6 April 1987.

Believes Wilson is skilled at "making sense of his anger" but feels playwright "asks too much" of the audience to expect them to believe some of the play's scenes. Commends James Earl Jones's performance as Troy.

Jarrett, Vernon. "'Fences' Gives Artful Look at Black Survival." *Chicago Sun Times*, 12 February 1986.
A glowing review of play that resurrects reviewer's childhood experiences living among blacks.

Johnson, Malcolm. "'Fences' Is Riveting at Yale Rep." *Hartford Courant*, 4 May 1985.

Kihn, Martin. "Wilson Builds Second Sturdy 'Fences' at Rep." *Yale Daily News*, 8 May 1985.
Very negative assessment of Yale Rep production as play about "drunks and losers."

Killen, Tom. "A Black Family's Struggle in Wilson Work at Rep." *New Haven Register*, 28 April 1985, p. D1.
Thinks Wilson writes for an audience of one. Candid conversation with playwright.

———. "Wilson Works His Way through Success." *New Haven Register*, 19 July 1987, pp. D1, D4.
Despite acclaim, Wilson wards off the distractions of fame and fortune by sitting at his typewriter doing what he does best.

Kissel, Howard. "One Man's Failure Is Another Man's Smash." *Daily News*, 27 March 1987.
Observes the irony of Troy Maxson's failed life giving Wilson success. Gives much credit to Jones.

Kroll, Jack. "Nine Innings against the Devil." *Newsweek*, 6 April 1987, p. 70.
Praises Jones's performance and commends Wilson as "one of those artists who can turn sincerity into a potent esthetic force."

Kuchwara, Michael. "Billy Dee Williams Breaks into Fences." *New Haven Register*, 21 February 1988, p. D14.
Discusses Williams's replacement of Jones and reveals Williams's background, which primed him for the role.

———. "Convictions of 'Fences' Producer Prove Lucrative." *New Haven Register*, 27 March 1988, p. D14.
Carol Shorenstein reminisces about her $850,000 gamble to sponsor *Fences* on Broadway against the warnings of naysayers who believed the play was not commercial.

Lesser, Ruth. "Yale Rep's Fences Is Well Done." *Journal Courier*, 8 May 1985, p. 44.
Compares *Fences* to *Ma Rainey*, which ran on Broadway when *Fences* opened at the Yale Rep; calls Troy "a man whose dreams are fated to go unfulfilled" and points out parallels to Dr. Faustus and Willie Loman.

Lida, David. "Fences: A Review." *Women's Wear Daily*, 27 March 1987.
Praises Wilson's "ear for language" and criticizes his "achingly melodramatic" plot and talkative characters.

Murphy, Thomas. "Fences Playwright Documents Black Experience." *New Haven Register*, 19 March 1989, p. D3.
A quick run-through of Wilson's vita on the occasion of play's San Francisco premiere.

Muse, Vance. "Building Fences: A Monumental Role for James Earl Jones." *Vanity Fair*, April 1987, p. 23.
Jones considers play important "way to make political statements."

Patrick, Michelle. "An American Voice." *Philip Morris Magazine*, March-April 1989, pp. 40–43.
Discusses saga of Paramount's production of *Fences*, tentatively starring Eddie Murphy as Cory Maxson; provides candid discussion of Wilson's years as a mediocre poet and an anonymous short story writer.

"Playwright August Wilson Working on Next Drama." *Jet*, 21 September 1987, p. 56.
Wilson anxious to begin another script even as *Fences* opens on Broadway.

Rich, Frank. "Family Ties in Wilson's 'Fences.'" *New York Times*, 27 March 1987.
Focuses upon the performances in Broadway production; he thinks Jones "has found the best role of his career" and considers Mary Alice's portrayal of Rose Maxson luminous.

———. "Wilson's 'Fences.'" *New York Times*, 7 May 1985.
Points to the play's 1957 setting as "a deceptively quiet eve" just before the furor of the Civil Rights Movement and race riots of the 1960s; commends Wilson's "monstrous and misdirected" portrayal of Troy but complains that there is little left for the other characters.

Richards, David. "The Powerful Confines of Fences." *Washington Post*, 27 April 1990, pp. D1, D4.
Commends Wilson's ability to raise the daily struggles of one black family to epic proportions; faults ability to sustain "dramatic momentum."

Rosenburg, Scott. "'Fences' Gives a '50s Black Family Poetic Voice." *San Francisco Examiner*, 13 February 1987, pp. D1, D16.
Notes that play does what mainstream American theater ignores—the drama of the African American experience; commends emphasis on voices and stories of individual characters.

Shannon, Sandra. "'Fences': August Wilson's Family Portrait." *America's Arena*, 8 June 1990, pp. 3–5.
Discusses *Fences* as domestic drama situated in the tradition of such classics as *Death of a Salesman*, *Long Day's Journey into Night*, and *Awake and Sing*.

Siegel, Joel. WABC-TV 7, 26 March 1987. *New York Theater Critics Reviews* 48 (1987): 321.

Staples, Brent. "'Fences': No Barrier to Emotion." *New York Times*, 5 April 1987, pp. 1, 39.

Notes audience reaction, especially in the second act when Rose strikes Troy, and discusses play from a black perspective, having grown up in an area similar to that which the play depicts.

Tallmer, Jerry. "Fences: Anguish of Wasted Talent." *New York Post*, 26 March 1987, p. C4.

Despite play's Pittsburgh setting and the rough similarities between Cory and Troy's relationship and Wilson's relationship with stepfather David Bedford, the playwright denies that the work is a transparent depiction of his life.

Taylor, Markland. "'Fences.'" *Variety*, 15 May 1985, pp. 96, 107.

Rejects idea that *Death of a Salesman* influenced play; doubts play original enough to reach Broadway.

———. "'Fences' Encompasses the Life of a Black Family." *New Haven Register*, 5 May 1985.

Feels play owes a debt to *Death of a Salesman*; also compares it to *Ma Rainey* and concludes both plays examine "the way blacks—the men in particular—react against years of bigotry and crushed dreams by lashing out not against white powers but against the people closest to them."

Taylor, Robert. "'Fences' Straddles Fine Line between Issues." *Tribune* (California), 13 February 1987, pp. E1, E12.

Notes attempt to "elevate front porch drama" to the level of myth and understands dilemma between emphasizing plot or the stories of characters.

Viagas, Robert. "Death of a Trashman." *Fairpress*, 8 May 1985, p. C2.

Draws parallels between play and *Death of a Salesman*, pointing to Troy's "soliloquies or apostrophes to Death, his infidelity and his self delusions."

Wallach, Allan. "Fenced In by a Lifetime of Resentments." *New York Newsday*, 27 March 1987.

Family conflict indicates Wilson's preference for emphasizing "a black man forced to come to terms with an unfeeling white world."

Watt, Douglass. "'Fences' Is All over the Lot: But James Earl Jones Is Its Saving Grace." *Daily News*, 3 April 1987.

Mixed review praising Jones but finding the story conventional and overlong.

White, Arnold. "Straddling the Fences." *City Sun*, 1 April 1987, pp. 11, 14.

Expresses problems with overdrawn protagonist.

Wilson, Edwin. "Wilson's 'Fences' on Broadway." *Wall Street Journal*, 31 March 1987, pp. 29 (W), 31 (E).

Commends Wilson's ability to create supremely tense moments.

Winn, Steven. "Larger-Than-Life." *San Francisco Chronicle*, 13 February 1987.
    Sees play as incoherent.


***The Piano Lesson***

"August Wilson's Broadway Bound Drama: *The Piano Lesson.*" *Kennedy Center
    Newsletter*, October/November 1989.
    Announces opening of play at Washington, D.C.'s Kennedy Center.
"August Wilson's 'Piano Lesson' to be Published in October." *New Haven Register*,
    24 June 1990.
Brustein, Robert. "The Lesson of 'The Piano Lesson.'" *New Republic*, 21 May 1990,
    pp. 28–29.
    As former dean of Yale School of Drama, questions fine line between commercial
    and nonprofit theater; in particular, bothered by Lloyd Richards's promotion of
    *The Piano Lesson.*
Caruso, Tom. "Direction, Cast Make 'Piano Lesson' Superb." *Journal Inquirer*,
    8 December 1987.
    Favorable review that calls for streamlining.
Christiansen, Richard. "'The Piano Lesson' Hits a Powerful Chord on Racial
    Injustice." *Chicago Tribune*, 18 January 1989.
    Acknowledges weakness in unresolved plot but praises rich scenes and powerful
    moments and use of language.
"Critics Honor 'Piano Lesson.'" *New York Times*, 15 May 1990.
    Announces Drama Critics Circle Award for play.
Dufresne, Beth. "Taking Pot Shots at Wilson." *New London Day*, 3 June 1990,
    pp. B1, B3.
    Reduces the Brustein-Richards controversy to jealousy, with racial overtones; also
    Wilson is holding something back by avoiding direct confrontation between
    white and black in his plays.
Friedman, Ted. "'Piano' Addresses Familial Conflicts." *Yale Daily News*, 4
    December 1987, p. 5.
    Praises play's dealing with the problem of heritage; doubts need for the "hocus-
    pocus."
Furman, Nancy. "August Wilson Wins Pulitzer Prize for Drama." *After Hours*,
    13 April 1990, p. 4.
Gale, William. "'Piano' Is Minor Work from Major Playwright." *Providence Rhode
    Island Journal*, 15 January 1988, p. B11.
    Finds play devoid of action.
Goodstein, Laurie, and Megan Rosenfeld. "Pulitzer Surprises: Getting the Word."
    *Washington Post*, 13 April 1990, pp. C1, C4.
    Includes brief background information on his life and his artistic agenda.

Henry, William A. *Time*, 30 January 1989, p. 69.

Notes Wilson's modesty.

Hummler, Richard. "Brustein: B'Way Tail Wagging the Yale Rep Dog." *Variety*,
16 May 1990, pp. 85–86.

Outlines controversy stemming from charges made by former Yale School of
Drama dean that Richards was more interested in turning a profit from *Piano
Lesson*'s Broadway run than in advancing Yale Rep's cause.

———. "Campaign Revamped before Piano Is Come and Gone." *Variety*, 16 May
1990, p. 309.

Advertising campaign to market Broadway play.

———. "The Piano Lesson." *Variety*, 18 April 1990.

Praises play and Wilson's "command for the black idiom."

Johnson, Malcolm. "'Piano Lesson' Hits Dramatic Keys Throughout." *Hartford
Courant*, 29 November 1990.

Mixed reviews of opening at the Yale Rep; complains of repetitive second act.

McFadden, Robert. "'Piano Lesson' Wins Drama Pulitzer as 21 Prizes Are Given."
*New York Times*, 13 April 1990, pp. A16–A17.

Includes quick overview of Wilson's background.

Nemy, Enid. "After the Pulitzer." *New York Times*, 20 April 1990.

Impact of Pulitzer on ticket sales.

Rich, Frank. "Broadway's Bounty: Dramas Brimming with Life." *New York Times*,
3 June 1990, pp. 1, 8.

Discusses play as part of annual roundup; seems particularly concerned about the
reaction of whites to the play.

———. "A Family Confronts Its Ties in August Wilson's 'Piano Lesson.'" *New
York Times*, 17 April 1990, pp. C13, C15.

Astutely comments on the presence of Africa in characters' conversations and in
presence of the piano; commends play for ensuring that the piano's music "is not
up for sale."

———. "Wilson's 'Piano Lesson.'" *New York Times*, 10 December 1987, p. C25.

Identifies ways Wilson charges plays with history, pointing out its presence in his
characters' "autobiographical tales" or their "chatty streams of associations";
praises Wilson for ability to include audiences in these staged lessons in history.

Rizzo, Frank. "State-Nurtured Drama Earns Author Pulitzer." *Hartford Courant*,
13 April 1990, p. A10.

Commends Connecticut for helping perfect play.

———. "Wilson, Richards in Running for Tonys. *Hartford Courant*, 8 May 1990,
pp. D1, D3.

Rothstein, Mervyn. "Helping a Serious Play on Broadway." *New York Times*,
5 September 1989, pp. C13, C15.

The Manhattan Theater Club plans to give its 12,000 subscriber tickets to play.

Scher, Herb. "Turning 'Profit': The Yale Rep on Broadway." *Theater Week*, 16–22 April 1990, pp. 20–25.
Examines economics surrounding the Yale Rep's Broadway production of play.

"Second Wilson Pulitzer Honors Yale Rep." *New Haven Register*, 15 April 1990, p. B2.
Notes roles played by New Haven, Yale, and the Yale Rep in play's Pulitzer.

Spillane, Margaret. "Wilson's Haunted Family." *New Haven Independent*, 3 December 1987.
Good critique of play: "This rich offering of musical and narrative testimony is not mere homage, not pastiche; it is an assemblage of healthy, on-going dialogues between present and past, in which horrors as well as treasures are brought to light."

Taylor, Markland. "Yale Rep's 'The Piano Lesson' Needs Considerable Fine-Tuning." *New Haven Register*, 29 November 1987, p. B5.
Summarizes plot; argues play needs clarifying, cutting, and less noisy, unsatisfactory ending.

"Tonys: Wilson Play 'Piano Lesson' in Contention after Yale Rep Start." *New Haven Register*, 8 May 1990, pp. 3, 5.

"Two-Timer: A Second Pulitzer Confirms August Wilson's Pre-eminence." *Time*, 23 April 1990, p. 99.
Considers the Pulitzer Committee's comparison of Wilson to O'Neill premature, but acknowledges Wilson's importance.

Viagas, Robert. "New Haven Audiences Had a Hand in Wilson's 'Piano Lesson' Pulitzer." *New Haven Register*, 22 April 1990, pp. D1, D2.
Both Wilson and Richards thank New Haven audiences for attending Yale Rep's performance of *The Piano Lesson* and for providing them with direct feedback on problems in the play.

———. "Tony Lunch Abuzz over Criticism Aimed at Yale Rep." *New Haven Register*, 17 May 1990, pp. 59, 61.
Reports controversy stemming from attack on Richards and Yale Rep by former dean Robert Brustein.

Weiss, Hedy. "Goodman Offers a Grand Piano." *Chicago Sun Times*, 18 January 1989, p. 36.
Concludes "'The Piano Lesson' needs a conductor more than a director," referring to the play's extraordinarily rich content; sees piano as a full-blown character.

Wilson, David. "An Unfinished Symphony: August Wilson's *The Piano Lesson* Opens But Doesn't Close." Review of *The Piano Lesson*. *New Haven Advocate*, 7 December 1987, p. 34.
Praises play while noting problems with excessive characters, a slow-moving and eventually unresolved plot, and apparent disregard for the audience's need to resolve play's major conflict.

"Wilson Awarded Pulitzer Prize for *The Piano Lesson*." *Yale Herald*, 13 April 1990, p. 2.

"Wilson Captures 2nd Pulitzer; Drama Premiered at Yale Rep." *New Haven Register*, 13 April 1990, pp. 1, 4.

### Two Trains Running

Ansen, David. "Of Prophets and Profits." *Newsweek*, 27 April 1992, p. 70.
   Explains that the play "is not a play about the '60s, but a form of oral history, in which we're invited to eavesdrop on the timeless continuum of the African-American experience"; believes Wilson's strategy is to leave it to the audience to connect interlocking themes of "economics, self esteem and spirituality."

Backalenick, Irene. "'Two Trains Running' Is Unique Despite Some Imperfections." *Westport News*, 6 April 1990.
   Observes very little action on stage.

Courtemanche, Eleanor. "August Wilson *Trains* His Sights on the '60s: The World Premiere of the Pulitzer Winner's New Work." *After Hours*, 6 April 1990, p. 3.
   Observes that characters "are concerned less with making history than with the eternal cycles of death, money, and luck"; considers the play's ending to be a "fluke."

de Barras, Paul. "August Opening: Wilson's Play Is Up to Par." *Seattle Times*, 3 January 1991, p. F3.
   Notes play is "almost all talk," but credits director Lloyd Richards with letting the play "elegantly rise on the strengths of its language."

Dufresne, Beth. "'Trains' Goes off Track Somewhere along the Line." *Day*, 5 April 1990, pp. 5–6.
   Objects to detached and static nature of characters; considers Hambone "too obvious."

———. "'Two Trains' Leaves Station." *Day*.
   Draws attention to the over-thirty age group that make up the cast of play; explains Wilson's reasoning behind creating these experienced characters "who offer some perspective."

Dworkin, Norine. "Blood on the Tracks." *American Theater*, May 1990, pp. 8–9.
   Sees play as continuation of *The Piano Lesson*; notes that it makes indirect references to the crucial error blacks made in leaving potentially strong economic base in South.

Erstein, Hap. "'Trains' Clicks along on Well-Laid Drama Track." *Washington Times*, 15 November 1991, pp. E1–E3.
   Thinks play needs trimming, but praises the "poetic jazzy narrative riffs."

Fleishman, Glenn. "Yale Rep's Two Trains Runs Aimlessly." *Yale Herald*, 6 April 1990.

Considers play "competent but not compelling," offering few insights.

Gale, William. "August Wilson's Vision of Light at the End of the Tunnel." *Providence Journal Bulletin*, 6 April 1990, pp. D1, 5.
Considers play to be talky, in need of sharpening and cutting, but still important.

Gerard, Jeremy. "Two Trains Running." *Variety*, 25 November 1991, pp. 46, 48.
Notes play's lack of action but plenitude of life and humor.

Goldberg, Bonnie. "'Two Trains Running' Is on the Right Track." *Bulletin Theater Circle*, 12 April 1990.
Comments perceptively on major characters.

Husar, Ruth. "Preachy Lines Slow Pace of 'Two Trains.'" *Evening Sentinel* (Ansonia), April 1990.
Regards play as "preachy" and thinks that the theme—going back to pick up the ball—is "thrust at the audience."

Isaacs, Robert. "'Trains' Needs Tuning for a Smoother Trip." *Waterbury Republican*, 6 April 1990.

Johnson, Malcolm. "New Wilson Play Needs More Work." *Hartford Courant*, 2 April 1990, pp. A9, A11.

Kelly, Kevin. "Heart and Mind Are in the Right Place in 'Two Trains Running.'" *Boston Globe*, 5 April 1990.
Complains about "odd lack of definition," but feels it is Wilson's "most natural play."

Matthews, Shirley. "'Two Trains' on the Right Track." *Bridgeport Post*, 4 April 1990, p. 16.
Praises Wilson's incorporation of numerous narratives in *Two Trains Running*.

Paglia, Robert. Review, "'Two Trains Running' at Yale Repertory Theater." WELI Radio, 2 April 1990.
Considers Wilson's latest production "extremely well done," pointing to its "journalistic precision" and its transcendant quality illustrating the universal phenomena of the conflict."

Penn, Roberta. "'Two Trains Running' Is Slow But Sure and Powerful." *Seattle Post Intelligencer*, date and page unavailable.
Praises *Two Trains Running* for addressing the unmined areas of the black experience avoided in Amiri Baraka's 1960s plays and downplayed by the "semipreciousness" of *Dreamgirls* and *For Colored Girls*.

Plemmons, Chesley. "'Two Trains Running.'" *Citizen News*, 11 April 1990, p. 6.
Very favorable review of opening at Yale Rep.

Rich, Frank. "August Wilson Reaches the 60's with Witnesses from a Distance." *New York Times*, 14 April 1990, pp. C13, C17.
Acknowledges the play's unrefined structure yet appreciates it as Wilson's

signature; considers the play to be "Wilson's most adventurous and honest attempt to reveal the intimate heart of history" and defends the rambling monologues as "not digressions; they are the play's very fiber."

Richards, David. "A People Face the Mirror of History." *New York Times*, 3 May 1992, pp. H5, H28.
Points to Wilson's avoidance of themes so typical of black playwrights of the 1960s and to the play's emphasis upon "the continuing struggle to survive in a system that has welshed on its promise of universal liberty and justice."

Rose, Lloyd. "'Trains' of Thought." *Washington Post*, 15 November 1991, pp. F1, F8.
Appreciates play's ability to sustain interest even though "there's nothing happening" and "there is no real story."

Rosenberg, David. "Parallel Tracks: Yale Rep Does August Wilson's 'Two Trains Running.'" *Fairpress*, 12 April 1990, pp. D1, D7.
Observes that Yale Rep production is too talky and lacks action but is optimistic about revisions.

Rosenfeld, Megan. "The Voices of August Wilson." *Washington Post*, 10 November 1991, pp. G1, G4.
Examines Wilson's mental exercises for creating characters for his plays.

Shannon, Sandra. "The Blues Cycle Continues: Wilson's Train Moves On." *Emerge*, April 1990, pp. 49–50.
Explains that the lethargy in play results from heavy influence of blues dynamic; considers lack of momentum to be intended and sermonizing to reflect African American oral tradition.

Swift, Orla. "'Trains' Interesting, But Rambling Work." *Record Journal*, 6 April 1990.

Viagas, Robert. "August Wilson's World Premiere: 'Two Trains Running' at Yale Rep." *New Haven Register*, 25 March 1990, pp. D1, D2.
Draws attention to play's opening while *The Piano Lesson* is still on Broadway; describes Wilson's artistic agenda once Richards leaves Yale School of Drama. Wilson also discusses the making of *Two Trains*.

———. "Dramatic John Henry's Pound Hard to Get Their Due." *New Haven Register*, 1 April 1990.
Praises Wilson's "ear for revealing speech" in Yale Rep premiere; believes Wilson has raised characters to the level of American archetypes.

———. "Season's Best Theater: Minority Plays, Players." *New Haven Register*, 27 May 1990, pp. D1, D5.
Comments on the unique success of plays written by and about minorities introduced during Connecticut's 1989–90 theater season; analyzes how and why

this success occurred in the midst of a traditional "old-money" white establishment in Connecticut.

Wilson, David. "A Train to Catch." *New Haven Advocate*, 9 April 1990, p. 41. Minimizes *Two Trains Running*'s flaws as typical for a work in progress but praises the play as "a stunning evening of theater"; gives a thorough background of the play's characters; heaps praise also on the direction of Lloyd Richards.

# NOTES ON CONTRIBUTORS

SANDRA ADELL is assistant professor of Afro-American studies at the University of Wisconsin-Madison. Her essays and reviews have appeared in *Diacritics, Comparative Literature Studies*, and *Transitions*, and her book, *Double-Consciousness/Double Bind: Theoretical Issues in Twentieth-Century Black Literature*, is forthcoming from the University of Illinois Press.

MICHAEL AWKWARD is associate professor of English and director of the Center for Afro-American and African Studies at the University of Michigan. He is the author of *Inspiriting Influences: Tradition, Revision, and Afro-American Women's Novels* and editor of *New Essays on "Their Eyes Were Watching God."*

HARRY J. ELAM, JR., is professor of drama at Stanford University and director of the Committee on Black Performing Arts. His essays have appeared in *Text and Performance Quarterly* and *Theater Journal*, and he is working on a manuscript entitled "The Ritual of Social Protest Theater."

JOAN FISHMAN is completing a dissertation on August Wilson at UCLA; she is also a motion picture producer whose credits include *The Prince of Pennsylvania, Age Isn't Everything*, and the forthcoming *Don't Stop Now.*

ANNE FLECHE, assistant professor of English at Boston College, teaches drama and film. She has just completed a book-length manuscript, "Mimetic Disillusion: Eugene O'Neill, Tennessee Williams, and U.S. Dramatic Realism."

MISSY DEHN KUBITSCHEK is professor of English and women's studies at Indiana University–Purdue University at Indianapolis. She is the author of *Claiming the Heritage: History and Female Identity in 20th-Century African-American Women's Novels.*

MICHAEL MORALES is completing a dissertation on August Wilson at Stanford University.

ALAN NADEL is associate professor of Literature at Rensselaer Polytechnic Institute. He is the author of *Invisible Criticism: Ralph Ellison and the*

*American Canon* and essays on twentieth-century American literature and film. He is currently completing *Containing History: Narratives of American Culture in the Atomic Age* for Duke University Press's New Americanist series.

MARK WILLIAM ROCHA is associate professor of English at California State University, Northridge. He has just completed a book-length manuscript, "August Wilson and the Quest for American History."

SANDRA G. SHANNON, associate professor of English at Howard University, has published a number of essays on African American literature and is completing *The Dramatic Vision of*

*August Wilson*, a critical biography, for Howard University Press.

JOHN TIMPANE teaches English at Lafayette College. He is the coauthor of *Writing Worth Reading* and is currently completing *The Renaissance Laugh*, a book about humor in sixteenth-century England.

CRAIG WERNER is chair of the Department of Afro-American Studies at the University of Wisconsin-Madison. He is the author of *Playing the Changes: From Afro-Modernism to the Jazz Impulse*, forthcoming from the University of Illinois Press, and several other books on Afro-American literature.

# INDEX TO THE PLAYS

This selective index—intended to assist the reader who uses this book to research specific plays or critical perspectives—identifies only the places where specific plays are *discussed*, not merely mentioned, and those critics and theorists used to advance an essay's argument. The index, moreover, refers to the texts of the essays, omitting references that appear only in footnotes or bibliographies and omitting the long annotated bibliography that concludes this collection.

## THE PLAYS

*Fences*, 7–8, 40–42, 67–68, 69–74, 89–95, 102–103, 137, 141, 154–156, 178–180, 183–184, 185–190, 213–226

*Jitney!*, 150

*Joe Turner's Come and Gone*, 4, 6, 11–14, 42–43, 95–102, 105–106, 111–113, 135–136, 142, 144, 156–159, 173–176, 183, 190–193

*Ma Rainey's Black Bottom*, 2, 3, 4, 15–18, 39–40, 51–65, 67–68, 74–79, 139, 151–154, 165, 169–173, 181, 183

*The Piano Lesson*, 2–3, 6, 9–10, 44–46, 105–111, 142–144, 159–161, 176–178, 183–184, 193–197

*Two Trains Running*, 4, 22, 46–47, 116–131, 139, 141, 147, 161–162, 165–168, 171

## CRITICS AND THEORISTS

Allen, Paula Gunn, 184, 185
Anzaldua, Gloria, 185
Baker, Houston A., Jr., 216–217
Baldwin, James, 208

Baraka, Amiri, 25, 28, 131
Bearden, Romare, 133–149
Benitez-Rojo, Antonio, 37–38
Benjamin, Walter, 53–54, 81
Bluestone, George, 206, 207
Brecht, Bertol, 11, 127
Brown, H. Rap, 119
Campbell, Mary Schmidt, 141, 145
Case, Sue-Ellen, 166, 168
Christian, Barbara, 178
Clifford, James, 209–210, 212
Coleman, Wanda, 22–23, 24, 26, 27, 30
Collins, Patricia Hill, 166, 167, 169, 179–180
Crouch, Stanley, 29–30, 31
Davis, Francis, 33
de Certeau, Michel, 88, 89, 100
de Man, Paul, 12, 13
Derrida, Jacques, 11
DeVries, Hilary, 175
Dolan, Jill, 167, 181
Drake, Sylvie, 129–130
Du Bois, W. E. B., 117, 126
Ellison, Ralph, 25, 26–27, 60, 88
Figueroa, Carlos, 33

Foucault, Michel, 69, 73, 81, 89, 94

Gates, Henry Louis, Jr., 117–118, 119, 127, 131, 213

Giddens, Gary, 33, 34

Gioia, Ted, 31–32

Harrison, Daphne, 170, 171

Harrison, Paul Carter, 22, 25

Heidegger, Martin, 62

Hernton, Calvin, 169

hooks, bell, 22–23, 25, 26, 180, 184, 185

James, William, 68, 71

Kent, George, 35–36

Larsson, Donald, 208

Locke, Alain, 23

Lukacs, George, 10–11

Marsalis, Wynton, 30, 32–33

Minh-ha, Trinh, 184, 185

Mitchell-Kernan, Claudia, 117–123

Mundle, C. W. K., 68

Murray, Albert, 28

Nietzche, Friedrich, 61–62, 63, 64, 69

Omi, Michael, 209–210

Radano, Roland, 33

Russell, Michele, 169–170

Shannon, Sandra, 57, 170–171

Sidran, Ben, 25

Sinyard, Neil, 206

Sollors, Werner, 211

Soyinka, Wole, 127, 133, 136, 145

Spender, Dale, 155

Spillers, Hortense, 55, 167

Szondi, Peter, 10–11

Tate, Greg, 31, 34

Thompson, Robert Farris, 25

White, Hayden, 89, 92

Williams, Martin, 33

Winant, Howard, 209–210